D1093219

# STAGING FASCISM

JEFFREY T. SCHNAPP

STANFORD UNIVERSITY PRESS    STANFORD, CALIFORNIA    1996

# 18 BL AND THE THEATER

## STAGING FASCISM

### OF MASSES FOR MASSES

Stanford University Press
Stanford, California
© 1996 by the Board of Trustees of the
Leland Stanford Junior University

Printed in the United States of America

CIP data appear at the end of the book

Stanford University Press publications are distributed exclusively by Stanford University Press
within the United States, Canada, Mexico, and
Central America; they are distributed exclusively
by Cambridge University Press throughout the
rest of the world.

## ACKNOWLEDGMENTS

It takes a village to make a book: in the case of *Staging Fascism*, a global village made up of electrical and optical pulses, fax and microwave transmissions, and E-mail messages, as well as of face-to-face communications. Among the many friends and colleagues to whom I have incurred personal and professional debts in the course of researching and writing the present one, I would like to single out Giovanni Tentori for his learned advice and generous help in obtaining various documents, and for reading portions of an earlier version of the manuscript; Sepp Gumbrecht for his shared enthusiasm for melding speculative flight with daily slogging in the archives; Timothy Lenoir who, along with Sepp, collaborated in the teaching of a memorable seminar entitled "Technological and Cultural Incubations of Fascism"; Claudio Fogu for his insights into fascist cultural politics and assistance in locating a couple of key archival documents; Corrado Sofia for his willingness to spend several long afternoons tediously poring over details from a half century ago and for his help in editing the interview in Appendix E; and Barbara Spackman for her always incisive criticisms and suggestions. I owe a very special debt of gratitude to Mara Blasetti for so generously making available to me the manuscript materials, drawings, and photographs in her collection, without which this book would have been impossible to complete. I am grateful as well to my friends Diane Ghirardo and Ruth Ben-Ghiat for their conversation, both in and out of the Roman state archives, regarding our many overlapping intellectual-historical interests; and grateful as well to Susanna Elm and Mark Seltzer for their wit and companionship during an inspiring year (1991–92) at the National Humanities Center. My thanks also go both to my friend and colleague Robert Harrison, for his intellectual companionship and tennistic prowess, which has always kept me literally and figuratively on my toes; and to George Mosse for his always thoughtful responses and encouragement. Claudia

Abbondanza undertook the onerous task of transcribing the interview with Sofia and was a superb research assistant during 1993–94; Judith Silverstein assisted me in compiling some of the appendixes. A harder debt to gauge, but a significant one nonetheless, is the inspiration provided by the participants in several graduate seminars on "Fascism and Culture" that I offered at Stanford and Cornell: students (now colleagues at various institutions) such as Chris Bongie, Erin Carlston, Heesok Chang, Alison Cornish, Cinzia Blum, Zakiya Hanafi, Elena Feder, Marcia Klotz, and Andrew Hewitt.

To Emily I owe a debt of a more incalculable sort, and to her this book is lovingly dedicated.

I also gratefully wish to acknowledge the support of the National Humanities Center and the Simon Guggenheim Memorial Foundation, which provided me with a leave year that was crucial to the completion of this book. I have also benefitted from a generous Hewlett Foundation travel grant and from a travel/research grant from the Mellon Foundation, both of which allowed for extended work in Italian archives. The Archivio Storico Fiat, the Getty Center for the History of Art and the Humanities, and several Italian libraries and archives offered invaluable assistance, as did my friend Pino d'Errico at the Biblioteca Nazionale Centrale in Rome. Last, but not least, I must thank Donald Raleigh and Lazar Fleishman for their help with the Slavic Studies portions of the book's argument, for whose deficiencies, of course, they bear no responsibility.

Several portions of *Staging Fascism* first appeared in "*18 BL*: Fascist Mass Spectacle," *Representations* 43 (Summer 1993): 89–125. I am grateful to the University of California Press for permitting their use.

J.T.S.

# ILLUSTRATIONS

# ABBREVIATIONS

| | |
|---|---|
| ACS | Archivio Centrale dello Stato, Rome |
| BA | Blasetti Archive, Rome |
| *CdS* | *Corriere della Sera* |
| CF | *Critica Fascista* |
| DN | Direttorio Nazionale |
| *GdP* | *Gazzetta del Popolo* |
| GUF | Gruppi Universitari Fascisti |
| *ILCA* | *I Littoriali della Cultura e dell'Arte: Rivista Mensile dei Fascisti Universitari* |
| *ILRM* | *I Littoriali: Rivista Mensile dei Littoriali della Cultura e dello Sport* |
| *LIL* | *L'Italia Letteraria* |
| *LIV* | *L'Italia Vivente* |
| *LN* | *La Nazione* |
| LUCE | L'Unione Cinematografica Educativa |
| *MdR* | *Meridiano di Roma* |
| OND | Opera Nazionale Dopolavoro |
| *OO* | *Opera omnia di Benito Mussolini*, ed. Edoardo Susmel and Duilio Susmel (Rome: Volpe, 1978) |
| PNF | Partito Nazionale Fascista |
| *PdI* | *Il Popolo d'Italia* |
| RAI | Reale Accademia d'Italia |
| SIAE | Società Italiana di Autori e Editori |

What is the ideal fascist? How might modern culture be mandated to mold this subject? And what is specific to the Italian version of this project? In this brilliant cultural micro-history of the fascist era, Jeffrey Schnapp addresses these questions as he reconstructs the most extreme attempt within the Mussolini regime to produce a mass theater. Named after the first truck to be mass-produced by Fiat, *18 BL* was conceived as a dramatic crucible of the new fascist subject. In technique and effect somewhere between a theater of war and a film production of epic proportions, the colossal spectacle was set outside Florence on a sculpted site the size of six football fields. Performed but once, it was pronounced dead on arrival, yet it lived on in disputes over its autopsy. In a reading that is both philological and symptomatic, Schnapp has now transformed this forgotten event into a lively exposition of fascist cultural politics in general.

What exactly was *18 BL*? As Schnapp tells the story, its origins are quite specific. On April 28, 1933, almost a year to the day before its performance, Mussolini lectured the Italian Society of Authors and Publishers on the state of theater, which he, like many in Europe at the time, considered to be in crisis. Il Duce called for a new kind of theater altogether: a theater *for* the masses if not *of* the masses.[1] The ground for a mass theater was prepared in Italy and elsewhere. Apart from open-air theaters, the thespian cars, a fleet of mobile modular theaters, were already in operation throughout the country. The primary purpose of these productions was hardly to advance the theatrical repertory. Rather, as Schnapp shows, it was to bind a disparate people into a linguistic group that was also a political mass, one national-ideological body. And in this binding, the medium was the message: these productions presented the fascist regime as a ubiquitous agent committed to modernizing the nation, to turning

Italy into a totality at once aesthetic, techno-logical, and political—in a word, spectacular.

*18 BL* was not just another entry in the spectacle sweepstakes opened up by Mussolini's speech; it was intended by its principal authors, the originator Alessandro Pavolini and the director Alessandro Blasetti, as the model of the new mass theater. After much debate, its testy committee of collaborators agreed on a concept. The performance would have three parts: act 1 would stage the struggles of World War I; act 2 the glories of the fascist revolution; act 3 the labors of the fascist reconstruction of the nation. This tripartite structure is typical of national epics (it plays on the common narrative of trial and triumph, death and resurrection). Not typical, however, is the protagonist here: in the words of Pavolini, "a truck as personage; as single and collective personage; as hero of the war, of the struggles of the fascist squadrons, and of building projects." *A truck as hero?* Obviously no mere truck, this 18 BL is loaded with allegorical freight. First of all, it is a she, indeed, a mother; more, this mother is dubbed "Mamma Giberna," or Mother Cartridge-Pouch, machinic matron of fascist subjects, mother truck to fascist mothertruckers.

In the first act, Mother Cartridge-Pouch is imaged as a combat nurse in World War I. She delivers supplies, comes under fire, brings reinforcements. Then, upon victory (the battle is that of Trento and Trieste), she honors the warriors in a parade with other 18 BLs. In the next act, set amid the labor strikes of 1922, Mother Cartridge-Pouch appears as a noble laborer attacked by a socialist mob. This scene is then doubled by an episode in a parliament full of fat and foppish members of liberal, socialist, and popular parties, all familiar caricatures from the time. As one exclaims, "But what do these fascists want?," Mother Cartridge-Pouch bursts in with her young troopers. Later, after these fascists are again attacked by a socialist mob, they regroup around the mother truck, and from on high the voice of Mussolini announces the March on Rome, the legendary founding of the fascist regime.

The last act of *18 BL* concerns the draining of the Pontine marshes in order to establish new farms and towns on the fascist model. In the first scene, formations of children and athletes pass in review, the first as the material, the second as the model, of fascist subject-formation—an image of human reclamation that interprets the allegory of physical reclamation that follows. Now old and battered, Mother Cartridge-Pouch breaks down at last; even she cannot satisfy the fascist demand for constant exertion. But since she is buried as landfill, her physical demise becomes the allegorical ground of the spiritual resurrection of the nation. And here a great figure on horseback, again assumed to be Mussolini, rises to command. The machinic mother goes under, but the metallic father takes over, and this is the peripeteic moment in the spectacle, the dramatic crux of identification for its audience.[2]

As Schnapp reconstructs it, then, *18 BL* is a family romance of the fascist revolution, an Italian version of *Birth of a Nation, October,* or *Triumph of the Will.* But the *individual* identification that occurs in the Oedipal family romance—that is, in the fantasmatic creation of new parental models—is here supplemented, even supplanted, by a *mass*

identification elicited by spectacular tableaux of the military, the party, and the nation. Again, it is these tableaux that punctuate the passage of the play: war followed by revolution capped by reconstruction. In a sense this transformation of family romance into national-origin myth, in which the party takes over for the family and the mass subsumes the individual, was mandated by Mussolini in his catalytic speech on theater a year before *18 BL* was performed. "Enough with the notorious romantic 'triangle' that has so obsessed us to this day," he declared at the time. The new mass theater "must stir up the great collective passions." This attack on bourgeois theater is thus an attack on bourgeois *psychology*, in which Mussolini joined not only politically suspect Futurists like Marinetti but politically correct modernists as well—a complicated point of convergence between fascism and modernism that is an important topic of this book. First to stir up and then to straiten the great collective passions is a fundamental project of fascist culture. And it is in relation to this project, which was pursued in related ways by different regimes of the time, that Schnapp contributes significantly to contemporary studies of mass politics, culture, and subjectivity.[3]

If the old forms of identity are inadequate, even resistant, to the new demands of fascist society, how might a culture be made to pose the necessary models? Moreover, if the old forms of identity are tied up with bourgeois individuality, how might this culture bind the masses to these new models in a way that does not rely on individualistic patterns of desire and identification? What collective rituals of national initiation might overcode the private scenes of Oedipal formation at work in bourgeois art forms? Moreover, what combination of archaic arts and modern media might "reestablish the values of sacred rituality within resolutely secular confines"? For Schnapp, these are the difficult questions that *18 BL* had to resolve, and this very difficulty suggests why it failed. Given these demands, *18 BL* could only become a total work of art too heavy to fly, a hybrid unable to reproduce. In order to engage the individual, it was still conceived in terms of theater, but in order to bind the collective, it also aspired to the condition of cinema. At the same time, it evoked both the choral aspect of Greek drama and the sacrificial dimension of medieval mystery plays, even as it also cited Soviet revolutionary films and pageants like *Potemkin* and *The Storming of the Winter Palace*, as well as Wagnerian opera (especially important for the phantamasgorical presentation of history as myth, another point of comparison with a national myth of origin such as *Triumph of the Will*).

In short, *18 BL* was a volatile compound of old dramaturgies and new technologies, which Schnapp describes as part ritual, part inaugural: a ritual designed "to bridge the gap between pre- and postrevolutionary generations and thereby to renew the revolution"; and an inaugural designed "to offer a preview of a future fully 'fascistized' society." It was an inaugural ritual, then, in which each new generation was to be sutured after the fact into the foundational moments of the fascist movement.[4] But even as this movement celebrated perennial youth and permanent revolution, it also evoked

**XV**

atavistic subjectivities and archaic communities. Finally, these tensions pulled *18 BL* apart, undid the very ideological suturing the spectacle otherwise performed: its own dramaturgical and technological stitching was too conflicted to hold up.

———————

Schnapp distinguishes his reading of *18 BL* from two tendencies in postwar histories of the fascist era: the first presents fascism as simply opposed to culture, whether traditional or modernist, the second as merely instrumental in relation to it. Again, in contrast to the first position, Schnapp regards culture as the laboratory of the fascist subject; and in contrast to the second, he sees the fascist involvement in culture as contentious and contradictory. These are important insights, and I want to underscore them here.

To take the second one first: in a neat formulation Schnapp argues that fascism required "an aesthetic *overproduction*—a surfeit of fascist signs, images, slogans, books, and buildings—in order to compensate for, fill in, and cover up its unstable ideological core." Here he concurs with recent studies of other fascisms that adapt the formula, devised by Fredric Jameson from Jacques Lacan and Louis Althusser, that cultural forms serve as imaginary resolutions of real contradictions.[5] However, focused on a single event, Schnapp is able to show that this resolution is never merely imaginary or completely resolved. In this way, he presents us with a fascism whose very conflicts fascinate: a fascism ambivalent about modernist art, attracted to its transgression of bourgeois culture but leery of its alienation of the masses; a fascism also ambivalent about media spectacle, eager to

exploit its technological advances but reluctant to sacrifice the communal basis of archaic arts; a fascism caught between the contradictory imperatives of the new mass subjectivity and the old heroic individualism, of the new mythic homogeneity of the people and the old elitist heterogeneity of the leader; a fascism also caught in a sibling rivalry with communism, envious of its political doctrine and cultural repertoire but contemptuous of the mechanistic aspects of its enemy twin. As Schnapp details the relationship of fascism to these different formations of modernism, spectacle, the masses, and communism, disciplinary oppositions favored by thinkers on the left *and* the right fall by the wayside. We see that fascism cannot simply be opposed to modernism (as triumphalist American accounts have it) *or* to communism (as triumphalist socialist accounts have it), that these old binaries no longer suffice in our world after the fall of the Berlin Wall. At the same time we see that the new conflations that have risen since the fall of the Wall—that communism only prepares fascism, that modernism was secretly fascistic all along—are even more inadequate. Indeed, from the *nouveaux philosophes* to post-*perestroika* critics like Boris Groys, this end-of-history story has been told again and again. Representative of American cultural studies at its critical best, *Staging Fascism* is an important corrective to this rhetoric that effectively continues the Cold War of cultural politics by other means.

But what of the first insight noted above regarding the cultural laboratory of the fascist subject? For me the failure of *18 BL* in this regard is focused in its climactic moment, when Mother Cartridge-Pouch falls and Mussolini rises. If the very first move of the spectacle was to displace the humanist hero of bourgeois theater with a machinic-maternal protagonist of fascist society, its very last move is to merge this military-industrial mother with the nationalist father. But the essential problem remains: *with whom or what is the audience to identify?* What is the offspring of mother truck and il Duce imagined to be? Or, again, how can a truck be a hero?

If an emblematic figure of machinic modernity was needed, why not use the train, the image of party discipline and state power? Yet the train, Schnapp tells us, could not evoke "the mythology of fascist squadrism" in military battles and political raids, nor could it capture the legend of fascist collectivity. Only the truck, "the proletariat/peasant vehicle par excellence," the icon of modern industry and agriculture, could do so. But then, how different is this fascist truck from the communist version (or, for that matter, the New Deal one)? These questions lead Schnapp to an important distinction between communist *mechanization* and fascist *metallization*. Politically, the communist figure of the mechanical poses the subject in functional mesh with a society conceived as an industrial factory, while the fascist figure of the metallic poses the subject in imaginary identification with a nation conceived as a militaristic party. Culturally, the communist figure of the mechanical is a trope of demystification: it seeks to *op*pose bourgeois individualism and illusionism and to *ex*pose a collectivist subject and culture that is rational, economic, classless, and sexless (think of Vsevolod Meyerhold's constructivist theater with its repertoire of biomechanical gestures and poses). The fascist figure of the

metallic is quite different. It is a trope of mythification that seeks to reforge the individual as mass and the mass as individual, not to break them down analytically and build them back functionally; its ideal subject is far from rational, economic, classless, or sexless. In the end, Schnapp argues, it is this metallic ideal that the audience of *18 BL* is asked to identify with, even to incorporate, and this ideal is embodied in the futurist-phallic figure of Mussolini.

Perhaps this is one reason why *18 BL* failed as a crucible of the fascist subject, for this metallic man remained only virtual in the production. "What the hell do *we* care about a truck?," some of the young in the audience cried out at the end of the spectacle. What could attract such men and women to a thing as strange as a marsupial mother truck? Mother Cartridge-Pouch had none of the death-drive desire with which the machine-guns of Freikorps mercenaries in the 1920's were invested or, for that matter, the bombers of American pilots in World War II. Schnapp argues that she had to be pure in order to ward off the sexual-political threats embodied in the contrary figure of the vamp. But why disregard desire altogether? One would not have thought that this is a mistake that fascists would make.

But then how strange a hero is Mother Cartridge-Pouch? Besides some communist relatives of the time, she has many capitalist descendants. (I read the manuscript of this book in June 1994, at a time when millions of Americans were captivated, first, by a white Ford Bronco escorted by a phalanx of police cars across the spectacular set of Los Angeles, and then by a Mother Bus-Bomb that rolled through this same network in a

**xvii**

movie with the futurist-fascist title of *Speed*.) *18 BL* may be best seen as one attempt by one regime to incite the masses to internalize a new subject of history, a subject, far more difficult than the proletariat, that even then threatened to overwhelm any definition of the human: the subject of military-industrial technoscience. In a sense *this* is the fantasmatic offspring that mother truck and il Duce were designed to conceive in the audience by the end of *18 BL*.

Of course, communism has had its avatars of this subject too, and capitalism continues to produce its brands as well. That is, capitalism continues to compel us to reconcile its new techno-commodities with our old body-egos. Were we not asked to identify first with our cars, then with our computers, in this way: to incorporate them psychically as well as physically? (Or should I say to be incorporated into them?) *18 BL* may have failed because it was too futuristic or too contradictory, but when one considers the psychophysical relays at work in our contemporary videodrome, the relays that course through an adult watching a *Terminator* or a *Robocop* movie, or a kid playing with a Transformer or a Power Ranger toy, this fascist spectacle may seem almost archaic, even simple, in comparison. All political regimes are involved in the business of subject-formation. In *Staging Fascism*, Jeffrey Schnapp gives us a detailed case study of one kind of subject-making, which can in turn be used to consider our own body politic, our own psychic nation.

**xviii**

Closing my eyes, I try to imagine this truly extraordinary symbolic scene: the dark mass of spectators, the cohorts of actors against the flaming backdrop of the heavens; overhead, the throb of airplanes . . . and the bright reflections cast by books crowned by muskets: fascism's magnificent civic and heroic dream.

—Yambo

The truck may not be chic, but it's more fascist than the latest Buick.

—Slogan posted in the Pisan *fascio* after the performance of *18 BL*

What a wondrous source of inspiration for the soul of an artist, an artist drunken with *national* greatness, to gaze upon this mass of human beings enraptured by melodious trills, inebriated by lyrical crescendos; an enthusiastic, frenetic, shouting, and applauding mass surrounded by an infinite natural landscape, a naked ambience with which the nation's struggles are renewed, its vast tide swaying to the impetus of music and song. Can you imagine the ecstasies, the overpowering spiritual visions, the fertile, deeply creative sparks that it makes available to the artist?

—Giuseppe Valenti on the stadium

The history of almost all such enterprises is . . . the history of as many errors and failures.

—Jacques Copeau on the Stanislavsky and Edward Gordon Craig *Hamlet*

# 1

Moscow or Rome? The question was posed with urgency throughout the 1920's and 1930's. Socialist pamphleteers drew up diagrams to illustrate the stark choice confronting all of humankind: "Fascism or Communism; Rome or Moscow."[1] Fascist syndicalists like Sergio Panunzio envisioned contemporary history as a clash between the two secular churches that had arisen after the death of God: the fascist "religion of spirit" and the bolshevist "religion of matter."[2] Massimo Bontempelli instead invoked funereal metaphors, speaking of "two burial grounds for nineteenth-century democracy in Europe: one in Rome, the other in Moscow. In Moscow the tomb is guarded by mysterious wild beasts scratching the earth. In Rome by young hawks, who, by staring into the sun, may succeed in altering its course."[3] The journalist Bruno Spampanato formulated the dilemma less as a choice between Rome *or* Moscow than between Rome *and* Moscow versus the old Europe:

Italy and Russia. . . . Two spatial unfoldings of history. Modern revolution is born in these gigantic *theaters*. The first, great in the spiritual grandeur of its universal mission. The second, great in the human grandeur of its numerous peoples. The political process that began in 1789 and extended into the capitalist phase now explodes and reaches its revolutionary epilogue, fusing together in equal measure the enduring vitality of Roman civilization and the fresh and primitive vitality of Moscow's anticivilization.[4]

Whatever the variations in emphasis, and even when Weimar Germany or New Deal America were thrown in as third or fourth terms, a common and widespread conviction subtends all of the views just cited: namely, that liberal democracy had run its full course in history. Industrialization had ensured the triumph of a new mass society and, so many believed (especially after the Great Crash of 1929), the demise of all liberal forms of social, cultural, political, and economic organization. And the bourgeois individual, the being who had once stood at the center of the universe of liberal democracy, had been

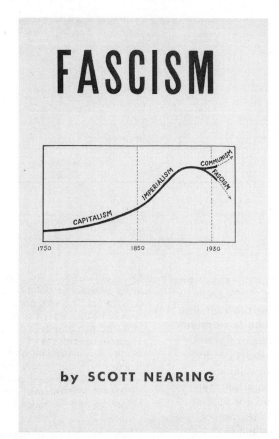

# FASCISM

by SCOTT NEARING

interred in the trenches of World War I. In the words of the socialist dramaturge Erwin Piscator:

The War finally buried bourgeois individualism under a hail of steel and a holocaust of fire. Man, the individual, existing as an isolated being, independent (at least seemingly) of social connections, revolving egocentrically around the concept of the self, in fact lies buried beneath a marble slab inscribed "The Unknown Soldier." . . . What came back [from the war] had nothing more in common with concepts like man, mankind, and humanity, which had symbolized the eternal nature of the God-given order in the parlors of prewar days.[5]

The question facing humankind was, therefore, less whether liberal democracy could or would survive, than one of *succession*. What sort of being would take the place of the bourgeois subject now buried in the tomb of the Unknown Soldier? What sort of mass society would arise out of the trenches' mud? Would the identity of the new subject and society be anchored in the concept of class or in that of the nation? Would their character be utopian, utilitarian, and collectivist, or instead mythical, aesthetic, and individualist? Did all roads lead to Moscow, or rather to Rome?

Irrespective of the answer, culture became one of the key domains with which Muscovite and Roman revolutionaries advanced their rival claims to political legitimacy and cultural modernity. Culture was the *laboratory* in which the new mass subject could be shaped and new forms of mass organization tested. I use the metaphor of the "laboratory" advisedly, not only because it pervades the cultural debates of the 1920's and 1930's, from Proletkult to the Bauhaus to the Gruppi Universitari Fascisti, but also because it underscores the inaugural role assigned by both revolutions to cultural artifacts. Works of fascist or communist art were conceived of as more than instruments of propaganda. Their task was to serve as messengers from the future, relays from the imaginary to the real, activating within the collective's mind and body the entire complex of the revolution's values *yet to be fully realized in history*. Since the values in question encompassed every area of human ac-

tivity—from work to leisure, from politics to ethics to individual psychology to a regime of bodily hygiene and exercise—culture was envisaged in total, even totalitarian, terms.

From the very start, the theater was the revolutionists' art of choice, much as it had been during the French Revolution. As a total art form, they felt, it alone could perform the work of integration once performed by religion. In precedents like the festivals of Unity and Indivisibility (1793), and of the Supreme Being (1794); in projects like Jacques-Louis David's for an immense theater designed to permit the French people to act out and view the great events of the Revolution, the revolutionists perceived the first glimmerings of a contemporary form of spectacle that might succeed in "adapting the spirit that gave birth to and animated the ancient Greek theatrical festivals to the special conditions of modern popular life."[6] The ancient origin to be reborn was variously imagined as Greek, Roman, Byzantine, or medieval. But its essentials were assumed to be the same between 1789 and 1922: accessibility, low cost, audience involvement, integration of all the arts, the mixing of all social classes, freedom from falsity and artifice, closeness to nature or to the real. The same went for its mission: the shaping of model citizens and a model society. The corrupt theater to be overcome had rent the domain of representation, just as the corrupt regime to be superseded had rent the social fabric. Actor and author had been disjoined from public, stage from auditorium, play from world, music from word, theater edifice from natural landscape.

The new/(ancient) theater would undertake the work of mending. The words of Georg

Fuchs, founder of Munich Art Theater, bespeak a century and a half of efforts by men such as Firmin Gémier, Maurice Pottecher, Romain Rolland, and Jacques Copeau, to revolutionize the theater and recover its popular and sacred roots: "Away with the footlights! Away with the wings, the backcloths, the flies, the flats, and the padded tights! Away with the peep-show stage! Away with the auditorium! This entire sham world of paste, wire, canvas and tinsel is ripe for destruction!"[7] To replace the sham worlds, first, of the aristocracy and, then, of the bourgeoisie, the revolutionaries of the theater devised a diversity of solutions, some populist, some avant-gardist, some populist and avant-gardist. Most were informed by a single ideal: that of placing the people on stage before the people, cast as itself and portraying its own life. The revolutionary theater thus aspired to fashion a collective Narcissus. It dreamt of all-absorbing forms of spectacle that would stage a sovereign collective subject gazing upon itself and shaping itself, as if constitutive of a fully autonomous universe.

The case of Soviet Russia is exemplary in this regard. Its value as a tool for mobilizing illiterate workers and peasants, its prestige as the preeminent fin de siècle art form, and its potential as a total spectacle blending all of the arts combined to bring about an explosion in the theater in the years following the October revolution. Hundreds of amateur and professional clubs sprang up throughout Russia and performed agitprop works, leading the critic Viktor Shklovsky to comment wryly that "the drama circles . . . are propagating like protozoa. Not lack of fuel, nor the lack of food, nor the Entente—no, nothing

4

can stop their growth."[8] Thousands of actors performed in open-air mass spectacles recreating the events of the revolution, worker and youth theaters proliferated under the guidance of Aleksandr Bogdanov's Proletkult, and avant-garde directors such as Vsevolod Meyerhold proclaimed a Theatrical October, launching a civil war against the bourgeois theater as millions starved and Russia battled through its own bitter civil war. By 1920, it seemed to Shklovsky that "all Russia is acting; some kind of elemental process is taking place where the living fabric of life is being transformed into the theatrical."[9] The purpose of this theatricalization of everyday life was understood by contemporary theorists as at once utopian and utilitarian. Through the revolutionary theater, it was hoped, "a new generation of harmoniously developed individuals" would be forged.[10] Or, in the words of Boris Arvatov, a leading theorist in the Lef group, the new mass theater aspired to become a school teaching "workers how to conduct themselves and how to master their own bodies," "a factory turning out people qualified for life."[11]

Italian fascism was in its infancy when Russia was decking itself out as a living stage. Originating from within the fold of socialism, the fascist movement emerged in 1919 from an ill-defined grouping of intransigent nationalists, irredentists, anarcho-syndicalists, futurists, and disaffected war veterans, drawn together by their militant opposition to Italy's parliamentary regime, to its politics of accommodation vis-à-vis a wave of strikes and factory occupations, and to the Treaty of Versailles. Although initially small, the movement was able to seize state power in October 1922. But it was not until the late

1920's that fascism's "cultural revolution" truly began: first, because Mussolini ruled over the old parliamentary state until 1925, when his dictatorship was declared; second, because fascism was an inherently unstable ideological formation. Fascist doctrine was constructed around a core of beliefs integrating the work of figures such as Georges Sorel, Sergio Panunzio, Paolo Orano, Enrico Corradini, Angelo Olivetti, and Roberto Michels. It proposed to merge nineteenth-century organic nationalism, as found in the literature of Italy's Risorgimento, with a Marxism stripped of its materialist underpinnings; and it proposed to do so in the context of a "communal, anti-individualistic, and antirationalistic" political culture that "represented at first a rejection of the heritage of the Enlightenment and the French Revolution, and later the creation of a comprehensive alternative, an intellectual, moral, and political framework that alone could ensure the perpetuity of a human collectivity in which all strata and all classes of society would be perfectly integrated."[12]

However consistent and comprehensive this body of doctrine, however, fascism never truly had at its disposal a philosophical system like that put forward by Marxism-Leninism as it struggled to actualize itself as a full-blown totalitarian state and to address such fundamental conflicts as those between its populist and elitist currents, and between its cult of heroic individualism and its institutional call to order. Nor did it always actively seek such philosophical underpinnings, despite the best efforts of philosophers like Giovanni Gentile and Julius Evola, who respectively sought to equip it with a

5

neo-Hegelian theory of the state and a metaphysics. Rather, fascism often amounted to little more than a complex of ethical principles, credos, myths, and aversions, held together by opportunism and rhetorical-aesthetic glue. Fascism was determined to remain a paradoxical creature: part doctrinal beast descended from the anarcho-syndicalist wing of antimaterialist Marxism, part chameleon. There was never much disagreement between its opponents and proponents on this point. The communist leader Palmiro Togliatti could thus fulminate from his Moscow pulpit "against considering fascist ideology as solidly constituted, finite, homogeneous. Fascist ideology is nothing if not a chameleon. Look at fascist ideology only in terms of the goal that fascism was aiming to achieve at that precise moment with that precise ideology." [13] Togliatti's words resonate with those of the fascist technocrat Camillo Pellizzi, who denied the possibility that fascist ideology could ever be reduced to a stable corpus of doctrines:

Above all else, fascism is and must ever-increasingly become a "way of life." To cast it as dogma, however the word is understood, means to bind it with a chain that, if it is not immediately sundered in the process of acting, can only end up shackling and perhaps killing off all future development. . . .

Our leaders [condottieri], and il Duce first and foremost, have been spurred on and inspired from above. From that "above" that resides in every man and from which gushes forth the will's creative surge. Dogma is unnecessary; discipline is enough. This is fascism's sole dogma. [14]

Improvisation, creative evolution, instinct reconciled with a higher intelligence, action in the service of life-force, infinite heterogeneity, introjected divinity: the (counter)-dogma of late Romantic art theory. The aesthetic tie-in is no accident. Unable or unwilling definitively to resolve the question of its identity by recourse to the utopias of theory and technology, haunted by its belatedness vis-à-vis its bolshevik rival, eager to make the nationalist redemption myths of the Risorgimento its own, fascism often sought answers to its identity crisis in the domain of culture. It required (and attempted to stimulate through the lavish patronage of modern art) an aesthetic *overproduction*—a surfeit of fascist signs, images, slogans, books, and buildings—in order to compensate for, fill in, and cover up its unstable ideological core. [15] Symbols—symbols like the fasces, open to an infinity of modernist, classical, or Romantic restylings, capable of sustaining a multiplicity of genealogical links between the new regime and the Roman imperial state, the *faisceau* of the French revolution, and the risorgimental *fasci*—were a privileged site of self-definition for fascism. This is one reason why image production and image management often took the place of actual economic and institutional reform during the fascist decades. The feature may be shared with other authoritarian systems: "In no democratic country," notes Igor Golomstock, "has the State valued culture so highly and devoted such constant attention to it [as under totalitarianism]." [16] However, it also helps to explain why the Italian regime, unlike totalitarian peers such as the Soviet Union, Nazi Germany, and Maoist China, tended towards an "eclecticism of the spirit" in its cultural policies, encouraging a proliferation of competing formulations of fascist modernity, among which Mussolini felt

3. Ferdinando Gatteschi,
poster for *18 BL*.

free to choose as a function of expediency or circumstance.[17]

In the pursuit of an adequately complex history of cultural modernism, this study reconstructs the climate of an entire era through the detailed analysis of one such formulation: an experimental mass spectacle that was engaged both in negotiating the fascist revolution's relation to its Soviet predecessor and in forging a fascist alternative to bolshevism's "mechanical" mass subject—the fascist ideal of "metallized man." Entitled *18 BL* (after the model name of its truck-heroine), the spectacle was the featured event of Italy's 1934 youth Olympics of art and culture: the newly founded Littoriali della Cultura e dell'Arte.[18] From the outset, the Littoriali had been promoted as *"a great illuminated stage* upon which converges the attention of the regime, of Italians, and . . . of an entire world that looks with extreme interest upon this new method of collective organization of youth in the difficult domain of culture." [19] And *18 BL* was to be the play within the play that would crystallize fascist modes of organization, coordination, and embodiment. The work was the creation of an editorial collective of eight young fascist writers, including the future leader of the Republic of Salò, Alessandro Pavolini. It was directed by a 33-year-old filmmaker, Alessandro Blasetti, and performed at night on the left bank of the river Arno in Florence before 20,000 spectators.

*18 BL* brought together 2,000 to 3,000 amateur actors, an air squadron, an infantry brigade, a cavalry brigade, 50 trucks, 8 tractor plows, 4 field and machine-gun batteries, 10 field ratio stations, and 6 photoelectric units in a stylized Soviet-style representation of the fascist revolution's past, present, and future. However titanic its scale, its ambitions were even greater: to launch a theater of the future, a modern theater *of* and *for* the masses that would once and for all end the crisis of the bourgeois theater.

Such an enterprise was not without important precedents. It would have been unthinkable without the utopic dreams of several generations of modern theater theorists, directors, designers, and architects: a list that would have to include names such as Richard Wagner, Edward Gordon Craig, Sheldon Cheney, Adolphe Appia, Jacques Copeau, Georg Fuchs, Nikolai Evreinov, Vsevolod Meyerhold, Max Reinhardt, Hans Poelzig, Erwin Piscator, Walter Gropius, Filippo Tommaso Marinetti, and Anton Giulio Bragaglia. Unthinkable also without the "interminable history" (as Jacques Rancière has aptly termed it) of efforts to forge an authentic "people's theater," variously sustained by Firmin Gémier, Maurice Pottecher, and Romain Rolland: a theater cast in the same mold as the revolutionary festivals of 1789, (although harkening back to Greek tragedy, Roman circuses, and medieval mystery plays), aimed at transforming the *demos* into a simultaneous maker and consumer of shows.

A product of these twin revolutions of the stage, *18 BL* sought to overcome the bourgeois theater's emphasis upon the individual psychology of protagonists, its reliance upon the star system, and its maintenance of a partition between interior and exterior forms of spectacle (for example, between theater's private dramas and the state's public acts of self-display), and between stage and auditorium. Against the traditional theater's piecemeal approach to representation, it elaborated both a total concept of spectacle and a total theater architecture in harmony with fascism's wholesale theatricalization of Italian public life. Moreover, within this theatricalized national setting, it aspired to fashion a distinctive mass hero for the new mass theater: a being cast in the image of the nation's leader at once individualized and mass-produced; a subject identified with the transnational values of industrialism, as well as with the new image and voice technologies, but in whom the principle of national difference could be modernized and preserved. In short, a mass protagonist who could represent the fascist revolution's continuities with its bolshevik double, but who, in so doing, could also embody the distinctive fascist ethos of constant exertion and fatigue endured by means of individual and collective discipline.

*18 BL* was an extravagant collective endeavor: perhaps the most extravagant theatrical experiment of its kind undertaken under fascist rule. Certainly, it was the most eagerly anticipated—and the most eagerly expunged from the annals of the regime (and, in consequence, from post–World War II historical memory). But however symptomatic *18 BL* may have been of the cultural-political climate of the period, with all its blind spots, ideological confusions, ambitions, tensions, and ambiguities, it was merely one small element within the larger grid of theatrical initiatives undertaken in the Italy of the 1920's and early 1930's. Accordingly, this study opens with an examination of the ways in which the Italian state attempted simultaneously to mobilize and to reorganize the contemporary theater world so as to find a central place within the regime's newly established corporative structures for it. The period in question marks the apex of fascism's half-hearted experiment with "corporative" forms of politico-economic organization: with institutional arrangements, that is, that brought together representatives of labor and capital within state-sponsored corporate entities, each responsible for a given sector of the national economy, as well as for coordinating their policies at the level of a National Council of Corporations. "The Italian nation is an organism having ends, a life, and means superior in power and duration to the single individuals or groups of individuals composing it" read the opening lines of the Labor Charter of 1927; "it is a moral, political, and economic unit which finds its integral realization in the fascist state." [20] So this study's first order of business is to show how the theater would find a central place within this corporate totality by means of institutional innovations, by expanding the traditional audience base of theater in order to promote the development of a national mass audience, and by ideologically inflecting the means by which theatrical works were delivered to this new mass audience in order to emphasize the fascist state's efforts to move "toward the people."

It begins with a synthetic overview of the event's broader cultural-historical context: a context made up of roving mechanized stages, proletarian repertory theaters, outdoor festivals, and newly centralized structures of production, funding, distribution, training, and coordination. After setting the stage in this manner, it turns to the circumstances and nature of Mussolini's call at the April 1933 congress of the Italian Society of Authors and Publishers for the creation of a "theater for 15,000 to 20,000" spectators. The central portion of the book concerns *18 BL* itself: a work that, its authors hoped, would respond to the need for a culture of the corporatist age. It provides a "thick description" (to employ a phrase borrowed by Clifford Geertz from the philosopher Gilbert Ryle) of how the spectacle arose amidst the theoretical debates unleashed by Mussolini's speech; how it was able to put itself forward as a solution to anxieties regarding the inadequacy of fascist culture and a growing gap between the pre– and post–March on Rome generations; how and by whom it was organized and realized; the work's aspirations, achievements, and failures. [21]

The detailed reconstruction of these various aspects of *18 BL*, however intriguing it might be in its own right, is nonetheless not intended as an end in itself. Rather, it serves as a springboard for an inquiry into the place of media, technology, and machinery in the fascist imagination, particularly in its links to fascist models of narrative, historiography, spectacle, and subjectivity. In this context, I map out a broader speculative genealogy of cultural modernism stretching back into the nineteenth century, which yields some unexpected pairings: the dandy and the dictator, the symbolist visionary moment and the fascist mass hallucination, the urban crowd and the industrial machine. The study concludes with a survey of the post–*18 BL* history of the fascist theater. The work's colossal failure created an equally colossal embarrassment for the parties directly or indirectly concerned. Ferocious and frank, the debate it unleashed contributed to an indefinite postponement of the once urgent matter of producing new and distinctive fascist cultural forms. It also reinforced the disjunction between experimental small-scale forms of spectacle and "popular" counterparts associated instead with mass open-air performances at historical or archeological sites, designed to transport works from the distant or recent past into the fascist present.

My principal object of analysis cannot be designated the official theater of the regime. A diversity of theaters coexisted during the 1930's, some traditional in character, some avant-garde, few propagandistic in the ordinary sense. So no simple correlation exists between state sponsorship and explicit political content. The few large-scale works that, like *18 BL*, endeavored to devise specifically fascist forms of theater have been ignored by historians or dismissed (and often properly so). I do not view the effort to dissect a work like *18 BL*, and to reconstruct and interpret the complex social choreography and myth-making that accompanied its staging, as an attempt somehow to rehabilitate a fatally flawed experiment, an experiment that, measured by any purely qualitative yardstick, might well be found wanting. Rather, I view it as a challenge to some of the modes of writing cultural history that have prevailed in the study of Italian fascism.

For reasons having to do with the urgent need to dismantle fascism's cultural and political claims, the first generation of postwar cultural historians was averse to an enterprise of this sort. Whether liberal or Marxist-affiliated, it took as axiomatic Benedetto Croce's notion, articulated in the 1925 "Manifesto of the Anti-Fascist Intellectuals," that fascism and the world of culture were diametrically opposed. Its historiography therefore emphasized apolitical or antifascist writing, turned a blind eye to the political commitments of major writers such as Ungaretti and Pirandello, and elaborated the fiction that neorealism—the characteristic cultural form of the 1930's and 1940's—represented a revolt against the unreality and manipulations of the fascist epoch.

Although its findings were often valuable, this historiographical model was gradually displaced by more complex second- and third-generation approaches determined to address a question that the first-generation historians either could or would not: namely, how did Mussolini's regime maintain a significant degree of support from the Italian populace during a period of over two decades? Terror and censorship were clearly inadequate responses, so, inspired by the groundbreaking work of historians such as Renzo de Felice (on Italian fascism) and George L. Mosse (on Nazi Germany), "consensus"-oriented historians turned their attention instead to the fascist state's instrumentalization of the realms of media, culture, intellectual inquiry, and leisure. Consensus studies have revolutionized the study of fascist cultural politics and yielded seminal works like Philip Cannistraro's *La fabbrica del consenso: Fascismo e mass media* (1975) and Victoria de Grazia's *The Culture of Consent: Mass Organization of Leisure in Fascist Italy* (1981). A necessary privileging of matters of governmental policy and a desire to provide a unified, top-down perspective on fascist culture lead them to emphasize principally how fascism shaped (or attempted to shape) men, women, youth, the media, workers, and so on, however, rather than how these shaping efforts were themselves practically or imaginatively shaped and deflected by individuals, groups, and broader historical forces.

For the same reason, studies concerned with the production of consensus shy away from sustained engagements with fascist aesthetic artifacts, with the result that the latter are usually reduced to the role of documentation confirming or confuting the intent of a given policy initiative. The imaginative worlds these works construct are rarely entered into, and the untidy process that permits prior materials, forms, and myths to be invested with fascist meanings is viewed, as it were, from the outside (paradoxically so, given the inaugural role that works of the imagination played in the rise of fascism). I believe it is precisely analysis of these imaginative worlds that is now beginning to be undertaken in the pursuit of a complementary, as it were, lateral perspective on the cultural history of the fascist decades. Cultural historians, that is, now need to do much as their colleagues in the field of architectural history have been doing for well over a decade: to look beyond the broad taxonomies—in the case of literature, based on confusing self-assigned labels such as *stracittà* and *strapaese* or on groupings by review—that have heretofore occupied them, in order to bring a broader set of methodological tools (psychoanalysis, reception theory, etc.) to bear on the reading of the period's aesthetic production.

In so doing, their task is twofold: on the one hand, to formulate alternate classification schemes and periodizations that help to account for the notable continuities between fascist-period culture and pre- and post-fascist aesthetic production, in order to explain, for instance, the remarkable ease with which categories, projects, and individuals drifted from radical right to left or radical left to right during the first half of the century; and on the other hand, to attend to the deeper question of how and why a generation of writers and artists, as well as substantial segments of their audience, not only heard and gave heed to the regime's call to forge an authentic fascist culture and society, but also expanded upon and reinvented this call, often transforming it into a personal calling.[22]

Fascism's interpellative success in post–World War I Italy, that is, points less to the efficacy of certain violent tactics and policy initiatives or to the crisis of the liberal state than to the fact, acutely understood by Georges Bataille, that fascism elaborated a myth far more powerful and psychologically astute than that provided by either its liberal or socialist rivals.[23] While Mussolini's policy efforts have been well described and documented, it is only in the past decade that the persuasive effects of this revolutionary myth or its ability to sustain a plurality of competing cultural formulations have begun to be accounted for in any detail. Here, I have in mind a research agenda aligned with a wide range of recent work, starting off with *Gli annitrenta; Arte e cultura in Italia*, a groundbreaking show and catalog assembled in 1982 by Renato Barilli and colleagues; Fredric Jameson's *Fables of Aggression* (1979), Pier Giorgio Zunino's *L'ideologia del fascismo* (1985), de Grazia's more recent study, *How Fascism Ruled Women:*

**11**

*Italy, 1922–1945* (1992); Giorgio Ciucci, Diane Ghirardo, Richard Etlin, and Thomas Schumacher's studies on architectural rationalism; Emilio Gentile's *Il mito dello stato nuovo dall'antigiolittismo al fascismo* (1982) and *Il culto del Littorio* (1993); Klaus Theweleit's psychoanalytic study of *Freikorps* officers, *Male Fantasies* (1977–78; trans. 1987–89), Hal Foster's recent inquiries into the modernist "mechanic" imaginary, Alice Yaeger Kaplan's *Reproduction of Banality* (1986), and the work of scholars such as Francesco Tentori, Laura Malvano, Barbara Spackman, and Pietro Cavallo.[24]

The event under consideration in this book, *18 BL*, put forward one distinctive redaction of this fascist myth. Although influential among intellectuals in the heady atmosphere of the early 1930's with its debates on the collective novel, rationalist architecture, fascist typography, muralism, the new objectivity, and realism, the redaction in question would prove less than successful in both the short and long run. In the short run, it yielded what its own director dubbed "the biggest fiasco in the history of international theater,"[25] although, in truth, it was just another fiasco to add to the modernist theater's lineage of grandiose errors and failures (a lineage that surely includes many far more distinguished works, by the likes of Rein-

hardt, Craig, Stanislavsky, Piscator, and Meyerhold). In the long run, it contributed to the collapse of the dream of an entire generation of fascist intellectuals who saw in fascism and fascist corporatism a revolutionary "third way." This failure makes *18 BL* all the more valuable a case study of the uncertainties of fascism in the making. In the pages that follow, I attempt to balance the properly philological demands of reconstructing a forgotten cultural experiment of the mid 1930's, as well as situating it within an appropriate cultural-historical framework, with the properly deconstructive demands of exploring *18 BL*'s conceptual fissures and blind spots. This first (and last) Italian fascist experiment with Soviet-style mass theater was many things to many people: to the fascist youth organizations, a training exercise that would build a bridge between the generations; to its young director and his supporters, a battering ram against cultural-political conservatives; to the theater community, a solution to the crisis of the traditional theater; to Mussolini's state, a potential answer to the vexing question of fascism's cultural identity; to the fascist right, an emblem of the enemy within. In this microhistorical study, this cluster of meanings is explored and their larger implications for a history of modernism are drawn out.

Viktor Shklovsky's remark, cited earlier, that in the wake of the 1917 revolution, the living fabric of Russian life was being "transformed into the theatrical" could well be applied to fascist Italy. To a degree unequaled in the nation's modern history, theater came to permeate the fabric of Italian life in the 1920's and 1930's, from the streets to the public squares to the factory floor to the corridors of the Palazzo Venezia, il Duce's headquarters. Among the fascist hierarchs, no fewer than six ministers or members either of the Grand Council or Directorate were involved to some degree in the prose and lyrical theater: Enrico Corradini, author of *Giulio Cesare* (Julius Caesar); Roberto Farinacci, who in 1926 penned a doggerel play entitled *Redenzione* (Redemption); Galeazzo Ciano, foreign minister between 1936 and 1943, and author of *La fortuna di Amleto* (Hamlet's luck) and a brief comedy, *Er fonno d'oro*, as well as of a body of theater criticism; Cornelio di Marzio, creator of *Uomini e giorni* (Men and days) and *Occhi di gufo* (The old owl's

eyes); Alessandro Pavolini, future minister of popular culture, author of *Le fatalone* (The vamps) and organizer of *18 BL*; and, finally, Edmondo Rossoni, head of the fascist labor unions and minister of agriculture between 1935 and 1939, co-author of *Il canto del lavoro* (The song of labor), with musical accompaniment provided by the composer Pietro Mascagni. Although not an author, Achille Starace, the dull-witted national secretary of the Fascist National Party (PNF), was also an avid patron and sometime sponsor of the Italian theater.[1]

Never one to be outdone by members of his entourage (however laughable the value of their contributions), Benito Mussolini himself dabbled frequently in the contemporary theater. During the 1930's, he collaborated with the playwright/librettist Giovacchino Forzano on a trilogy of historical tragedies depicting the lives of Napoleon, Cavour, and Julius Caesar, respectively entitled *Campo di maggio* (Champ de Mai; 1930), *Villafranca* (1931),

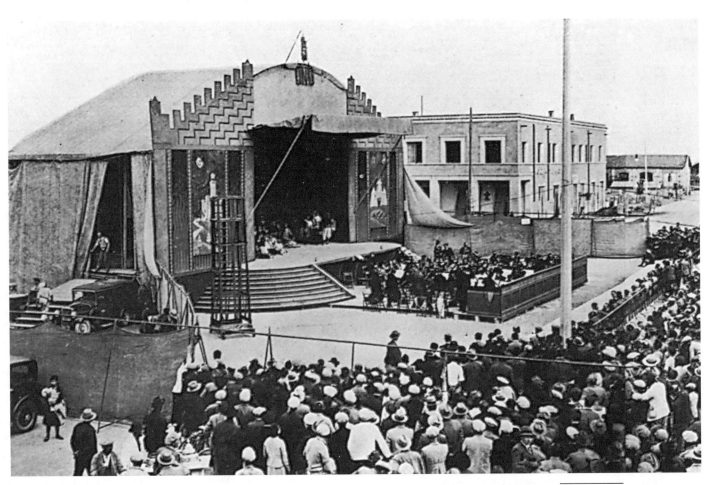

4. Thespian car theater, performance of Verdi's *Il trovatore* in Littoria; from the OND pamphlet *Carro di Tespi* (1936).

and *Cesare* (1939).[2] To these modest exercises in playwrighting one must add a vigorous participation in debates concerning state patronage of the theater and opera. On at least one occasion, il Duce even found the time to make detailed suggestions for the revision of a dramatic text: the tragedy *Simma*, by the much-admired Francesco Pastonchi, to whom he offered the closing thought (borrowed from Anatole France) "Caressez votre phrase: elle finira pour [*sic*] vous sourire" ("Caress your sentence: she will end up smiling back at you").[3]

The fascist hierarchs' involvement in theater must be viewed against the backdrop of a widely perceived, and even more widely decried worldwide crisis of the traditional theater during the 1920's and 1930's. "We have not yet produced a dramatic aesthetic to express our age," proclaimed the French director-founder of the Vieux Colombier theater school, Jacques Copeau. The situation was so catastrophic, Copeau and many others felt, that "in order to save the theater, we must leave it. Those who want to stay in it will be condemned to being nothing but entertainers or aesthetes. As for us, we are not afraid to admit that we are tired of keeping alive a cult whose deity is absent, and we are going outdoors, on the road, to try to meet him there."[4] Whether imagined by Copeau or by contemporary Italian theater critics, the crisis was thought to be one of inadequate facilities, of an aging community of actors and authors, of a diminishing contemporary repertory, of a faltering star system and patronage network, and, first and foremost, of audiences in decline because (or such at least was a widespread perception) of growing competition from movies and

sporting events.[5] It was as an expression of the fascist leaders' personal commitment to theater and in response to the latter crisis that the Italian government adopted a series of cultural policy measures in the later 1920's, designed to achieve four interrelated goals:[6]

*First*, to absorb the fragmented and regionally based world of theater into the regime's fully centralized corporative structures: structures that were first being put into place during this very period, and that were accordingly identified with fascism's alternative to socialist and liberal approaches to institutional reform and modernization.

*Second*, to expand the traditional audience of theater and music, whether from the standpoint of topography or of social class, in order to promote the development of a genuine mass and national public. This goal was to be pursued both on the regional level, where dialect theater would be viewed, at least for a time, as acceptable, and on the national level, where efforts would be made to popularize the national cultural heritage—all this in the interests of forging a mass society "individualized" both internally (through a recognition that there exist natural hierarchical distinctions between the elite and the mass) and externally (through a sense of shared national identity and difference).

*Third*, to alter and ideologically inflect the means by which and the context within which theatrical and musical works were delivered to this emerging mass of individuals in order to emphasize the fascist state's vigorous efforts to move "towards the people."

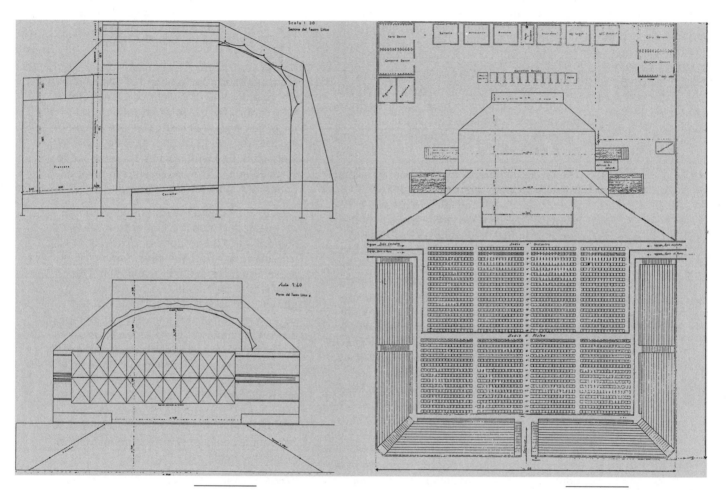

5. Cross-section and frontal
diagrams of stage, operatic
thespian car; from OND,
*Carro di Tespi* (1936).

6. Diagram of theater including auditorium, operatic
thespian car. From OND,
*Carro di Tespi* (1936).

*Fourth*, to encourage the development of specifically "fascist" cultural forms, forms that would allow fascism's distinctive redaction of modernity to crystallize fully.

The first of these aims was addressed via the establishment in December 1930 of the Corporazione dello Spettacolo (Corporation of Spectacle), a centralized national entity bringing together individuals at all levels of the music, theater, and film industries (and, later, all professional athletes), with the express aim of harmonizing all conflicting interests in the service of the national good.[7] The second and third objectives were addressed via the creation and promotion of philodramatic associations, "theatrical Saturdays," thespian cars, and open-air festivals. The fourth was undertaken in a variety of manners, from public appeals to the artistic community that it forge "an art of fascist times" to playwriting competitions, sponsored by governmental entities such as the Opera Nazionale Dopolavoro (OND) and Gruppi Universitari Fascisti (GUF), "for a theatrical work written by an Italian citizen, dealing with a theme imbued with the fascist atmosphere."[8]

Like open-air festivals, Italian philodramatic associations predated the March on Rome, but it was under fascism that they came into their own. They were amateur drama clubs that trained workers in the theater arts, now under the aegis of the fascist after-work organization, OND.[9] Such clubs had been far scarcer before the fascist era and had often been linked to socialist "people's houses" (*case del popolo*), as in the case of the Socialist Workers' Theater of Milan. But by 1938 they numbered over 2,000 and performed in 1,200 theaters all over Italy, in addition to which they staged 360 open-air performances on thespian cars before audiences totaling nearly 200,000 spectators. If the philodramatists' repertory and stagecraft remained for the most part traditional (and embarrassingly so in the eyes of fascist and nonfascist intellectuals alike), their intended intellectual horizons were hardly provincial.[10] The juries of the annual philodramatic contests always included major contemporary critics like Silvio d'Amico. The movement's standard reference manual—authored by no less a figure than Antonio Valente, one of the designers of the 1932 Exhibition of the Fascist Revolution and inventor (along with Forzano) of the thespian cars—called for a modern theater cast in the image of "our era of the masses": a theater suited to the "skeptical and, in a way, atheistic spirit of the modern world" and founded, not on individual protagonists, but instead on an "aesthetics of the company" (*l'estetica dei complessi*).[11] Such qualitative considerations aside, however, the sheer scale of the movement is striking. As early as 1931, the philodramatists performed 13,733 plays in a single year. By 1938 the number of regular philodramatic actors had surpassed 32,000, and the movement was administering 45 acting schools, 10 directing schools, and 469 regional theater libraries.[12]

In addition to this mass mobilization of amateur dramatists, there were initiatives focused on the professional theater. So-called theatrical Saturdays, reduced-rate matinee performances in smaller cities, reached over 400,000 workers and peasants in 1936 alone. But the thespian cars and open-air spectacles were far more indicative of the regime's determination to forge a national mass audience. Thespian cars were mechanized traveling playhouses modeled both on native touring companies and on precedents such as Pavel Gaideburov and N. F. Skarskaya's Peredvizhnoi teatr (Mobile theater) in Russia and, especially, Firmin Gémier's French Théâtre National Ambulant (National itinerant theater). The former dated from 1903 and enjoyed considerable success during the early years of the Soviet revolution, closing only in 1928; the latter, a collapsible theater transported by steam tractors, designed to hold 1,600 spectators, had begun its wanderings across France on Bastille Day 1911.[13]

Although the original idea was sometimes attributed to a young writer named Goffredo Ginocchio, the thespian cars were designed by Antonio Valente and first developed in the late 1920's by the OND under the guidance of Giovacchino Forzano and the watchful eye of Augusto Turati, the PNF's national secretary.[14] (As of May 1927, the PNF had assumed direct control over the OND.) They were partly inspired by the success of mass sporting events, at least to judge by the following anecdote recounted by Forzano:

I had never been to a soccer match, so I accepted [Giuseppe Bottai's] invitation. At the stadium, Bottai introduced me to Augusto Turati, the party secretary. At a certain point in the match, observing the crowd's enthusiasm for this battle of feet, I exclaimed: "If only they would get so enthused at open-air theater performances!" Turati responded: "My dear Forzano, the OND is looking into the construction of a small transportable theater that will be able to reach small towns [paesetti] where there are no permanent theaters. Why don't you take charge of this initiative?"[15]

A first prototype was developed by Valente, Forzano, and (it would appear) Aristide Rotunno in 1928–29. It was inaugurated with performances of Vittorio Alfieri's *Oreste* and Leopoldo Marenco's *Il falconiere di Pietro Ardena* in Rome's Piazzale del Pincio (attended by Mussolini), Piazza Navona, and PNF stadium, after which there followed a highly successful national tour, involving 67 shows in 35 cities and towns. Over the next two years, four squadrons of thespian cars were built. Larger and more technically refined than the prototype, each had its own company of up to 400 actors, dancers, musicians, and staff. Three were dedicated to performances of plays by such authors as Goldoni, d'Annunzio, Forzano, Rosso di San Secondo, Chiarelli, Bonelli, and Pirandello; a fourth specialized in performances of operas from the current lyric repertory, principally by established composers such as Puccini, Verdi, Leoncavallo, Rossini, Giordano, and Mascagni.[16]

For close to ten years, these four companies crisscrossed the entire peninsula every spring and summer, performing in public squares before small-town audiences ranging in size from 2,000 to 15,000. Their 1937 schedule, for instance, took them over 10,000 miles, with the drama cars performing 124 times before 170,000 spectators and the opera car performing 75 times before 430,000 spectators. The tours' immediate purpose was to bring provincial audiences into the fold of Italian high culture. They were intended to further fascism's "spiritual and intellectual reclamation" of Italy and to propagate the national language "in those areas where dialects still hold our marvelous language in the thrall of deformity."[17] But

7. Thespian trucks, from *Comoedia* 15.7 (July 15–Aug. 15, 1933).

8. (opposite) Thespian car under construction. From OND, *Carro di Tespi* (1936).

"national ambulation" was at least as important to their mission as "cultural dissemination." "Nomadism," Frederick Brown observes of the French Théâtre National Ambulant, "went hand in hand with an ideal of tribal oneness or of unindividuated mass for whose sake [Gémier] marshaled all the technology provided by a civilization that he did not suffer gladly, the movable stage recalling David's floats of 1793 while prefiguring those that would ride on the [Popular Front's] human tide of 1936."[18] Similarly, the thespian cars embraced technology as the hallmark of a fully modernized and rationalized future Italy.

On a deeper level, thus, *the medium was the true message*. Mobile and modular, capable of rapid assembly and disassembly by teams of skilled technicians, and featuring up-to-date stage and lighting designs, the thespian cars functioned as vehicles for fascist values.[19] Their arrival in a city already constituted something of an event, thanks to the anticipation stirred up by media coverage, by posters, and by efforts on the OND's part to coordinate transportation of rural workers and peasants to the show. Such expectations would come to a head on the day of the performance as the trucks rolled into the city's public square, whereupon an army of assembly technicians (assisted by hundreds of hired hands) would set about the task of erecting the canvas and steel armature; positioning lights, curtains, and sets; and filling out the seating areas.[20] Always well attended, this pre-performance show was meant to display the efficiency achieved through corporative organization and was celebrated for this by the regime's propagandists. Modular modes of construction and

organization were new to Italy, and here the modular utopia is emphatically architectural *and* human: "The scientific discipline of work is applied with the most rigorous automatism. Every gesture has a function and is brief, resolute, firm. Hands and shoulders turn to pieces whose position in the construction is known precisely. Suddenly, the scaffolding of tubes rises solidly up into the air. Every worker is a technician; he lives and masters the sector of material for which he is responsible."[21] Broken down into specialized and segmented tasks that could be mastered by individual laborers working in close collaboration, the "scientific discipline of work" displayed in the building process may sound like just the sort of Taylorist ideology espoused by Henry Ford and embraced by Lenin during the first phase of the Soviet revolution.[22] And in large part it was. But the end product towards which it strove was not just a technological utopia founded on an ethos of functionalism and emancipatory automatism. Rather, it aspired to realize an aesthetic totality (identical to the nation): a totality amounting to *more than the sum of any given set of individual parts, functions or elements*. In the case of the thespian cars, the totality in question was at once human, mechanical, aerial, and electrical. Explicitly associated with the advent of beauty, it was alleged to result from fascism's "miraculous" overcoming of human nature, time, and space—an overcoming whose authenticity was guaranteed, however, by its being nature-, time-, and space-bound:

Everything is intelligence and certainty and precision. The skeleton takes shape before the ecstatic eyes of onlookers; it becomes walls, pillars, and vaults. From the hammer to the bolt to the pulley to the dynamo to the generator that distributes and multiplies and interrupts the electrical current for purposes of lighting: the entire gamut of devices, as well as the full range of technicians, stand before the people. A people who see and learn just how rapidly and easily fascism's school of innovation transfigures crude matter into style, harmony, and beauty. Here then is the miracle of transformation, of construction, of making things men time space obey: the miracle, that is, of the corporative age.[23]

The rapid and easy passage described here from crude matter to art, from mere technology to a transfigured totality (the corporative age), was central to the mythos of the thespian cars, the political style of the fascist state, and, as will soon be seen, the concept of spectacle elaborated in *18 BL*. It was also integral to the design of the stage and, in particular, to the stage's most evocative feature: the Fortuny cupola.[24] Invented by the Catalan–born but Venice–based designer, painter, and lighting engineer Mariano Fortuny, this ellipsoid cupola constituted the structural core of the mobile theaters. It consisted of a nearly ten-meter-tall canvas sack hung from an armature of tubes and held taut by a powerful electric vacuum attached from the back.[25] Horizonless, seemingly infinite luminous fields could be created by casting indirect light against its smooth surfaces: fields representing skyscapes, moving clouds, starlight, and sunsets so effectively that they might easily be confused with the actual vault of the heavens overhead.[26] Indeed, such confusions would become essential to the dramaturgy of the thespian cars. Just as the assembly process had dramatized the passage from mere technology to an aesthetic totality, so the spectacles would manipulate the interplay between the circumambient sky and the illusions produced within the cupola by technical wizardry in order to hint that the theater itself had become the site of a vertical opening: an opening through which, figuratively speaking, the collectivity might be lifted heavenwards.

One could go on detailing other technical features on the thespian cars: their complex electrical control booths, their use of longitudinal tracks for rapid set changes, and so forth. One could also document their increasing use as platforms for political propaganda: the fascist anthems "Giovinezza" and "The Hymn to Rome" were sung at the conclusion of the opera car's shows in 1937, for instance, a year during which "the most significant epic lyrics concerned with the Fascist Empire" were recited during intermissions.[27] But the key point would remain much the same: through these and other aspects of their design, construction, and staging, the cars portrayed the fascist government (however disingenuously) as a ubiquitous, active, and disciplined agent of cultural and political modernization reaching out directly to attend to the needs of the Italian masses and to forge the nation into a unified whole. Moreover, the vision of fascist modernity conveyed by the cars and by their stagecraft was not to be contemplated in isolation. Rather, the "marvelous reality" they would bring to the provinces was to resonate not only with the open sky but also, and most especially, with the classical, medieval, and renaissance architectural backdrops provided by Italy's towns and cities, so as to imply a genealogical link between the nation's past and present grandeur.[28]

Such oblique allusions to cultural tradition would give way to more direct ones during

9. Photomontage of Mussolini profiled against thespian car theater under construction. From OND, *Carro di Tespi* (1936).

the period of Mussolini's imperial adventures in Ethiopia, when open-air festivals brought as many as two million spectators a year to sites such as the Baths of Caracalla, the Basilica of Maxentius, and the Roman arena in Verona. The history of theater performances at ancient Greek and Roman archeological sites is a long and rich one in Italy, predating the March on Rome by sev-

eral decades and, in at least one instance, centuries.[29] But there is no disputing the fact that, if fascism did not discover these sorts of spectacles, it adopted them as its own and was instrumental in ensuring their diffusion and popular success—a success that endures to the present day. Before 1922, only a small handful of Italy's ancient theaters had been in even occasional use (mostly thanks to the efforts of Alessandro Romanelli). By the late 1930's, so many ancient theaters and performance sites had been restored (and, when necessary, "reconstructed") that the list of sites in either occasional or regular current use had swollen to include Paestum, Siracusa, Verona, Fiesole, Ostia, Taormina, Pola, and Sabratha, in addition to which one would have to count renaissance settings like Milan's Castello Sforzesco and Florence's Boboli gardens, which were employed for special open-air performances. The precise circumstances that led to the recovery of each site varied, as did the use to which each was put. There was also considerable variation in the degree of central government involvement, particularly in the start-up phase. But, as the cases of Paestum, Siracusa, and Verona demonstrate (the special case of Sabratha will be considered in this study's closing pages), the entire web of initiatives formed an eminently modern, cohesive politics of spectacle that sought to provide "hygienic" outdoor alternatives to the "sickly" interiors of the bourgeois theater, to popularize elite forms of culture (much as television would do in subsequent decades) and to forge a new sense of nationhood both by promoting interregional tourism and by placing the Italian masses face to face with the past, present, and future "Mediterranean solar genius of their race."

The ruins of the ancient Greek city of Paestum (modern Pesto) were first excavated in 1830. Excavations resumed in 1907 but were interrupted again in the years following World War I. So it was only during the mid 1920's that a full-scale restoration of the city was undertaken and undertaken within the symbolically charged framework provided by the *bonifica integrale* program: the fascist government's campaign to increase agricultural production by reclaiming wastelands, building new irrigation systems, and reforesting areas suffering from soil erosion. The concept of a national *bonifica* (derived from the Latin *bonus*, "good," and *ficare*, a late variant of *facere*, "to make") evoked at once the artificial conversion of useless lands to productive purposes, the clearing of mines and unexploded projectiles from a battlefield, an act of beautification through the removal of impurities, the cashing in of bonuses or bonds, and, perhaps most telling of all, the operation of tempering steel to ensure hardness. Fascist oratory played upon the full range of meanings as it gradually extended the notion into the domains of demographics and culture, such that the program became "integral" also in the sense of all-embracing. Perhaps nowhere was it able to do so with greater ease than at Paestum, where land and theater reclamation went hand in hand. Silting in the mouth of the river Silarus had long placed this portion of Basilicata at the mercy of malaria-bearing mosquitoes, as a result of which the recovery of the surrounding farmlands was a necessary precondition for the transformation of Paestum's temples into a performance site. The first such spectacle took place in 1932 and involved a dramatization of two idylls by Theocritus, *The Amorous Colloquy* and *The*

10. (opposite) Electrical control booth for operatic thespian car theater, inside view. From OND, *Carro di Tespi* (1936).

*Sorceress*, translated into modern Italian, and a mime by Herodas, *The Shoemaker*, translated into Sicilian, all three accompanied by dance and contemporary music (composed by Arthur Honegger, Giuseppe Mulè, and Ildebrando Pizzetti). Like its successors, this first event was organized by the Istituto Nazionale del Dramma Antico, a public entity founded in 1925 with Mussolini's support, which passed under the direct authority of the Ministry of National Education in 1929 and coordinated its efforts with entities like OND. Its mission was described as being "to gather the people together at classical celebrations that point to the [people's] past and unveil anew the beauty of our simple and serene art; and to summon the new intellectual classes to collaborate in this work of regeneration, making them look backward, so that when they look forward, this vision of the past greatness of our race will infuse with greater amplitude and, therefore, dignity their vision of our artistic and political tomorrow." [30] At Paestum this backward/forward-looking task was interpreted as an invitation to create dramatic "reevocations" of classical festivals: *modern* imaginative reconstructions mixing choreographies, music, poetry, and choruses. Accordingly, subsequent programs would include stagings of the Panathenaea, the Athenian festival honoring the goddess Athena, of additional Theocritan idylls, and even of a "Dionysian Mystery" (loosely based on Euripides' *Bacchae*).

Paestum was the younger and smaller sibling of Siracusa, the principal ancient Greek theater managed by the Istituto Nazionale del Drama Antico. Whereas the former was employed for adaptations of minor genres

and festivals to the stage, the latter was reserved for the large-scale presentation of ancient tragedies, comedies, and satiric dramas. The Siracusa amphitheater's modern history stretches back to 1914, when, only six years after its restoration was completed, Count Mario Tommaso Gargallo organized a successful production of Aeschylus's *Agamemnon* under the direction of Ettore Romagnoli and with sets by Duilio Cambelotti. The theater returned to life in 1921 with a Romagnoli/Cambelotti staging of *The Choeforoi*, after which time its performances grew in frequency and number, particularly after the Istituto assumed control and became a state-supported entity. By 1939 its success was such that the fascist theater historian Mario Corsi could exult:

The number of spectators has grown noticeably every year, as has the involvement of the great popular masses, who have been able to attend from every corner of Sicily and Italy thanks to the help provided by the regime's institutions. The OND organizes convoys for every play cycle, thereby contributing with great efficacy to the diffusion of classical drama and to the coming into being of the mass theater that is one of the regime's most brilliant intellectual accomplishments. Only a few years back this form of spectacle would have been thought of as an erudite form of entertainment of interest only to the privileged elite. Now that it has been made available to the people, it has proven of such beauty and artistry that it moves the soul of a humble artisan no less than that of an intellectual. In the Greek Theater of Siracusa, Greek tragedy, which was created for the people and its spiritual edification, has thus recovered its exalted originary function. [31]

However hyperbolically phrased, Corsi's main claim is mostly borne out by the facts. Price reductions on tickets, visits for youth and worker groups organized by entities

11. Euripides' *Bacchae* performed among the Greek temples of Paestum. From Corsi, *Il teatro all'aperto in Italia* (1938).

like the OND, special performances, transportation discounts: all doubtless helped to shape a new public for Greek tragedy. But an equally important key to the popular acclaim garnered by the ancient theater festival at Siracusa (and, for that matter, Paestum) was the interpretation of Greek culture that it presented to this audience: namely, one that was antihistoricist in tone. The 1914 *Agamemnon* had still been shaped around philological and archeological considerations. It strove to present Aeschylus's tragedy much as it might have been in the fourth century before Christ, on the basis of the best available scientific data. During the ensuing decades, the Istituto underwent a modernist turn of mind: "It sought forms of expression better suited to modern aesthetic norms. It set out to banish even the slightest attempt at archeological reconstruction in decor and aimed to put forward a contemporary interpretation of the spirit that animates the masterpieces of the Greek theater, in such a way as to render them the living patrimony of humankind once again."[32] The shift from a cult of historical accuracy (however speculative) to one of "living" actuality, or from science to myth, was symptomatic

12. The Greek theater at Siracusa during a performance of Aeschylus's *Agamemnon*. From Corsi, *Il teatro all'aperto in Italia* (1930).

**27**

of the epoch as a whole. In this particular case, it was masterminded by Romagnoli, an eminent and prolific classicist, ardent fascist, and ally of Filippo Tommaso Marinetti (both were members of the Italian Academy). From his earliest translations of ancient dramatic works, Romagnoli had championed forceful approaches to updating antique culture and rejected narrowly antiquarian or scientistic types of historiography. Hence the ease with which, in the course of a 1930 inaugural speech given in the Campidoglio in commemoration of the bimillenarian celebration of Virgil's birth, he could identify Augustan imperialism with its Mussolinian counterpart, and ancient agrarianism with the fascist "Battle for Grain."[33] Romagnoli's goal was to resuscitate the classical past by reinventing it and embedding it in the present, in keeping with which objective his Siracusan collaborations with Cambellotti were never passéist or backward-looking. They sought to transform the literary monuments of the Greek past into living monuments that could breathe anew through innovations like the addition of contemporary sets and music, or through changes like the reassignment to actors, ballet dancers, and an on-stage

13. The stage of the Siracusa Greek theater during a performance of Euripides' *Hippolytus* (1936). From Mario Corsi, *Il teatro all'aperto in Italia* (1939).

singing chorus of the functions traditionally reserved for the tragic chorus.[34]

Much of what has been said about Paestum and Siracusa could also be said of the Roman arena in Verona, despite the difference in repertories. With a capacity of up to 20,000 spectators, it was easily the largest ancient theater in regular use during the fascist decades. It was also the most venerable, having hosted a wide variety of shows throughout the eighteenth and nineteenth century. In the words of the Venetian dramatist Carlo Goldoni: "Spectacles are performed in the central area: races, bullfights, and, in the summer, comedies are presented without any other light than that of the sun. For which purpose a wooden theater is erected upon robust trestles in the midst of the arena for the summer and dismantled in winter; and the best of Italy's companies alternate in coming to show off their talent."[35] The tradition was sustained into the second half of the subsequent century with the so-called "Diurnal Theater," where the sixteen-year-old Eleanora Duse made her debut in Shakespeare's *Romeo and Juliet*. The arena's recent history began on August 10, 1913, when the first of eight performances of Verdi's *Aida* was held in celebration of the composer's 100th birthday. Enormously successful, it established an operatic tradition

14. Verdi's *Aida* performed in the Roman arena in Verona (1913). From Mario Corsi, *Il teatro all'aperto in Italia* (1939).

that has continued to this day (despite interruptions during both world wars).

Between 1913 and 1929, the Verona festival was organized and sustained by private promoters, receiving only limited state support. By 1930, however, the economic malaise brought on by the Depression had changed the situation. Attendance had begun to waver, and the festival promoters had suffered repeated losses. This led the city of Verona to step in and to place the arena under the management of the Ente Autonomo della Fiera di Verona (already responsible for organizing the Veronese trade fair).[36] The arrangement lasted four years, until a specialized entity, the Ente Autonomo per gli Spettacoli Lirici nell'Arena, was created under the authority of Ciano's Ministry of Press and Propaganda (later redubbed the Ministry of Popular Culture). This reshuffling did not produce any surface shifts. The repertory remained much the same: overwhelmingly nineteenth-century Italian, often with nationalistic overtones, complemented by the occasional Wagnerian swerve (one in 1937 probably conditioned by Mussolini's impending Berlin journey). Likewise, the scale and grandeur of the productions: the limit having already been reached back in 1930 through the addition of a modern lighting system and the recovery of all remaining "dead" spots in the coliseum either for seating or for sets. But it did ensure the arena's future via its full integration into the fabric of initiatives I have been surveying in this chapter. Group voyages were organized through local fascist organizations, special ticket packages were made available to encourage certain social groups to experience melodrama firsthand: an art form in which, as the pamphlets never tired in repeating, Italian primacy was indisputable. A national and international campaign was orchestrated by various state agencies so as to transform the vast arena into a privileged tourist destination: a destination that identified the great mass theaters of Roman antiquity with the new mass civilization being forged by fascism.

# 3

The initiatives just described reached as many as 3 million Italians a year and helped to bring total annual ticket sales for the theater and musical performances up to a peak of around 20 million (or to about one ticket purchased per 2.2 citizens).[1] But they were never intended as anything more than a preparatory stage. A second phase was always envisioned (although its fulfillment was regularly postponed) in which the prefascist repertory would yield its place to an authentically fascist repertory made up of works that would convey the "revolutionary spirit" of the times.[2] Ancient tragedies and comedies, the operatic repertory of the prior century, no matter how audaciously modernized or magnificently staged, simply would not do. A political revolution required a revolution in the theater, or so it was thought. And any political revolution that could not breed a revolution on stage ran the risk of being seen as no revolution at all.

The campaign for a new repertory was led by the likes of the futurist director/stage designer Anton Giulio Bragaglia, who had called for a state-supported revolutionary fascist theater and denounced the too tradition-bound dramaturgy of the philodramatists, outdoor festivals, and thespian cars. "The fascist revolution remains antirevolutionary in the theater," Bragaglia complained in an open letter to Mussolini that served as a preface to *Il teatro della revoluzione* (The theater of the revolution; 1929), "no man has been transformed, none of the fascist era's directives have been carried over into the theater; il Duce goes to see *Norma* staged as it would have been in the time of Belli [*sic*], or *Traviata* at the time of Napoleon [III] and his goatee."[3] These criticisms translated into an urgent call for a cultural-political revolution: "The hour of fascist revelations in the theater has sounded for us at last. Our contribution marks a crucial moment in the regeneration of the scenic arts that fascism can and will accomplish."[4] Small experimental theaters like Bragaglia's own Teatro degli Indipendenti, Luigi Pirandello's Teatro d'Arte, and Dario Niccodemi's Teatro Sperimentale di Bologna (all of which had received government subventions during the 1920's) were no longer adequate vehicles for fascist values. Bragaglia's solution, however, remained equivocal. On the one hand, he argued that true fascist theater would have to address the masses: "Beyond defending our technical laboratory, we want to offer our definitive [product] to the people, without having to worry about commercial constraints, so that we too can do things on a grand scale. Generally speaking, art cannot be made without protection; all the more so antitraditional art, which, when made outside the revolutionary's lair, is only possible with the regime's power [behind it]."[5] On the other hand, in concluding remarks to a six-month referendum in *La Fiera Letteraria* on the virtues of small versus large theaters, he supported the majority vote for small experimental theaters.[6]

Whether discussed by avant-gardists, cultural moderates, or by PNF bureaucrats of various stripes, this future fascist repertory was rarely conceived of in narrowly propagandistic terms. Propagandistic intent, crude didacticism, and an excessive reliance on mechanization were among the attributes of the Soviet and Weimar revolutionary theaters most regularly decried in the cultural debates of the early 1930's, to the point where in 1932 Mussolini went so far as to turn down a proposal for the building of two national theaters on the grounds that "the belief that modern facilities [alone] will save the prose theater" is "a typically mechanico-positivist, materialist error."[7] Socialism, it was claimed by many, had confused propaganda with art, the material context with the spirit of the artwork. Fascism would promote a more exalted art: an art conjoining the real and the ideal, total in its scope and transformative in its impact on the audience; an art free from the obligation to educate or to persuade, so that it could educate and persuade on a higher/deeper spiritual plane.[8] The precise formula would be worked out by the first generation of fascist dramatists. But there was general agreement that it would conjoin an elemental form of "realism" with something more: magic, mystery, myth, a sense of secular, but nonetheless sacred, rituality.

Numerous playwrights took on this mission even before it was formally announced. A trickle of overtly fascist works had begun to appear during the mid 1920's by now justly forgotten authors: works like Ernesto Forzano's *Rapsodia Fascista* (Fascist rhapsody; 1926), a symbolist play of d'Annunzian inspiration whose three acts are envisioned as a sequence of sacrifices leading to a revolutionary holocaust under the aegis of "The Genius of Rome" (Il Genio di Roma) and "Italicus—the animating spirit of fascism."[9] They were succeeded by only slightly more dignified attempts at political theater on the part of emerging writers like Vitaliano Brancati, author of a one-act play entitled *Everest* (1928) and of the patriotic drama *Piave* (1932). The first of these texts is typical of the earliest attempts to codify the genre. Defined by its author as a "myth," a literary genre like the "fable" favored by the later Pirandello, it is enveloped in a densely mystical, visionary atmosphere. It recounts the tale of a city 2,000 years in the future, built high on the slopes of Mount Everest, whose inhabitants succeed (after many travails) in freeing the summit of its encumbering foliage, only to discover the colossal portrait of Mussolini sculpted beneath and facing the orient. The unveiling provokes a recognition on their part that their exalted existence—exalted, because here, as in Nietzsche, height implies moral sublimity—is the direct product of His monumental will. In Brancati's own words, spoken during a visit to the Palazzo Venezia: "*Everest* is inspired by an instinct for high mountains upon which vertigo has become the normal climate. This feeling can be adequately conveyed only if the work is performed outdoors. If done so on a grand scale, the result will be a classical spectacle, well-chiseled [*scolpito*] in a mythic sense, closing with a dance." [10]

Brancati's youthful myth trades in the same brand of Duce-worship found in a wide variety of contemporary works, two cases in point being Saverio Grana's *Il mito di Roma* (The myth of Rome; 1927) and Mario Bonetti and Lelio Montanari's *L'artefice* (The artificer; 1932)—one of a number of plays permeated by the presence of an unnamed, and therefore all the more godlike, commander.[11] Several government-sponsored play and scriptwriting contests with obligatory fascist themes tried to promote a higher caliber of products, but none yielded a single entry deemed acceptable by the contest judges. To summarize: various attempts were made to create a "theater of fascist times" between 1925 and 1932. Just about all were found wanting, whether by the regime's cultural-political arbiters or by its opponents.

So it was to Italy's authors that Mussolini turned in April 1933 during the fiftieth anniversary congress of the Italian Society of Authors and Publishers (SIAE), insisting that, while it can promulgate good laws and integrate writers within its administrative structures, "a state cannot create its own literature." [12] He then went on officially to summon them to become interpreters of the era's collective passions:

I have heard reference made to a crisis of the theater. This crisis is real, but it cannot be attributed to the cinema's success. It must be considered from a dual perspective, at once spiritual and material. The spiritual aspect concerns authors, the material aspect the number of seats. It is necessary to prepare a theater of masses, a theater able to accommodate 15,000 or 20,000 persons. La Scala was adequate a century ago, when the population of Milan totaled 180,000 inhabitants. It is not today, when the population has reached a million. The scarcity of seats creates the need for high prices, which keep the crowds away. But theaters, which, in my view, possess greater educational efficacy than do cinemas, must be designed for the people, just as dramatic works must have the breadth the people demand. They must stir up the great collective passions, be inspired by a sense of intense and deep humanity, and bring to the stage that which truly counts in the life of the spirit and in human affairs. Enough with the notorious romantic "triangle" that has so obsessed us to this day! The full range of triangular configurations is by now long exhausted. Find a dramatic expression for the collective's passions and you will see the theaters packed.[13]

The "theater of masses" evoked in Mussolini's speech rehearses a number of ideas that were already in wide circulation from the publication in 1903 of Romain Rolland's *The People's Theater* through the November 1919 opening of the Berlin Großes Schauspielhaus (Great Spectacle Hall). On the one hand, the phrase envisaged a physical plant more like a modern sports arena than like the great theaters of the nineteenth century: an arena like Reinhardt's "theater of 5,000" where large numbers of spectators could be accommodated at sharply reduced cost within the confines of a space specifically structured in accord with the new realities of industrial mass society. In keeping not only with fascism's cult of the oceanic mob, but also with ancient Roman precedent, Mussolini's arena would have a capacity, not of 5,000, but of 20,000 (this was, as noted earlier, the capacity of the amphitheater at Verona after its modernization in 1930). On the other hand, the phrase designated a popular theater, cast in the mold of Rolland's historical dramas, that would forego the representation of romantic triangles, boudoir dramas, and the like, favoring instead "the great collective passions" that characterized life in the new century. "Cherchez la foule" (seek out the crowd) would be the motto of this new fascist theater. Not uncharacteristically, Mussolini left to others the task of determining the precise nature of the modern crowd's passions and what dramatic form and forum would be appropriate for works of the requisite scale and breadth.

Although short on details, Mussolini's SIAE speech provided general guidelines for subsequent debate, as well as a suggestive set of slogans—always one of il Duce's strong suits: theater for 20,000, theater of masses, theater for masses, theater of masses for masses. Far more detailed proposals were formulated in the wake of the SIAE congress as rival cultural forces leapt at the opportunity to connect the new labels with old projects carried over from earlier campaigns for the foundation of national theaters or from debates—like that, already referred to, in *La Fiera Letteraria*—over the virtues (or vices) of large-scale theaters. Some of these proposals would fall squarely within the bounds of Mussolini's "material" perspective: the case of Gaetano Ciocca's mass theater and a rival proposal by Telesio Interlandi. Others, like Bontempelli's musings on theater, myth, and sport, would adopt a more "spiritual" orientation. Still others would combine or oscillate between both perspectives, involving both a new type of spectacle and a new space of performance, as in Pietro Maria Bardi's proposal for a fascist mystery play. I begin with the first.

Ciocca was an industrial engineer who in 1930 found himself entrusted with construction of a ball-bearing plant near Moscow as part of a business agreement between Fiat and the Soviet government.[14] This was Ciocca's first encounter with Soviet Russia, and his fascination with certain aspects of Soviet collectivization led to the writing of *Giudizio sul bolscevismo: Com'è finito il piano quinquennale* (Judgment on Bolshevism: How the five-year plan ended up; 1932), a critical account of his work experiences that was well received by the fascist press, and *Economia di massa* (The mass economy; 1936), a study of industrialization and economic rationalization in which the Soviet and the American lessons were adapted to the specific needs of western European economies. Neither book reveals any deep curiosity about cultural matters, although the first laments at length the deadening effects upon the human spirit of Russia's "idolatry" of the machine: a form of worship that Ciocca explains in terms of the young nation's desire to ape that other great representative of materialism and "class capitalism," the United States.[15] Nor does Ciocca's later work, which included a Le Corbusier–inspired project for field-workers' homes "conceived of and constructed as if they were machines" and a futuristic proposal for a national transportation system based upon the application of rail-type concepts to automobile and truck transportation.[16] In recognition of the postindividual nature of fascist society, the latter project attempted to reconcile public and private transport, the state's need for regimentation and the individual's need for freedom of movement, through a fusion of train and automobile that Ciocca referred to as "the guided street": a street where all vehicles travel in convoys from station to station along self-guiding rails (in reality cement dividers). This because the new mass economy dictates a reduction of labor through the "judicious use of machines," not in order to augment individual wealth, but rather "to increase the nation's power, a power measured according to the number of arms, hearts, brains, made available for the pursuit of the highest collective aims by being freed from ordinary economic duties."[17]

Inspired by Mussolini's SIAE speech, Ciocca seems to have become deeply interested in the technical requirements of stadium-sized theaters (an interest that, with Bardi and Bontempelli's energetic support, would extend well into the late 1930's). For him, a mass theater was one that offered the maximum number of spectators the best possible spectacle at the least expense. As such, and much like nearly everyone else involved in the design of mass theaters, from the Americas to eastern Europe, he conceived of his role as that of democratizing elite forms of culture:

An ordinary operatic spectacle at Milan's La Scala costs 100,000 lire. If there are 2,000 spectators, the cost is 50 lire per person. If there were 20,000, the cost would descend to 5 lire per person. Now it is far easier to find 20,000 citizens able to spend 5 lire than 2,000 able to spend 50. The entire gist of the theater's crisis and of the social need for mass spectacles is summed up in these little figures.[18]

Like Soviet predecessors such as Evreinov and Meyerhold, and Weimar ones like Reinhardt, Gropius, and Piscator, Ciocca recognized that a shift in scale would not be adequate in and of itself. An aesthetic revolution would be necessary: "The enormous theater requires an enormous stage. The scenic demands of holding [*incatenare*] the crowd's attention, of striking its imagination, of exciting its passions, are irreconcilable with restricted stage spaces."[19] In a subsequent essay on the rural house as a machine for fascist living, Ciocca designated this revolutionary aesthetic as a corporatist one, merging individuality with discipline and uniformity, Italy's Roman past with its fascist future:

A collective gymnastic exercise, a parade of militias, do they not possess a singular, profound, and suggestive beauty? Fantasy and variety are wonderful things when they are spontaneous, but when they aren't and hide, like so much architecture, a melancholic absence of originality, they repel. Repel. Repel especially the disciplined, the simple, the sincere, the peasant. The new world arising on the basis of discipline will have its own aesthetic, *the aesthetic of discipline*: an aesthetic that was hardly born today. It was born with the pyramids, [and] shone forth in Roman military encampments, aqueducts, and in Roman civilization as a whole.[20]

The codification of this venerably ancient, yet ultramodern, aesthetic remained the special province of directors, set designers, and authors. Ciocca's was instead the "exquisitely geometrical problem of maximums and minimums. Maximums of capacity, comfort, and representational potential; a minimum of expense."[21] In a series of technical statements and plans published in *Quadrante* from July 1933 onward, Ciocca addressed problems of visibility, acoustics, capacity, and efficient crowd flow in the process of refining his designs. Inspired less by Italian predecessors such as the mass theater presented at the 1928 MIAR exhibit than by contemporary Soviet experiments such as Grigoriy Barchin and Yevgeniy Wachtangoff's Meyerhold Theater, he came forward with plans for a stadium made up of two intersecting circles: one large—representing the concentric seating area; one small and centered on the perimeter of the large one—representing a rotating bipartite stage.[22] If his theater's overall shape was meant to echo ancient Roman coliseums, the latter feature was almost surely borrowed from Russian designs, since his first *Quadrante* article had praised the "excellent effects obtained with mobile stage platforms and high-relief backdrops in Soviet theaters."[23] Fascist theaters of masses would far exceed all Soviet predecessors, however, and not just because of their links to classical antiquity. They would achieve "infinitely better effects by introducing on stage *absolute reality*. . . . We shall

get used to seeing the stage spectacle now from in front, now from the side, now from behind, just as we are used to seeing the spectacle of life."[24] But the accent on realism and on the fusion between the scenic representation and reality does not necessarily imply a hyperrealist aesthetic: "The theater of masses will not exhaust its mission by presenting plays; rather, it will also and most especially be employed for parades. . . . In mass theaters, the potential for parades is phantasmagoric. While 20,000 admiring and applauding spectators cram the hall 30,000 others, gathered backstage and under stairwells, file across the stage amid bright lights and flashing screens: a prize to men of goodwill, an incitement to tepid souls, a warning to doubters."[25] In short, like many other members of his generation of architect-engineers, whether in Italy or abroad, Ciocca's fantasy was to crossbreed the avant-garde cabaret and variety theater projects of futurism, Dadaism, and Bauhaus with the mass athletic stadia of early 1930's Europe.[26]

Telesio Interlandi was even more of an architectural outsider than Ciocca. But he was a political insider and played an instrumental role in shaping Mussolini's vision of a "theater for 20,000." An emblematic figure of the period in his passions and contradictions, Interlandi was at once a militant fascist, an anti-American, a crude anti-Semite, a cultural modernist, a xenophobe, and an open admirer of the Bolshevik Revolution who maintained close ties to the Soviet embassy in Rome. As the editor-founder of the intransigent newspaper *Il Tevere* (and, subsequently, from the pages of reviews like *Quadrivio* and *La Difesa della Razza*), he ex-

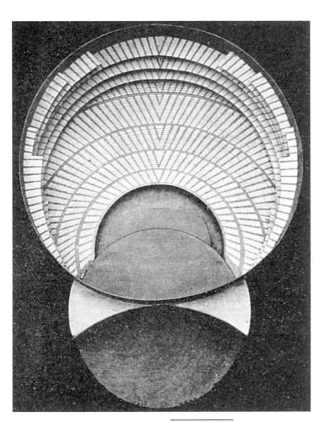

15. Gaetano Ciocca, theater of masses, overhead view of model. From RAI, *Atti—Convegno di lettere* (1935).

16. Gaetano Ciocca, theater of masses, orthogonal view of model. From RAI, *Atti—Convegno di lettere* (1935).

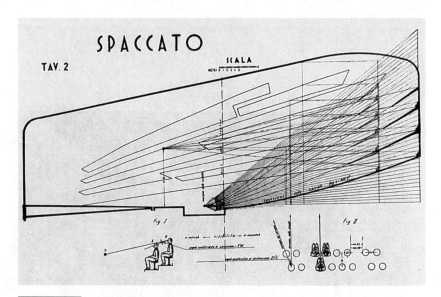

SPACCATO

TAV. 2

SCALA

Fig I          Fig II

17. Gaetano Ciocca, theater of masses, cross-section diagram. From RAI, *Atti— Convegno di lettere* (1935).

ercised considerable sway over contemporary cultural debates, particularly in the domain of the theater. Interlandi's thespian interests dated back to an early acting career and were sustained into the mid 1920's, when he collaborated with Corrado Pavolini on *La croce del sud* (The Southern Cross), a play staged by Pirandello and roundly dismissed by critics.[27] Already, in advance of Mussolini's SIAE speech, he and Vitaliano Brancati had launched a fierce polemic entitled "Theaters Against the Theater," blaming the contemporary crisis on antiquated facilities: "Our theaters are positively bestial vis-à-vis modern needs. All the innovative fury of architects who would have us live in clinic-like homes ceases, as if spellbound, at the threshold of the theater; it is as if the theater were a relic one is forbidden to touch, even to effect a more rational restructuring."[28] The supposed neglect of architects prompted Interlandi to devise a response

of his own in the form of a theater-in-the-round seating 15,000 spectators, covered, like the 1927 Gropius/Piscator Total Theater, by a metal-gridwork-supported dome. Like Ciocca's, the design was meant to echo that of Roman amphitheaters (even if allusions to the visionary architecture of Claude-Nicholas Ledoux or Etienne-Louis Boullée seem equally weighty). It was also explicitly modeled on contemporary sports stadiums: "The stage is no longer at the end of the hall, but at the center. It becomes the 'focal point' of visual and acoustic attention, as do the boxing ring and the football field."[29] The seating areas would be structured so as to reflect the new social realities of the mass era: "There are no longer variations in types of seating; not even between seats in the sun and shade. Everyone finds a place in the sun of electrical lighting."[30] This technological flattening out of social differences in the name of discipline and democracy would also extend to the theater's acoustics and sight lines, all of which would be equalized via the application of the most advanced modern practices, so as to dictate only minimal variations in an always low ticket price.[31] Similarly, there was to be a reversible relation between stage and auditorium. After each act of their performance, the mass of actors on stage and all their props would recede into the floor (thanks to hydraulic machinery). The stage area would then be transformed into a public gathering place, where the mass public was free to congregate and move about.

Despite their enormous scale, the theaters proposed by Ciocca, Interlandi, and others did not appear extravagant to contemporaries. On the contrary, they were dwarfed

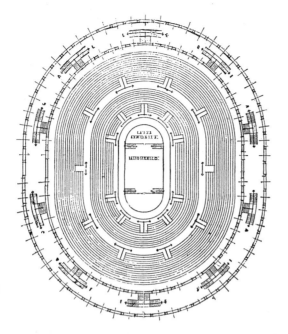

by the many "stadiums for 100,000 spectators" dreamed up by the era's architects. Realized in the Los Angeles Coliseum (expanded for the 1932 Olympics to accommodate 125,000 spectators) and the 1936 Berlin Olympic stadium (capacity 100,000), these reinforced concrete arenas were always envisaged as modern, hygienic, and fully rationalized mass environments, environments shaped in accordance with newly developed scientific crowd-management and traffic-flow techniques. A symptomatic case in point is Le Corbusier and Pierre Jeanneret's 1936 project for a 100,000-seat stadium for popular events (*réjouissances populaires*) in Paris, complete with a huge stage, cinema screen, track, and orator's podium. The product of its authors' Popular Front sympathies, and derived from their prior work on the 1932 Palace of Soviets competition, it envisaged "the creation of a entirely new kind of facility that responds to new needs arising out of society's present evolution." "Such a

18. (right) Telesio Interlandi, theater of masses, overhead diagram. From *Il Tevere*, June 26, 1933.

19. (below, right) Telesio Interlandi, theater of masses, cross-section diagram. From *Il Tevere*, June 26, 1933.

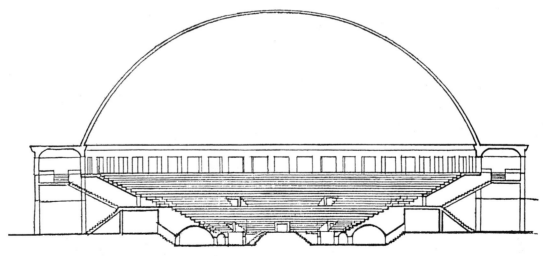

20. Le Corbusier and Pierre Jeanneret, project for a national center for popular celebrations involving 100,000 participants (1936). From *Oeuvres complètes, 1934–1938* (1939). In the accompanying text, the architects describe the complex as having "the look of a natural occurrence." They continue: "Such a center must be national in character. There are many circumstances today in which the masses must be able to commune through the unanimity bred by the emotions provoked by art. Music, speech, theaters, mime, sets, and plasticity find new and unlimited prospects extending out before them. New creations will arise."

[national] 'Center,'" they argued, "opens up to animators [*animateurs*] creative opportunities of a grandeur hitherto unknown: speeches, theater, gymnastics, music, dance, sets, the participation of a mass of 100,000, grouped together, shaped into a unit by the [stadium's] architecture." [32] Fantasies of this kind had inspired Italy (like most of its western and eastern European peers) to embark on an ambitious program of stadium building in the early 1930's. The decade was launched with the construction of Enrico del Debbio's austerely classical Mussolini stadium (now the Stadio Olimpico) and Pier Luigi Nervi's brilliant rationalist Berta Stadium in Florence (now the Stadio Campo di Marte), the proposed site of Bardi's mystery play. The next few years saw either the construction or the planning of a Mussolini Stadium in Turin (architects Bianchini, Fagnoni, and Ortensi [1933]); a Mussolini Forum reworking Milan's Napoleonic arena (architect Giuseppe de Finetti [1933]); a mass stadium in Rome (architects Nervi and Cesare Valle [1933]); and smaller stadiums in places such as Como (architect Gianni Mantero), Bologna, Lucca (architects Bianchini, Fagnoni, and Mannozzi), and Livorno. Designed to increase the scale of mass sporting events like soccer games—Italy's enduring fever for the game is a contemporary by-product—these stadiums were always also conceived of as sites for political rallies and mass choreographies much like the later Soviet-bloc Spartakaiads. They found their complement in mass auditorium projects like the ones put forward by Muratori/Fariello/Quaroni, Griffini/Faludi/Cavaglieri, and Nervi/Valle/Guidi during the 1935 competition for a hall to be built in Rome's Circus

Maximus area "able to seat 5,000 spectators, but expandable to a much greater capacity." [33] One entry, by Luigi Vietti, even included an ovoid open-air *megatheater*— "a typical mass theater," according to one commentator, with a total capacity of up to 15,000, and featured a Ciocca-inspired tripartite stage that rose, descended, and rotated thanks to "the same quick and easy pneumatic system employed in the undercarriages of trucks." [34] Such proposals continued at least through 1940, when Giuseppe Terragni seems to have drawn up plans for a spiral-shaped mass theater and for a "total cinema" hall (doubtless modeled after the Gropius/Piscator Total Theater). [35]

The theater, stadium, and auditorium projects of the period, whether responding directly to Mussolini's SIAE speech or not, whether by professional architects or engineers or men of letters, found their greatest source of "spiritual" inspiration in the theoretical writings of Bontempelli, published, among other places, in *Quadrante* and *La Gazzetta del Popolo*. [36] In the eyes of the noted novelist and editor-founder of the journal *900: Cahiers d'Italie et d'Europe* (whose editorial board included Ilya Ehrenburg, Ramón Gómez de la Serna, and James Joyce), it was clear that the supreme leader "had not been speaking only to architects, but most especially to authors." [37] To authors like himself who had long been spreading the gospel of a turn away from avant-garde experimentalism in the name of a return to the popular and religious roots of drama, "Spectacle has always and everywhere been a popular form in the broadest sense, it has always been 'a theater for 20,000'; and theater began its decline from the very moment

it was imagined that the theater could be made for the elect alone."[38] As instances of prior theaters for 20,000, Bontempelli invoked Greek tragedy, the medieval mystery plays, Elizabethan drama, the *commedia dell'arte*, and, in the modern period, Wagner's musical theater, Verdi's melodramas, and the Russian ballet. But the latter were the last efflorescence of a declining age—the so-called "Romantic age" extending from Christianity to the avant-gardes—that had ended with World War I. Thanks to the war, the past had been swept away, and a new "primordial atmosphere" had descended upon the West: an atmosphere that had made it once again possible for authors to forge new myths and heroes. Two contemporary settings could serve as incubators for a new theater in this transformed setting. The first was mass politics: "[The new] vast theaters will work admirably for public ceremonies of a celebratory or political nature. And, indeed, isn't it possible that from these the seed of a new theatrical form could come into being? It wouldn't be the first time, if we keep in mind that the remote origins of the theater . . . reach back to popular religious ceremonies, and that even the most recent of comedies descends in a direct line from the Dionysian mysteries."[39] The second incubator was mass athletics: "I believe (and have been arguing for years) in the advent of a theater for masses: a theater of primordial

**41**

21. Pier Luigi Nervi, Berta stadium, stairway to grandstand. From *Architettura* 11.3 (Mar. 1932).

passions and linear actions whose counterpart and most intense collaborator will be that excessive and overflowing public that we have begun to get acquainted with in sports stadiums." [40]

Whether in the domain of politics, of sports, or of the theater, the key issue for Bontempelli was the activation of the mass spectator within the spectacle. In action—not the superficial "agitation" of, say, the futurists, but instead the sort of deep physical, emotional, and spiritual "action" resulting from a direct confrontation with elementary natural forces lodged in the darkest recesses of the real— lay salvation and, much as in Heidegger's *Being and Time*, the recovery of human existence's otherwise lost metaphysical dimension. [41] In action's absence, there were only alienation, inauthenticity, and unreality. In action's presence, there was magic. The mass spectator would have to be swept up by the immensity of the new theater's perspectives, heed its appeal to primordial sentiments, and be transformed from a "tired and cold judge" into a vigorous protagonist. [42] A synergy could thereby be established linking fascist politics to fascist dramaturgy. To the former's intensified collaboration between citizenry and state would correspond a dynamic equilibrium between audience and stage. Both represent efforts to reinvent the category of the sacred and reestablish the values of sacred rituality within resolutely secular confines.

Bontempelli's theorizations were to prove extraordinarily influential. Whether in his formulation of the ideal of magic realism, his meditations on the modern monumentalism, his call for a return to primordial values in art and architecture, it was Bontempelli who set the intellectual tone for the entire era. Occupying a parallel (although not identical) terrain was one of the period's most lively forums: Nino d'Aroma's important bimonthly *L'Italia Vivente*. Much as *Critica*

22. Luigi Vietti, photomontage of "megatheater" and surroundings. From *Architettura* 14.12 (Dec. 1935).

**43**

*Fascista* had done back in 1926 on the subject of fascist culture, *L'Italia Vivente* launched an "Inquiry for an Art of Our Times" in the immediate wake of Mussolini's SIAE speech. In this context, it polled writers and critics like Enrico Pea, Camillo Pellizzi, Umberto Barbaro, Ugo Betti, and Pier Maria Pasinetti on the links between works of art and their sociohistorical context; on the adequacy of contemporary art as an interpreter of the fascist spirit; and on the future prospects for developing an "art of our times." The results of the poll were published in three successive issues (May 30, June 15, and June 30) accompanied by essays explicitly dealing with Mussolini's call for a mass theater.[43] In August 1933 the journal followed up on this initiative with the first of several special issues bearing titles such as "In Favor of an Experimental State Theater"

and "A Fascist Theater for Fascist Italy." The former, characteristically, amounted to an extended plea for the creation of a new state theater under the directorship of Bragaglia: a petition underwritten by a cast of stellar contributors that counted, among others, Marinetti, Curzio Malaparte, Bontempelli, Luigi Bonelli, and Corrado Pavolini. The issue's lead essay was by Augusto Consorti and declared that "for [the theater] there has been no fascism, no revolution; neither has there been nor is there this Italy of today, all vibrant and alive, eager to hoist the banners of its spirituality above all the civilizations camped on the globe."[44] This negative judgment was followed by a denunciation of one of Bragaglia's main conservative rivals: "If ideas were thrushes and words were *crostini* then one could content oneself with Forzano's rotisseries and pass off *Villafranca* as a work of the new era, as a work of our revolution. But fascism's ideas and words were not meant for the *rosticceria* and thus are ill suited to Giovacchino's spit."[45] No less indicative of the journal's modernist interpretation of Mussolini's "theater for 20,000" were articles by Luigi Bonelli and Corrado de Vita, both of which invoked precedents such as the Lef, Zon, and Tram theaters, as well as other state-supported Soviet theaters, in arguing for the establishment in Italy of an experimental state stage. Finally, in "Notes Towards a Mass Theater," Sandro de Feo, soon to become (with Bonelli) a co-author of *18 BL*, addressed the material side of the SIAE proposal, calling for the preservation of a distinctively fascist sense of hierarchy in theater architecture: "It is absurd," he averred, "to consider, as I read somewhere, abolishing the distinction between different kinds of seating in these theaters-to-be;

this is the usual facile rhetoric of our home-grown bolsheviks, who prepare American cocktails in rationalist salons while discussing mass psychology." [46] He concluded by sounding a warning against the confusion between artistic and political merit: "I would at first prohibit authors from treating the revolution, not because it cannot be adequately dealt with, but because effective treatments would be far outnumbered by inadequate ones, which would, nonetheless, gain acceptance." [47] De Feo was almost certainly alluding to the poor quality of the submissions generated by the OND's 1933 national competition for the composition of plays that directly reflected the fascist climate (so poor that none gained either "acceptance" or the OND prize). The warning would of course go unheeded by de Feo himself later in that same year.

De Feo's hesitations about an overtly political fascist theater were not shared by Bardi, who, alongside Bontempelli, was the era's most significant culture critic. A prolific journalist, editor, and curator, and tireless defender of modern art and architecture against the fascist *arrière-garde*, Bardi responded to the SIAE speech with a proposal of his own for a "fascist sacred pageant" (*sacra rappresentazione del fascismo*). The drama would be performed in Florence's Berta Stadium, because "stadiums will be the birthplace of the theater of masses." [48] It would consist of three synthetic tableaux, the first portraying World War I, the second the fascist revolution, and the third the "peace and power of fascism," employing artillery, airplanes, an artificial canal, a bridge, and an actual railway meant to encircle the entirety of the oval stage. Its pro-tagonist would be the masses: masses made up of students, fascist youths, and OND members (Bardi explicitly banished all professional thespians from his sacred theater, Forzano being personally singled out for exclusion). The action was to be stylized, hinging upon the transformation of the bridges from a symbol of war and division into a symbol of social unity and peace. The high degree of stylization was not, however, meant to erect a barrier between the "sacred" world of the drama and the "secular" world that lay outside the stadium. Much as Ciocca had hoped would be the case in his mass theater, the play would end with a disruption of all barriers separating the ideal from the real. The actors would raise a flag atop the stadium's *fasces*-girded tower and march out of the stadium into the streets of Florence.

Like the many fascist intellectuals who contributed to the debates in *Quadrante*, *Quadrivio*, *L'Italia Vivente*, *Critica Fascista*, and other journals and newspapers, Alessandro Pavolini, the originator of *18 BL*, also heard Mussolini's speech as an invitation to create a theater modeled on fascism's most immediate contribution to Italian national life—namely, mass rallies, parades, and ceremonies, with their elaborate rituals, choral chants, and Homeric war cries (borrowed from d'Annunzio) of *Eia eia alalà*, which had become a common feature of daily life since the March on Rome. "It is an incredible sight to glance down upon the sea of humanity that gathers before the Palazzo Venezia to pay homage to Il Duce," one foreign drama critic would explain. "In truth a theater of the masses!" [49] This common interpretation would have been buttressed by il Duce's frequent self-styling as the dramaturge of the Italian masses: a self-styling the contemporary press, conditioned by a generous system of subventions, was only too eager to parrot.[50] In the phrase "stir up the great collective passions," Pavolini and his young cohorts doubtless also heard echoes of the cultural war cry of Marinetti's 1909 Manifesto of Futurism: "We will sing the great crowds stirred up by work, pleasure, and revolt; we will sing the multicolored and polyphonic tides of revolution in modern capitals."[51] Since futurism had played an inaugural role in the rise of fascism, for Pavolini there could be little doubt that the "multicolored and polyphonic tide" best suited to the requirements of both the futurist leader and Mussolini was the fascist revolution. Here, then, was a fitting subject matter to be sung in the new mass theater. And who better to sing it than Italy's youth: the first generation raised in the bracing climate of the fascist era, the first generation untainted by the prefascist past? The choice would have seemed all the more obvious given that youth held, not only the key to the perpetuation of fascism's "permanent revolution," but also, as had often been intoned during years of debate over the crisis of the traditional theater, the key to the resurgence of the Italian theater.[52] Several generations of theater theorists, from Edward Gordon Craig through Jacques Copeau, had argued much the same: the theater of the future would be a theater of, by, and for youth.

Pavolini had risen with exceptional speed through the ranks of the PNF to become the federal secretary of the Florentine *fascio*, a member of the party directorate, and a delegate in the Italian parliament, all by the age of 31.[53] Too young to have fought in World War I, he had joined the fascist movement within days of his seventeenth birthday and had the good fortune to find himself in Rome a year later (pursuing studies in political science) when the blackshirts marched on the capital. His pedigree as a "fascist of the first hour" was, therefore, solid enough, even if he truly belonged to the first "successor" generation. As for his career as a fascist official, it began modestly with responsibilities in the local GUF and Balilla (fascist boy scout) organizations. Soon enough it began to soar thanks to his family's connections and influence. (His father, Paolo Emilio, was a noted Sanskrit scholar, a professor and dean instrumental in the fascistization of the University of Florence, and, later, a member of the Accademia dei Lincei and Accademia d'Italia; his older brother Corrado was a well-respected dramaturge and critic.) In this early phase, Pavolini distinguished himself by his radical intransigence, demonstrated in polemical articles for *Battaglie Fasciste, Rivoluzione Fascista,* and *La Montagna,* and by his leadership role in actions like the 1925 assault on Gaetano Salvemini's university lecture hall.[54] The crucial event that would set the stage for his transformation from party militant to fascist hierarch was Augusto Turati's accession to the secretariat of the PNF in March 1926. Turati's secretariat brought a decisive shift away from the unruly squadrism his predecessor Farinacci had encouraged (and that young militants like Pavolini had supported), and introduced in its place a move towards party discipline, hierarchy, and coordination from the center. One of Turati's prime concerns was with the development and training of a new leadership cadre: a concern that conferred special

45

importance upon groups such as the GUF, within which the young Pavolini was emerging as a prominent figure. The future head of the Ministry of Popular Culture embraced this new line just as enthusiastically as he had earlier advocated squadrist violence and turned his journalistic sights towards cultural and artistic arguments, intervening in the *Critica Fascista* debate on fascist culture and Pirandello's *italianità* ("Italianness"), as well as publishing short stories (in *Solaria*), a play (in *Comoedia*), and a "sporting novel" (*Giro d'Italia*).[55] In 1929 he was named to the rank of federal secretary and assumed the directorship of *Il Bargello*, whose pages he and Gioacchino Contri, the journal's editor-in-chief, opened up to some of the period's leading literary and artistic lights, including Bilenchi, Rosai, Vittorini, and Pratolini.

Pavolini's tenure at the helm of *Il Bargello* is emblematic of larger contradictions within fascism's cultural politics as the regime completed its first decade of existence. Feverishly antibourgeois in its rhetoric, nostalgic for the movement's revolutionary beginnings, heterogeneous on its cultural page, combining regionalist and populist themes, the journal nonetheless stuck close to the party's program. In the words of Marco Palla: "The moralizing exigencies of building up a disciplined and compact mass party that is extremely active and present in the nation's life; the totalitarian penetration of all sectors of Italian society; the determining role of the fascist party's labor, welfare, and propaganda organizations: all these motives, formulated by Augusto Turati, were embraced by Pavolini as if his own." [56] This high degree of orthodoxy did not impede *Il Bargello* from adopting panrevolutionist or

"universalist" positions, as, for instance, in a series of articles from 1930 through 1932 concerned with Stalin's five-year plan, fascist corporatism, and the rise of German national socialism. In one such article, Pavolini expanded the *Critica Fascista* Moscow/Rome debate to encompass also Berlin (uncannily so given his close allegiance to Hitlerian Germany during the Republic of Salò):

Revolutionary mobs—disciplined and fiery—fill the squares and stadiums of Rome, Moscow, and Berlin. Black shirts, Soviet shirts, brown shirts. Lictorial fasci, red stars, swastikas. . . .
In Moscow, Berlin, and Rome, the vast and compact mobs raise their impassioned faces, their banners, their unanimous songs. The spotlights of history and of world attention brightly illumine them, while the rest of the globe is consigned to shadows cast by the mediocre and tragic adventures caused by deep disorientation. But once again, among the vanguards of tomorrow, among the most enlightened spirits, it is Rome that appears at the leading edge.[57]

That the metaphor of the spotlight should surface here amid rival uniforms, stadiums, symbols, and choral songs cannot be accidental, as *18 BL* would soon confirm. It suggests, rather, the close interconnection between political and cultural themes in the young Pavolini's imagination. More than a figure of speech, the theater of revolution was for Pavolini a quite literal theater: a theater that the most advanced cultural forces would have to bring into being, even at the risk of generating scandal and opposition. This conviction helps to explain later polemics like, for example, his apologia for the invitations extended to the painters Mario Sironi, Felice Casorati, and Giorgio de Chirico (who in 1929 had designed sets and costumes for Diaghilev's Ballets Russes) to contribute set designs to the first Maggio Musicale Fiorentino (1933) and, likewise, to Max Reinhardt and Jacques Copeau to direct, respectively, a performance of *A Midsummer Night's Dream* in the Boboli gardens and *The Miracle of Saint Uliva* in Santa Croce; invitations for which the festival organizers were attacked by cultural nationalists and conservatives like Ugo Ojetti.[58] In his and their defense, Pavolini sounded the populist-avant-gardist themes that would inspire his next great theatrical endeavor. He insisted that the recently redesigned Teatro Comunale was "one of the most modern, comfortable, and best equipped; not only the largest in Italy and one of the largest in Europe, but also the best adapted to today's needs because of its ability to accommodate both an elegant and a mass public, whether local or made up of economy-class tourists."[59] It therefore was fitting that "the Maggio Musicale should serve as an innovative testing ground for Italian set design and as an experimental center for European scenographers, permitting new and brilliant elements to express themselves for the first time, not on worthy but inadequate experimental stages, but instead in a large and fully up-to-date theater."[60] To stage a close encounter between the new mass audience and the cultural "vanguards of tomorrow"— between two worlds, that is, that bourgeois society had kept segregated, this was Pavolini's formula for cultural revolution, and this would also be his response to Mussolini's SIAE summons. His wager was that, standing face to face, the vanguard and the mass would recognize that each was the mirror image of the other.

Owing to his political prominence, his youth, and his visibility as a literary-cultural arbiter (not to mention his skills as an excellent tennis player), the Florentine federal secretary was entrusted in 1934 with organizing the first "Lictorial Games of Culture and Art" (Littoriali della Cultura e dell'Arte): a national competition among university students in fields such as painting, poetry, narrative, theater criticism, music, translation, film, fascist doctrine, scientific studies, and political science.[61] Pavolini seemed ideally suited to the task inasmuch as the games were a key component in the regime's overall strategy for "at all costs avoiding a rift between the generation that fought the war and the revolution, and subsequent generations."[62] Modeled on similar youth festivals and cultural Olympiads in the Soviet Union (like the 1931 Theatrical Olympiad), the Littoriali were initially envisaged as a spiritual appendage to the physical Littoriali: the Littoriali dello Sport, first held in Bologna in 1932 alongside the Lictorial architecture competition (Littoriali di Architettura).[63] An "appendage" because the cultural-political redemption of Italy that fascism set about accomplishing was from the start conceived of as a (re)anchoring of mental life in renewed material bodies. Hence, for instance, the recurrence of a constellation of motifs linking youthful bodies to athletic competition to the modernist theater in theoretical writings by Marinetti, Bragaglia, Sofia, Bardi, and Bontempelli, and in such decisions as that taken in 1932 to absorb all professional athletes into the Corporation of Spectacle.[64] Hence, also, such experiments as Vitaliano Brancati's 1931 *L'urto: Un dramma da rappresentare all'aperto in uno stadio* (Clash: A drama to be performed in an open-air stadium) and

23. Birth-Mother of the Rev-
olution: an 18 BL truck.
From Archivio Storico Fiat,
Turin.

Pirandello's show honoring the boxer Primo Carnera for his June 1933 victory over Jack Sharkey.[65] Nation-building depended upon a spiritual rebuilding, which depended, in turn, upon bodybuilding. So the Littoriali of Culture and Art were meant as a mental counterpart to the Littoriali of Architecture and Sport. In Pavolini's own phrasing, they constituted the "free, solar gymnastics of the brain."[66] By training brain and body together, it was hoped, they would shape the future fascist elite: an "aristocracy of command" cast in the image of the supreme commander and the first generation of blackshirt revolutionaries.[67]

Concern had been growing within society at large regarding intergenerational strife as the fascist revolution neared and passed the ten-year anniversary mark. The review *Il Saggiatore*, for instance, felt the matter urgent enough to merit an "Inquiry into the New Generation."[68] Its editors asked prominent figures like Betti, Bontempelli, Bardi, Evola, Bottai, Marinetti, Corrado Alvaro, Adriano Tilgher, and Mario Missiroli to address three questions. First, was it possible to speak of a "decisive and definitive gap" separating today's youth from their elders? Second, did the new generation possess "a well-delineated spiritual vision that could infuse culture and life" with a new spirit? Third, if the answer to question 2 was affirmative, what would the respondent identify as the telltale signs of this complete spiritual renewal?[69] The majority answer was that there was indeed a decisive (although not definitive) generation gap: the result of youth's rejection of idealism, religion, abstraction, tradition, and bourgeois individual-

ism in the name of realism, amorality, sports, and an activist/collectivist ethos. A new world was in the making—a world in which "the old liberal culture is in decline; politics rules over modern life; a collective (but non-bureaucratic) order is put in place; individuals are no longer considered privileged spiritual subjects; [and] work is the measure for differentiating among individuals"—and, in a subsequent triple issue, *Il Saggiatore* gathered together 57 "contributions to a new culture" by young writers, artists, and journalists.[70] As one participant in the inquiry would put it in a front-page article in *Corriere Padano* published one day after the performance of *18 BL* and bearing the alarmist title "Individuality and Collectivism: Dangerous Orientations," contemporary youth culture constituted "an apocalyptic sort of ambiance, a tabula rasa, within which the most representative youths are raised to be well equipped for practical action, to be new and ancient, unprejudiced and spontaneous, half twentieth-century Russian bolsheviks and half Machiavellian or Guicciardinian Florentines of the Renaissance."[71]

Similar concerns had been felt within the upper ranks of the PNF for a number of years before the *Il Saggiatore* poll, not so much because the "realist" ethos stood in contradiction to fascist values, as because the existence of a decisive generation gap posed practical problems for a regime becoming preoccupied with its long-term survival. In a party circular dated January 20, 1930, Mussolini had thus felt it necessary to reassert the credo that "the regime is and intends to remain a regime of youth" and to insist that "the young and youngest, which is to say those who were unable to fight in the war or revolution, should be resolutely led along the path of apprenticeship within the hierarchies that shape the political, administrative, labor, journalistic, cooperative, scholastic, military, athletic, afterwork, etc., spheres, *without inane jealousies or preconceived fears.*" [72] In this context, he reshuffled the fascist youth organizations and commissioned a report on university groups, which reached his desk in mid-July 1931, just as the controversy his 1930 circular had provoked in the pages of Bottai's *Critica Fascista* was beginning to give way to the Rome/Moscow debate. [73] The report concluded that "the university masses are not yet as il Duce wants them." This was especially the case with "students in law, letters, philosophy: the abstract ones," who, unlike their "exact" peers in medicine and engineering, demonstrated "an acute sense of autonomy vis-à-vis the party, and an extremely lively intolerance of all disciplinary and hierarchical ties." [74] The solution proposed by the report's author, Carlo Scorza, commander of the Fasci Giovanili, was twofold: a fascistization of university youth (the "abstract" in particular) and "the development of a myth for university youth, because youth needs to believe blindly in something and feel itself at the center." [75] Scorza found students at present "spiritually bewildered to the degree that they found themselves grappling with two great events—the war and the revolution—in which they did not participate and to which they did not contribute." [76] Just as their predecessors during the Risorgimento had been able to rally round the myth of the redemption of the Fatherland, just as during subsequent decades myths like socialism, irredentism, and futurism had conferred meaning upon their existences, so today's students needed a new secular faith: a religion founded upon the cult of Mussolini, who equaled "LOYALTY-COURAGE-THOUGHT-LIGHT-BEAUTY-HEROISM-ETERNITY," and according to which entry into the Promised Land was equivalent to membership in the PNF. [77]

Primary responsibility for propagating this "myth" rested with the Littoriali of Culture and Art, but they were to do so in an underhanded fashion. In the words of Achille Starace, national secretary during the 1930's, "the goal of the Littoriali was and is to directly influence youth, spurring them to reflect seriously (and outside of the classroom) on the most exquisite and pressing problems of contemporary political and spiritual life, in order to have a decisive impact on their training as a ruling class." [78] But the success of the Littoriali as a breeding ground for the future fascist vanguard would depend in large measure upon the granting of a considerable degree of intellectual freedom. *Serious* reflection had to be possible; serious reflection and serious experimentation. It was this atmosphere of relative permissiveness that, in Pavolini's view, rendered these "Olympics of the spirit" a natural setting for the triumphal debut of the first theater "born and realized by forces with no prior experience of theater of spectacle: conceived by youth, directed by youth, and acted out by youth": il Duce's dreamed-of theater for 20,000 spectators. [79]

The project was set in motion sometime in December 1933, when Pavolini convened a series of meetings at the Casa del Fascio in Florence that were attended by eight fascist critics, playwrights, directors, and set

**PROPULSORI**

24. "Propellants": corporatism and the fasces bound together to form the monumental state-in-motion. Cartoon from *Il Popolo d'Italia*, June 9, 1934.

designers (including himself): Luigi Bonelli, Gherardo Gherardi, Sandro de Feo, Nicola Lisi, Raffaello Melani, Corrado Sofia, and Giorgio Venturini, ranging from youth to middle age.[80] (Called in at a later point were the composer Renzo Massarani, the choreographer Angela Sartorio, and Ugo Ceseri, the corpulent movie actor who would play the driver of the principal 18 BL truck.) The spectacle took shape as a group creation in a period of intense debate over the so-called "choral" or collective novel. As Pavolini describes it: "Each of us contributed. First the physiognomy of the spectacle was discussed, then ideas for its plot were put forward, and finally the idea of articulating the whole around an 18 BL truck was seized upon: a truck as protagonist; as single and collective personage; as hero of the war, of the struggles of the fascist squadrons, and of building projects."[81]

The era of the masses, it was thought by members of this "half-bolshevik, half-Machiavellian" new generation, required new collective forms of art and new collective heroes, whether human or mechanical or both. Two models were assumed as normative: on the one hand, the collective modes of writing, organization, and production required by the cinema; on the other, the possibility envisaged by Stalin's first five-year plan (1928–33) that, as "engineers who are building men's souls," writers could collaboratively document and thereby contribute to the nation's heroic new economic life—a fantasy variously realized in works such as Boris Pilniak's *The Volga Falls into the Caspian Sea* (1930) and Valentin Kataev's *Time Forward!* (1932), as well as in collective narratives like that documenting the construction of the White Sea canal (later dubbed by Solzhenitsyn "the first [novel] in Russian literature to glorify slave labor").[82] The fascist revolution, too, it was thought, demanded that the psychologism and "intimism" of the naturalist, or *verista*, novel be abandoned in the pursuit of a new mass epos that, miming recent communications technologies such as the radio and following the lead of novelists such as John Dos Passos and the Soviet writers' collectives, would commingle "the infinitely vast and the infinitely minute, the voice of the individual and the howl of the mob."[83] The fragmentary and intertwined realities of urban experience, the heroic trials and tribulations of the modern individual, the great collective enterprise of industrialization and national reconstruction, the conquests of modern science, could be represented by pressing modernist techniques, like the insertion of external objects into the narrative stream and the

SOCIAL DEMOCRAZIA

**LA SOLA BONIFICA**

25. "The True Reclamation": the fascist tractor, once an outlaw, now a lawmaker, plows the fields left fallow by social democracy. Cartoon from *Il Popolo d'Italia*, Mar. 10, 1934.

merce; 1932) and *Il piano quinquiennale Sovietico* (The Soviet five-year plan; 1931). It remained to be seen, however, whether the proposed collective construct would be a matter of process or simply of product. In Pavolini's experiment, the answer would be "both." Every phase of the creative and production process—from the crafting of the script to the selling of tickets—would put on display fascism's culture of collective discipline and collaboration. And the spectacle itself would place masses of actors and machines on stage before a mass audience: "Born of the masses, it has as actors the masses and as spectators the Italian and Florentine masses."[84] Hence the label coined by Venturini: theater of masses for masses—a phrase that, at least for Venturini, alluded to the country that "first felt this necessity and constituted a theater of propaganda and of masses, from which, thanks to hard work and no little sacrifice, magnificent accomplishments have resulted."[85] (The country in question being Soviet Russia.) It goes without saying that this thoroughly collectivist interpretation of Mussolini's SIAE speech was, as *18 BL*'s authors would later be forced to admit, at once obvious—given the cultural-political context just evoked—and far from obvious—given Mussolini's omission of any reference to the mass as actor.

Among the plots considered by Pavolini's collective were a sequence of five battles from World War I, the so-called Empoli massacre (a 1921 incident in which nine sailors lost their lives), and the murder of the young fascist Giovanni Berta at the hands of Florentine communists (an event featured in Bardi's mystery play).[86] The last of these three themes, championed by de Feo and

use of multiple narrative voices, into the service of a distinctively fascist form of realism. This was the theory behind the "choral novel" as formulated, albeit rather muddily, by the editor-playwright Valentino Bompiani, the publisher also of numerous divulgative works about the Soviet Union including Ciocca's *Giudizio sul bolscevismo* (Judgment on Bolshevism; 1932) and Bardi's *Un fascista al paese dei Soviet* (A fascist in the land of Soviets; 1933), as well as translations of René Fülöp-Miller's *Il volto del Bolscevismo* (The face of Bolshevism; 1931) and Hubert Renfro Knickerbocker's *La minaccia del commercio rosso* (The menace of Red com-

26. Seventy-four Pavesi tractors at the starting line. From *La Conquista della Terra* 3.4 (Apr. 1932). The original caption reads: "From the grandstand, built for the occasion, *Il Duce* attends the magnificent spectacle" ("Dal palco, appositamente costruito, Il Duce assiste al grandioso spettacolo").

**53**

Sofia and favored by the performance site, prevailed at the very beginning. As deliberations proceeded, however, the fascist martyr was shunted aside in favor of a Fiat 18 BL truck (Pavolini's idea, although supported by Bonelli and Venturini).[87] Especially given the prominence of the national train system in the fascist imagination, the selection of a truck as martyr/hero may not from a postwar perspective seem a self-evident choice, and understanding of it is of some importance to any interpretation of the period. Since the late nineteenth century, trains had become a privileged symbol of modernization and progress throughout the world—and this was particularly true of Italy, where they had come to signify three much-vaunted fascist

"conquests": the reimposition of discipline after the labor disruptions of the postwar period, the forging of a centralized national state, and the democratization of modes of transport that had once been a bourgeois luxury. This rendered trains a highly effective symbol of central governmental power, to be contrasted with the automobile, identified from the time of the Founding Manifesto of Futurism (1909) with modern individualism, particularly in its transgressive, desublimatory aspects. Accordingly, when an engineer like Gaetano Ciocca set about imagining a fully rationalized fascist Italy, an Italy that would reconcile individual needs with those of a totalitarian state, he envisaged a

27. The head trucker at the wheel: Mussolini on a Fowler steamroller. From *La Conquista della Terra* 3.4 (Apr. 1932).

and air traffic, of merchandise and cargo, of electricity, of images on screen and on paper, of telegraphic messages, of voices carried over the telephone and radio, and to do so within the context of an intensive flow of figurative electricity between leader and mass: this was the stuff of which modern states would be constructed.

Suspended between the domains of train and automobile lay the realm inhabited by trucks. Trucks emerged as symbols of the collectivity early in modern transportation history because of their links (along with buses) to industry and to the urban proletariat, on the one hand, and (along with tractors) to modernized agriculture and the peasantry, on the other. Unlike in the case of trains, the collectivity in question cannot readily be identified with the state, because of the exceptional degree of autonomy and freedom of movement granted by truck travel—so exceptional that, from the start, trucks and truckers were always associated less with society than with the "off-road" world of the outlaw proletariat. The notion explains a diversity of relatively recent phenomena, from Carlo Quartucci's leftist Camion theater, which toured Italy during the 1960's and 1970's, staging site-specific "revolutionary interventions" in the form of theatrical actions, video presentations, demonstrations, and shows, to the psychedelic bus of Ken Kesey's Merry Pranksters, celebrated in Tom Wolfe's *The Electric Kool-Aid Acid Test*.[88] It is perhaps most familiar to us thanks to American adventure films such as Steven Spielberg's *Duel* (1971) and Hal Needham's *Smokey and the Bandit* (1977), films in which the trucker is always cast as the member of an outlaw tribe at war with a

mechanism integrating automobile and rail transport into a single, rail-based system. For all its apparent eccentricity, Ciocca's guided-street project embodied an important insight. From the latter half of the nineteenth century onward, the state's power had increasingly become identified with the building and controlling of rail and roadway traffic. No longer imagined as a stable arbiter of forces to which it was external, or as a conservator and accumulator of the national patrimony, the state was being seen as an agent that aggressively coordinated, generated, and accelerated movements along the interconnecting grid of vectors and flows, to which its relationship was one of simultaneous immanence and transcendence. To manage ever-growing streams of vehicle

28. The Albereta dell'Isolotto, Florence, before *18 BL*. From *BA* (1934).

masses for masses," the members of Pavolini's authorial collective found it easy to reach agreement. The fascist revolution and the world war that immediately preceded it could best be embodied in a truck—by definition, the vehicle of the "proletarian nation." [89] They made this choice with a full awareness of the mythographic framework just described. When asked about the precise identity of the truck-protagonist of *18 BL* in a radio interview, Giulio Ginnasi, the secretary of the Florentine GUF, responded: "Anonymous." When interrogated about the identity of the work's authors in a follow-up question, he connected the truck with the authorial collective, and the authorial collective, in turn, with the national collective: "Anonymous as well: [it includes] all Italian soldiers, all fascist squadrists, all the youth of the new Italy: in brief, Mussolini's entire people." [90] The truck was the fascist everyman and everywoman, a humble and heroic soldier as well as soldier carrier, capable (or so *18 BL*'s authors hoped) of eliciting the same empathic reaction as the martyred body of Giovanni Berta.

The selection of an 18 BL as mass hero of Pavolini's spectacle was clinched by the fact that this particular truck was already enshrined in the iconography of fascist squadrism. Featured during the 1920's on PNF postcards, as well as in the works of artists such as Mario Sironi, the 18 BL merged the domains of industry and mechanized agriculture—it was one of Fiat's first mass-produced trucks—with the dual evocation of fascism's outlaw origins and of World War I. [91] Pavolini stated the point explicitly in "Two Fascist Exhibitions," a May 1932 essay filled with premonitions of the spectacle to

mediocre universe of restricted roadways, traffic rules, police forces, lawyers, and merchants, because of his adherence to a higher moral law. Stripped of its rhetoric of individualism and of its vision of superhighway networks as extensions of nature, the myth harkens back to numerous bolshevist, fascist, Maoist, and even New Deal precedents. In its standard version, it imagines the foundation of a new state in terms of the transformation of outlaw truck(er)s into revolutionary lawmakers. The passage is marked by a shift away from random off-road wandering towards integrated (and usually geometrically ordered) mass-convoy movements.

In the case of fascism, the evocative power of this myth was so strong that, when it came to representing the revolution's beginnings in the context of the first "theater of come. "In October, at the Roman Palace of Expositions," he wrote, referring to the upcoming Exhibition of the Fascist Revolution, "we shall see the slender, frayed, and fierce pennants of old squadrons, the red banners pillaged from gutted Chambers of Labor, the relics of Martyrs, our weapons as ultracivil savages—cudgels and bullwhips, double-barreled guns and illegal knuckles—and *the unforgettable truck*, carroccio *of avenging raids, troop-carrier within which our songs were born.*" [92] After this allusion to the truck as birth-mother of the revolution, came a comparison with an exhibition of agricultural machinery and a celebration of the *bonifica integrale*: "a program that, by reason of its imposing contours and revolutionary value, can only be compared with the all-too-famous 'five-year plan' of the bolsheviks." [93] The moral of the story took the form of an

29. *18 BL*: map of the theater and its surroundings. From *La Nazione*, April 18, 1934.

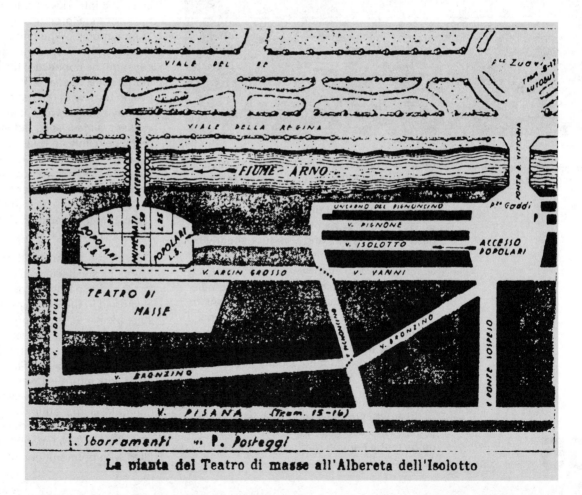

La pianta del Teatro di masse all'Albereta dell'Isolotto

appeal to contemporary artists: "Movie makers, men of theater, find a way to comprehend the aesthetic [consequences] of these enormous events. . . . we await an Oriani who will dedicate pages of an epic timbre to the *bonifica integrale*, to the entire agricultural battle fought by fascism, just like those in [Oriani's] *Lotta Politica* [Political Struggle] that recount the building of the Italian railway system."[94] One and a half years later, Pavolini would oversee the collective drafting of a martial epic fitting this description.

These sorts of imaginings were shaped by contemporary man/machine choreographies like the ones that accompanied Mussolini's second visit to the Pontine marshes on April 5, 1932. Six months later, il Duce would return to inaugurate Littoria; on this occasion, his task was to survey the entire complex of land-reclamation works. The highlight of the tour was a spectacle combining racing, drama, and farming (not unlike contemporary American tractor pulls): 110 industrial vehicles—74 Pavesi tractors and 36 steam-driven Fowler trucks—lined up for what was described by organizers as "the greatest rally of agricultural machinery that humankind has ever seen."[95] Atop a grandstand built for the occasion, Mussolini gave the starting signal, waving a flag that was also mounted at the helm of every truck:

The machines, shuddering impatiently as if ready to rear up like horses of steel, begin advancing simultaneously. The front-line of tractors, extending for nearly a kilometer, sets out along a single sweeping axis to break up land once condemned by the swamp, land that for centuries has been awaiting the plow's wounding and fertilizing action. Clods of earth are pushed to the furrow's side and offered up to the sun's kiss.[96]

The spectacle of penetration, insemination, and postcoital kissing was, at least in the mind of Vasco Patti, co-director of the journal of the Opera Nazionale per i Combattenti (a state-supported veterans' association instrumental in the reclamation of the marshes), simply an external manifestation of the inner workings of Mussolini's fertile mind: "The gaze of il Duce, deeply satisfied, rests upon the majestic gathering of machines created by man in order to redeem the earth, and it is easy to imagine the vision that glimmers forth in the Chief's eyes: that of the imperial destiny of Rome resuscitated through the furrow's fertilizing powers."[97]

A first treatment entitled *18 BL* was developed from the brainstorming sessions held at the Casa del Fascio against the backdrop just described.[98] Each author was assigned the task of fleshing out a subsection of the work and, after revisions and collective discussion, some five or six contributions were passed along to Alessandro Blasetti, the distinguished young filmmaker whom Pavolini had chosen to direct the spectacle.[99] Regarded by some as the Sergei Eisenstein of the new Italian cinema, Blasetti, only 33 years old, had just completed a suite of historical open-air films involving large numbers of nonprofessional actors, notably *Sole* (Sun), *Palio, Terra madre* (Earth Mother), and, the masterpiece of the early fascist cinema, *1860*. From these directorial experiences, Blasetti would bring to *18 BL* a battery of techniques for mounting battle scenes and achieving complex twilight lighting effects, as well as a stylized realist mode of narration always open to allegorical intimations. Blasetti reworked the collective's texts with the demands of staging such a large spectacle in mind, carrying over from his films numerous formal and thematic elements.[100] During the ensuing months of preparation, he adopted, for instance, *Sole*'s Manichean dialectic of darkness and light, representing the Pontine marshes as embodying the values of "darkness and old age" and the reclaimed swamps as containing the promise of "sun and youth" (not to mention the figurative link the film established between frog croakings and voices of antifascist doubt).[101] He borrowed from *Terra madre*'s mass open-air ceremonials and myths of rural virtue and urban vice, as well as exploiting its use of long intervals of silence as a dramatic device. From *1860*, he carried over, among many other ingredients, the film's vast landscape settings; its mass choreographies; its use of bugle calls, songs, flags, and banners; its tendency to create dislocated relations between bodies and voices; its oblique presentation of Garibaldi through the masses converging towards unity under his leadership;[102] and the parade featured in its epilogue: a "bold vision of the fascist phalanxes marching before the Garibaldian recruits against the imperial backdrop of Mussolini's forum."[103]

There exist numerous other bridge elements between Blasetti's prior work and *18 BL*, but it is important to note that there was another cinematographic precedent of some importance, although of less distinction: Forzano's *Camicia nera* (Black Shirt; 1933).[104] Initially referred to as *Il Decennale* because of its direct ties to the decennial celebrations, this crude propaganda film (whose definitive title was supposedly assigned by Mussolini himself) was the Istituto LUCE's first full-length feature. It therefore received extravagant

publicity, not to mention official praise, and was obligatory fare in all public schools and for all fascist university groups. *Camicia nera* does not lend itself readily to a reconstruction of *18 BL*'s origins, since it freely recycles motifs from Blasetti and several other directors (among these motifs the juxtaposition of socialist orators with croaking frogs featured in *Sole* and reprised in *18 BL*). Like most younger fascist artists and intellectuals, *18 BL*'s authors felt nothing but contempt for the librettist-playwright, now turned director. Nevertheless, it seems improbable that Forzano's film had no formative impact on the authorial collective, if only for its distillation of fascist commonplaces. Much like Bardi's mystery play and Pavolini's spectacle, *Camicia nera* narrated the epic of the *bonifica integrale* in three distinct "acts": World War I, the fascist revolution, and the fascist reconstruction of the nation as embodied by the foundation of Littoria, which is to say, the Lictorial Era. It attempted to implement what was then dubbed a "realist" (and only later a "neorealist") aesthetic: employing 10,000 amateurs and only one professional actor, mixing documentary with nondocumentary footage, emphasizing the heroism of the common man and the sacrifices endured by the Italian peasantry. As is typical of the period, these "realist" ingredients coexist with the use (however maladroit) of montage, animation, maps, graphics, songs, text, and headlines, much as they would in *18 BL*. Last, but not least, there would seem to be an abundance of borrowings: the young gymnasts who appear in the opening of the third act; the satirical banquets (in one case directed at the corrupt bourgeoisie, in the other, at corrupt politicians); the withholding of Mussolini's pres-

30. *18 BL*: Act 1, scene 2. From *Scenario* 3.5 (May 1934).

ence until the final half of the action; the celebration of the links between squadrism and 18 BL trucks.

Whatever the precise significance of *Camicia nera* in the genesis and narrative structure of *18 BL*, the first challenge facing Blasetti was less the script than the design and construction of an outdoor theater: an arena, as per il Duce's orders, "able to accommodate 15,000 to 20,000 persons." Assisted by Venturini in matters of stage design, Flavio Calzavara in blocking out the mass choreographies, several dozen workers, and a team of 30 bulldozers, Blasetti set about the task

with barely six weeks at his disposal.[105] Drawing his inspiration from contemporary projects like the Gropius/Piscator Total Theater, Norman Bel Geddes's "theater of the future," and Ciocca's mass theater, the young director had initially dreamed of building an amphitheater that would turn the conventional Greco-Roman theater inside out, placing the audience at the center of a crater, surrounded by a circular upward sloping stage.[106] Practical considerations led to the adoption of an alternate plan. The site selected for *18 BL* was on the left shore of the Arno, across from the Cascine, Florence's principal public park. The location was at

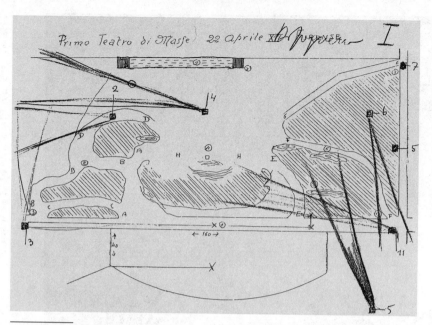

Primo Teatro di Masse 22 aprile XII Jurnecca — I

31. Alessandro Blasetti, stage drawing showing beacon positions for Act 2, scene 1. From *BA* (1934). Numbered squares refer to beacon and searchlight positions; numbered circles refer to staging areas and telephone emplacements; letters designate roadways.

32. (opposite, top) Alessandro Blasetti, stage drawing showing beacon positions for Act 2, scene 2. From *BA* (1934).

33. (opposite, bottom) Alessandro Blasetti, stage drawing showing beacon positions for Act 2, scene 3. From *BA* (1934).

**60**

once urban and pastoral: "urban," however, only inasmuch as it overlooked the great monuments of medieval and renaissance Florence; "pastoral" inasmuch as the land lay beyond the outer reaches of the city and was putatively agricultural.[107]

Contemporary photographs suggest, in fact, that the principal use of the site had been as a dump, which is to say that Blasetti's construction project must itself be viewed as a kind of suburban land-reclamation project. The point is crucial and embeds the construction of Blasetti's theater in fascism's central redemptive myth. The nation's wastelands, whether produced by human neglect or natural adversity, simply *had* to be recovered if the national body politic were to be restored to an integrity that was at once identifiable with the Roman imperial

past and with a future in which the Italian nation would form a mobile, electrified whole. No matter how evanescent its results, the process of recovery was to be undertaken according to the laws of an accelerated new temporality and by tapping hitherto unavailable human energies.

The terrain in question was known to locals as the Albereta dell'Isolotto. It was cleft in two by a deep gully (Via Argin Grosso), which the municipal authorities agreed to expand so that Blasetti could transform it into a command post and lighting pit. The gently sloping riverbank to the north was chosen as a seating area; the steeper incline rising up to the south as a stage.[108] The stage fulfilled one of the main criteria that Romain Rolland had established for the People's Theater: that it "be so constructed as to allow masses of people to act on it: fifteen meters wide . . . and twenty deep."[109] One must, however, multiply these figures by a factor of ten to arrive at the elephantine proportions of Blasetti's stage: roughly 150 meters deep and 200 meters wide (an area equivalent to six American football fields).[110] Blasetti had a series of artificial hills carved into this canted platform (which he leveled and reshaped): a three-stepped hill to the left, a two-stepped hill to the right, and, at the center, a 300-foot-long ridge with a basin hollowed out in its middle, behind which rose a conical hilltop—the stage's highest point. Some twelve staging areas were cut into the various hillsides for the preparation of the spectacle's scenes, as well as a circuit of roads, trenches, and pits, for moving actors, artillery, horses, and trucks. A network of field telephones was installed to ease communications between the lighting em-

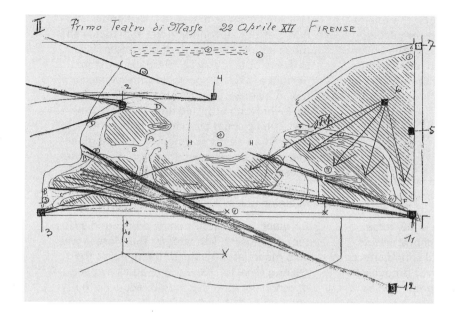

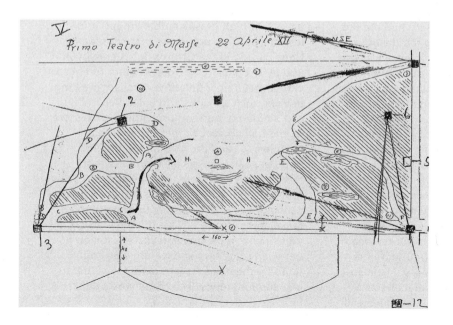

placements, staging areas, and the director's headquarters.[111]

Since this was a stage without the traditional curtain, Blasetti determined that the action should migrate from one area to another, following the movements of Ceseri and his truck. While the spectacle unfolded within these sharply illuminated zones, new scenes could be prepared in the darkened areas: "During pauses, thunderous sounds and luminous effects must draw the spectators' attention towards zones extraneous to the action, and at the same time they must develop, extend, and hold together the dramatic design of the action from one moment to another."[112] Given that both the front and back sides of the stage sloped steeply downwards, Blasetti envisaged *18 BL* as a kind of shadow play in reverse, with figures rising up and disappearing rapidly over the horizon line. The actors and machines, that is, would be viewed in profile from below, as in the films of Carl Dreyer, Eisenstein, and Aleksandr Dovzhenko. Their abstract silhouettes, cut out either against the night sky or against fields of light produced by means of pyrotechnics, battery-powered beacons, and powerful industrial and military searchlights, would thereby appear to have been elevated to a higher, more volatile plane of existence: a plane defined by the propensity of these sharply outlined bodies and machines to suddenly emerge out of or dissolve into seas of darkness or brilliant light.[113] Immense chiaroscuro tableaux would form the heart and soul of *18 BL*, much as in Adolph Appia's "living theater," where light was to "pour living colors through space, render the picture flexible, control the Sign . . . and thus immerse the actor in an atmosphere designed for him."[114] They took on the role reserved for dialogue and character development in the traditional theater, so the bulk of Blasetti's energies (if one is to judge by his notes) were devoted to programming the interplay of shadow and light.[115]

In addition to lighting, there was a second key element that would have to sustain dramatic tension in *18 BL*: the alternation between silence and the "thunderous sounds" alluded to above.[116] The scale of Blasetti's stage was such that microphones had to be planted throughout the landscape to ensure the diffusion of the work's few terse monologues, dialogues, and choral shouts.[117] The musical score, songs, and sound effects were all recorded in advance for broadcast over the same loudspeakers employed by the microphones. The procedure was not unlike that adopted in *1860*, where, in order to avoid the limitations imposed by cumbersome sound equipment, Blasetti had the film shot as if silent, post-dubbing the dialogue and sound effects over what, in essence, was a silent film. This recourse to microphones and a recorded soundtrack would later prove controversial,[118] but its principal aim was to simplify rehearsals and performances by freeing the actors to move about without concern for whether they could or could not be heard.[119] It also permitted the amalgamation of "natural" and "artificial" sounds: mechanically reproduced music, voices, and machine sounds could thereby be intermingled with the live noises produced on stage by actors, weapons, and trucks, creating the sense of an unstable boundary between the real and the imaginary.[120] It also allowed for some original spatial effects: "a customized network of loudspeakers will be installed so as to create a vast sonic field that, besides surrounding the audience, can move sounds, songs, rhythms, and noises close up or far away."[121] Perhaps most important of all, in a spectacle within which a few individuals would speak for the nation as a whole, it permitted amplification: Ceseri's voice could be made to boom more loudly than a firing cannon.[122] A vocal gigantism could be achieved that would grant the occasional dialogues exchanged among the human protagonists priority over the sea of machine noises.[123]

So much for Blasetti's stage and sound system. Because this theater *for* the masses was also meant as a theater *of* the masses, the seating area, too, was designed as a space of representation that would reconcile the competing demands of fascist populism and elitism. Shaped like a broad rectangle with a curved back, surrounded on all sides by a ten-foot-high grassy embankment, it followed a scheme not unlike that adopted by Hans Poelzig in the Großes Schauspielhaus and by Gropius in the Total Theater to the extent that it abandoned vertical segmenting devices such as loges and balconies in favor of a single-tier auditorium within which there would be "no special rostrum for the authorities. . . . and the arrangement of the popular seating areas is so rational that there can be no differences in visibility."[124] Its aim was "the fusion of thousands and thousands of souls within a single framework of ideas and events."[125] This drive towards unicity of perspective and ecstatic fusion between stage and auditorium was countered by the need for lateral forms of hierarchy and difference. The result was a separa-

34. The boat bridge under construction. From *Comoedia* 16.6 (June 1934).

tion between the more expensive reserved seats (5,000 places sold at 10, 20, or 50 lire apiece), which, much as in contemporary football stadiums, were situated along the theater's central axis, and the "popular" seating areas (15,000 places sold at 3 lire each), relegated instead to the flanks. No free tickets were distributed, and the sole discount was for OND participants. The distinction between numbered and unnumbered seating areas may seem perfectly ordinary (and indeed it was). But as indicated by de Feo's earlier-cited complaint about cer-

tain "home-grown bolsheviks" wanting to "abolish the distinction between different kinds of seating in theaters-to-be" the symbolic implications of the stadium's hierarchical organization must be taken seriously. All the more so when one observes that the separation between seating areas corresponded to an elaborate social choreography, reflected in turn in the play's staging of the dialectic between mass man and the heroic individual. Blasetti had originally intended a double boat bridge illuminated by

35. Giannetto Mannucci and Maurizio Tempestini, drawing of entrance to theater of masses. From *BA* (1934).

torches to be the sole entryway to his mass theater, but an inadequate supply of military riverboats led to his adoption of a dual entrance solution. The entrance on the Oltrarno side of the river was restricted to the holders of "popular" tickets, who were obliged to assemble in the Piazza Gaddi and descend a blind alleyway known as Via Isolotto: a "natural" itinerary given that many of them would have been arriving from the adjacent proletarian neighborhood of San Frediano (site of Giovanni Berta's "martyrdom"). As they entered the mist-filled stadium, these often illiterate working-class spectators would have been dazzled by ten massive open books topped by bayonets: canvas and wood constructions designed by Ferdinando Gatteschi and built in a ring around the stadium's periphery. Powerful floodlights were directed at the books' white pages so as to bounce light back out into the stalls. Amid these pages, soon to be inscribed by the first generation of fascist youth, the "popular" sector of the audience would have gazed upon the procession of dignitaries entering the theater's middle section, including writers like Ugo Ojetti, Corrado Pavolini, and Massimo Bontempelli, most of Italy's theater critics, and fascist hierarchs like Ciano. An equation would thus have been implied between fascist faces, fasces, weapons, and books.[126]

36. *18 BL*: the audience of 20,000 spectators. From *Comoedia* 16.6 (June 1934).

The "elite" members of the audience would reach their numbered seats by following an itinerary restricted to the city side of the river. Having traversed the ambassadorial and upper-class neighborhoods of nineteenth-century Florence, they would have reached the Piazza Zuavi, proceeding down the dark and spacious tree-lined promenades of the Cascine (Viale del Re and Viale della Regina) up to the theater's genuine entrance: a bridge of riverboats, designed by Mannucci and Tempestini, illuminated by torches held by boatmen.[127] Boat bridges were one of the most ancient forms of military bridging, employed from the time of Xerxes through World War I, so the symbolism of moving across the river towards a "theater of war," as if one were a soldier, could not have been lost on the audience. The primary aim was surely symbolic. I quote from a contemporary source:

For this new type of theater, a new method of entry was essential. The theater of the Albereta is a kind of inaccessible hermetic temple: will it be, amid the night lights, a phantasmagoria recreating the myths that Wagner conceived for the Bayreuth stage, but with entirely new means than those of which he disposed? Here we are dealing, not with myth, but with contemporary history. Nevertheless, the latter is sufficiently poetic to partake of the appearance and fascination of myth.[128]

Traversing this magical bridge, standing under a celestial *X* formed by beams of light projected from opposite sides of the Arno, spectators would have gazed down the river and over the city's rooftops upon such monuments as the cupola of the Duomo, Giotto's bell tower, and the tower of the Palazzo Vecchio. They would then have completed their walk on the water, ascended a broad stairway, and passed through a triumphal gateway of fasces marked with the Roman numeral XII (dating the spectacle according to the fascist revolutionary calendar). Beyond the gateway lay the canvas books with bayonets and, beyond them, the misty swirl of the assembled crowd surrounded by the Tuscan landscape and under the night sky. There, the heart of this outdoor hermetic temple would at last have been reached: a place of mass communion where, bathed in the wartime smells of gunpowder and burnt magnesium, the distinction between members of the priesthood and mere believers was maintained, even as they rubbed shoulders and merged into a single charismatic community; a healthful Italian Bayreuth where the national body politic could be reconstituted in harmony with the values of fascist ruralism.

*18 BL* was originally scheduled to be performed on April 22 as the crowning event of opening-day ceremonies at the 1934 Littoriali, but logistical difficulties—including, it would appear, a noticeable lack of zeal on the part of his young cast of actors—led Blasetti to seek a one-week delay as early as the middle of March; to which Pavolini objected on the grounds that "the human material (young fascists) could not be so *well* employed . . . and news of a postponement would be demoralizing."[1] Several weeks of torrential rains ensured that Blasetti had his way. Expectations had been raised to a fever pitch by a month of press coverage in such newspapers and reviews as *La Stampa*, *L'Ambrosiano*, *Corriere della Sera*, *Il Giornale d'Italia*, *La Tribuna*, *La Nazione*, *Il Nuovo Giornale*, *Il Lavoro Fascista*, and *Il Cantiere*; and the delay hardly diminished the public's conviction that "the good success of *18 BL* is something that, in these times of impassioned discussion of collec-

tive art, individualistic art, etc., etc., transcends in importance even the Lictorial Games themselves."[2]

It was the organizers who contributed the lion's share of hyperbole, however, and what had once been billed as a mere experiment soon began to take on an air of permanence. By mid-April, a scriptwriting contest for future spectacles had already been announced, with prize monies of 17,000 lire: 10,000 for the first-place winner, 5,000 for second, and 2,000 for third.[3] These future spectacles would grant "maximum prominence to scenes of mass movement sustained by technical resources unavailable on the ordinary stage (lights, searchlights, loudspeakers, motor vehicles, etc.), while dialogue is to be kept to a minimum. Historical reevocations are not excluded, even if the spirit of the Littoriali discourages the pursuit of actual choreographic effects and timeworn commonplaces (pageants in period costume, etc.)."[4]

37. Poster for *18 BL*. From *BA* (1934).

In order to guarantee that *18 BL* (and not historical pageants) would become the absolute point of reference, a call was issued to all artists: "The organizing committee of the Littoriali attributes great importance to the participation of Italian artists in this first mass spectacle (i.e., *18 BL*), so that the experiments and successes of tomorrow may be guided by this particular experience. The event will make it clear how the war scenes included in the spectacle (artillery in action, columns of trucks, troop movements, etc.) could be of special interest to all artists participating in the contest."[5] In the meantime, Pavolini and Blasetti were already envisaging the Isolotto theater as a permanent structure, predicting that it would be the crucible

within which the first genuinely fascist art form would be forged, a school for the directors of the future, and an academy where, "if one experiment follows another and a tradition forms, there is no reason why a new Aristophanes or Aeschylus cannot arise tomorrow."[6] The exuberance of the moment is best captured by the Florentine theater critic Cipriano Giachetti, writing on the eve of the performance:

Today it is war, revolution, reconstruction. Tomorrow it could well be the great events of history, reconstructed along essential lines, lines whose veracity exceeds that of the cinema, where artifice prevails over reality. Tomorrow it will be the most celebrated poems (a few days ago Blasetti suggested [Giosuè] Carducci's "Song of Legnano") and perhaps fantastic creations. Because nothing that speaks to spectators' sensory organs and emotions is precluded in this new theater.[7]

It was against the backdrop of such lavish expectations that the first "theater of masses" opened its doors on April 29, exactly one week after the inauguration of the Lictorial games and one year after Mussolini's SIAE speech. The sell-out audience assembled according to plan, if one exempts the persistence of certain high-bourgeois theatergoing habits: "ladies in evening dresses, dancing shoes, coats made of young and delicate fur, gold and silver jewelry."[8] Despite (or, indeed, because of) such affectations, this portion of the spectacle would be judged a success by all. As intended by the organizers, the bridge, the various massing points, and the book-lit auditorium, all seem to have infused the assembled spectators with the sense that they themselves were the protagonists of Mussolini's mass theater.[9] "There were not 3,000 actors," observed many audience members, "but 23,000."[10] To this extent, *18 BL* can be said to have fulfilled Robespierre's dream of a theater in which the spectator himself is the principal source of spectacle: "the most magnificent of spectacles is that of a great people assembled."[11]

The two-hour performance commenced with the entire landscape as well as much of the seating area veiled in a curtain of white smoke. At the appointed hour, a call to order sounded over the public address system, the lights were extinguished, and the smoke dissipated, exposing to view the immense stage, the surrounding landscape, and the night sky. The first of the play's three acts began with the trumpet calls from the solemn opening bars of maestro Renzo Massarani's orchestral score, *Trumpet Calls and Dances for 18 BL*.[12] Then came the broadcast of the spectacle's leitmotif, "The Captain's Testament": a World War I hymn associated with the daredevil Alpine brigades instrumental in Italy's victory over Austria in the battle of the Piave river and, later, in the rise of fascism. The action may be summarized as follows:

*Act 1, Scene 1*. The location and volume of the chorus of singing voices oscillates as a searchlight scans the right portion of the stage, finding bodies, networks of barbed wire, running soldiers, sandbags, galloping horses, artillery being hauled into position.[13] Suddenly the rumble of an 18 BL Fiat truck is heard, and, as it crosses over the horizon line, artillery barrages light up the night sky. A spotlight reveals the truck's destination: a troop of several hundred second-line Italian soldiers, to whom its jovial Tuscan driver, Ugo Ceseri, delivers good humor, rations,

and mail. The truck's nickname, "Mother Cartridge-Pouch" (Mamma Giberna) is repeatedly shouted out in the course of a brief dialogue between Ceseri and the soldiers.[14]

*Scene 2*. New volleys of rockets are fired in the distance by the enemy forces, and a spotlight points to the middle hilltop, where a fierce machine-gun battle has front-line Italian soldiers pinned against the barbed wire. The truck now rumbles up the slope, its armored shield (borrowed from a 75-millimeter artillery battery) riddled by bullets. A firestorm rages as it clears the crest of the hill. Snippets of dialogue and song can be heard, interwoven with mechanical sounds and explosions. The driver heaves two sacks of food into a communications trench and continues down the back side of the slope out of the public's view. An Austrian artillery shell explodes where it has disappeared.

*Scene 3*. Confused voices are heard in the dark. The truck reappears around the corner of the third hill, its roar resounding with redoubled force. The twilight reveals that it is brimming over with young soldiers being transported to the front. Several dozen 18 BL's follow in its wake and unload their soldiers, who join in the assault across the top of the ridge. Searchlights scan the horizon. Artillery and machine-gun battles start and stop until, at last, victory is at hand. Far behind the top of the first hill, an Italian flag is hoisted against the brilliant white light of a sign announcing the conquest of Italian Trento and Trieste. Ceseri's truck, buried under a collapsed wall in the middle of the stage, reemerges from the rubble to lead a parade of 18 BL's over the horizon towards the flag, accompanied by triumphal shouting

**69**

and song. End of Act 1. The stage lights are extinguished, the stadium lights turned on.

The transition between World War I and the labor strikes of 1922 is marked by a fade out of the cannonades and by a fireworks display designed by Blasetti and pictured as follows in his notes:

After the victorious cries and chants will come an original pyrotechnic show, festive in its frequency, its showers, and its bright colors (white, yellow, blue, pink) to be fired in rapid alternation from the left and right sides of the stage. Lasting as long as needed to complete all requisite set changes, this display will gradually diminish in frequency and in the festiveness of its colors and sounds to the point where it becomes, in the end, an isolated but abundant rain of deep blood-red hue, echoed by a howl issuing from the stage.[15]

The intermission was carried out precisely as described, so when *Act 2, Scene 1* begins and the stadium lights are turned off, the public finds itself beneath a fiery curtain and assailed by the electronic growl of a howling mob. Beyond the red rain, the repositioned stage lights reveal a new landscape on the lower left-hand side of the stage. Strewn across it are abandoned work implements, battered haystacks, rotting produce. Factory sirens sound, but their wail is soon distorted into the squawk of rusty gears. Ceseri and his mechanic are attempting to unload their 18 BL's cargo. They preach against the strike and call out for help. But they become the target of a roving mob of gray strikers, brandishing pickets and a bright red flag. The mob's "mechanical howl"—the phrase belongs to the script—increases to deafening proportions as the strikers surround the truck (symbol of World War I) and batter it with sticks and stones, leaving the mechanic

38. *18 BL*: Act 1, scene 2. From *Comoedia* 16.6 (June 1934).

39. *18 BL*: Act 1, scene 3. From *BA* (1934).

unconscious. At this very instant, the truck's engine starts up and begins to roar above the chorus of shouts. The circle of strikers opens up, and Ceseri can be overheard crying out for revenge as the truck escapes into a gully.

*Scene 2*. An immense banquet table bearing the word PARLIAMENT appears atop the central hillock bathed in red light. Seated at the table is a group of geriatric politicians representing the liberal, socialist, and popular parties, as well as the Freemasons. Some are elegantly dressed in black tuxedos. They wear oversized top hats, which hang down over their eyes, and are engaged in conspiratorial whispering. Others are fat, sloppily but brightly dressed, and full of rhetorical bluster. The strikers gather around them, remaining silent except for an occasional chorus of "Long live the people's representatives!" and "Down with the army!" Soon all conversation has ceased and the only noises that can be heard are those of a banquet. Knives and forks clang on plates; the old men chew, belch, and cackle. A few minutes later, applause rings out. A socialist politician has stood up to begin a speech. Instead of a voice, however, the sound of a barrel organ issues from his mouth: a wind-up barrel

40. *18 BL*: Act 2, scene 3.
From *BA* (1934).

organ, like that employed by beggars with monkeys, playing the Dance of the Seven Veils from Richard Strauss's opera *Salomé*. Behind him, hundreds of slogan-bearing multicolored balloons rise up into the sky filled with empty promises. The barrel organ churns away for several minutes, after which it begins to wind down as a newsboy cries out headlines announcing the foundation of fascist groups. The balloons vanish and the music stops. One of the elders croaks loudly the fateful words of Luigi Facta before the March on Rome: "But what do these fascists want?" At this precise instant, Mother Cartridge-Pouch, loaded with young fascists, appears unexpectedly over the hilltop and sends everyone scampering. She thunders down the hill and overturns the table of parliament. In the aftermath of her intrusion, Ceseri harangues the mob: "Seven million paychecks lost due to the railway strike! One hundred and thirty million in damages to farming thanks to the socialist dictatorship in

41. *18 BL*: Act 2, scene 3, From *BA* (1934).

the Bologna region! Everywhere dead men sacrificed to the demagogic beast! Workers, when will you free yourselves from your mystifying leaders? Italians, your salvation lies in your daring!" [16]

*Scene 3.* Fire alarms ring out. Fascist hymns are sung by choruses far away and nearby. Ceseri's admonitions have failed, evidently, since a factory is ablaze in the left corner of the landscape. His 18 BL, filled with blackshirts, goes to the rescue but is ambushed by an armed socialist mob, from which issues the usual mechanical howl. Bullets fly in all directions. Other fascist brigades douse the fire. When the ambush is over, darkness descends again, and in the twilight one can see the fascist dead and wounded being heaped onto the platform of Ceseri's truck, as if on an altar. The truck rolls up to the

summit of the stage's central crest, and 200 fascists converge upon it, arranging themselves in a square formation and standing mutely at attention. Over the horizon, a bright white light glows with increasing intensity. Projected from out of the light, a "metallic and clear voice" (Mussolini's) interrupts the funereal silence, calling out: "Heroes of the war and martyrs of the revolution!" "Present" they respond. "To whom does Italy belong, to whom Rome?" continues the metallic voice. "To us!—To us!—To us!" they respond. [17] But the chorus of voices is no longer isolated. From all sides of the auditorium and stage, 1,000 blackshirts, including members of the audience, shout out, "To us!" Led by a convoy of several dozen trucks, they parade out across the landscape and converge over the horizon line, where their silhouettes vanish into the white light. Act 2 has ended; fascism's putative revolution, the March on Rome, has begun.

The final act of *18 BL* concerns one of the centerpieces of fascist domestic policy and perhaps the most revealing of fascism's redemptive myths: the draining of the Pontine marshes, the reclamation of marshland for purposes of agriculture, and the construction there, always at breakneck speed, of fascist new towns. [18] Since these events project the action of *18 BL* ten years forward, Blasetti devised a second interlude to mark the transition from the early 1920's to 1932. First, as the sounds of the March on Rome begin to taper off, the stage's searchlights turn away from the marchers towards the night sky, which they scan nervously. Suddenly several airplanes—doubtless in formation, according to the conventions of the contemporary mass flight—appear and repeatedly swoop

73

down over the stadium, showering the crowd
with broadsheets from *Il Popolo d'Italia* pro-
claiming Mussolini's seizure of power and
celebrating the principal phases and accomplishments of fascist rule. At the same time,
young fascists dressed like newspaper boys
run up and down the aisles, shouting out the
headlines and distributing newspapers. Once
the time allotted to carry out set changes
has elapsed, the newspaper boys vanish and
the airplanes peel off to the right and left
of the stage.[19]

*Act 3, Scene 1.* The lights drop, and Massarani's heroic dance music sounds. The stage
is aswarm with hundreds of near-naked
children, who wend their way up over the
horizon following furrows cut into the land
by a handful of peasants, whose wagons
and tools are in view. The children are followed by 100 athletes in formation, who perform a gymnastic dance with lances and
bows: emblems of the "human reclamation"
accomplished by fascist education.

43. *18 BL*: Act 3, scene 3.
From *BA* (1934).

steely words: "Here . . . landfill" (*Qui. Colmata*). A legion of trucks roars up alongside the center-right lip and begins to fill in the swamp. The Commander rotates 180° and issues a command to a squadron of bulldozers on the right side of the stage: "In three days, the road to Littoria will cross this void. We shall work all night."[22]

*Scene 3.* The entire stage is lit. On the left, the filling operation continues; on the right, the bulldozers carve out a highway. Here and there packs of workers can be seen plowing and planting the land. Trucks crisscross in the background. The agitation continues until a factory whistle sounds, marking the end of the night shift. Tools are abandoned, the trucks head back to their sheds, songs of war and revolution are sung. The stage is left empty, except for a few stragglers whose banter is overheard as they await a ride from Mother Cartridge-Pouch, now rebaptized *Old Cartridge-Pouch*. Still driven by Ceseri, she arrives from offstage right, battered and torn. Although she is able to transport them halfway across the stage, her motor is blown and soon begins spewing steam and smoke. All efforts to revive her fail, and, instead of abandoning her, they decide to push her right up to the lip of the first swamp. As she wobbles towards the precipice, two columns of trucks filled with workers arrive on the scene. They surround her and shut off their engines. The left hillock is now ablaze "in the mode of dazzling transfigurations or the head of Moses"; there is dead silence.[23] Ceseri stands at the center of this funereal composition and proclaims in a mournful tone: "She has fought the war, the revolution, and the battle of land reclamation. Now she will eagerly support the highway to Littoria."

*Scene 2.* Off in a hollow to the left of the stage, a swamp comes into view under a faint greenish spotlight. Filled with reeds and bubbling with mud, it emanates steam and froglike croakings intermingled with voices of rumor, calumny, and doubt.[20] As the gymnasts depart, one of the frogs mutters, "Billions and billions spent to uglify the race! Violent and ignorant generations are being fashioned, hungry for war, slaughter, and excess." "They tell me the holy youth of Milan have risen up in the name of pagan tyranny," croaks another. "How true, how true! In Naples too," responds a third.[21] The rumormongering continues until, above them on the horizon, atop the highest point on the stage, a monumental figure on horseback (identical to the Garibaldi of *1860*) appears in profile against intersecting beams of light: the Commander. He utters only two

The old truck is pushed over the precipice into the swamp and buried in the mud, as Ceseri prophesies her return (with a characteristically fascist, not to mention blasphemous, conflation of the secular and sacred orders): "In three days she will return to her duties anew, my old lady. Forever!"[24] The lights darken and focus on her carcass. The double column of trucks departs and passes above her, barely visible. The sound of marching drums is heard, blended with music. White buildings flicker in the distance as Italy marches off towards the city of the future: Littoria (now renamed Latina), first of the fascist new towns. A heroic trumpet call is heard far off in the distance and echoes back with redoubled force. The stadium lights come on.

War—revolution—reconstruction: here were the three great themes of *18 BL*'s theater of and for the masses. However crude its unfolding of these themes may seem, the spectacle aspired to elevate contemporary history to the status of myth by means of a hybrid stagecraft merging hyperrealism with allegory, and even political caricature.[1] In an era when the transition from silent to talking films was being completed, it tried to adapt to the stage the use of layered soundtracks, cinematic lighting tricks, and editing techniques such as montage and the rapid crosscutting of scenes. This it did in an effort to supplant the values of the nineteenth-century theater: whether the latter's emphasis upon the individual psychology of protagonists, or its reliance upon the star system, subjection to the limitations imposed by indoor stages, and dependence upon the sonority of the spoken word. In a pre-performance interview, Blasetti would thus declare: "Movies have accustomed spectators to seeing things on a grand scale; they

habituated them to a sense of realism, to rapid shifts between scenes, to a vastness of spaces and horizons that the theater cannot provide. Here, precisely, it is a matter of creating a theater that can offer those sensations to the public."[2]

For all its attempts to transport cinematic sensations to the stage, *18 BL* also set out to transcend the cinema and forge a hallucinatory dramatic form not unrelated to the Wagnerian *Gesamtkunstwerk*, at once hyperreal and superreal in character. It set out to achieve a higher, more distinctively fascist form of tragic pathos: "to embody the real and the symbolic simultaneously, creating a kind of actualized mystical experience [*una specie di misticizzazione di atto*] . . . of a heroic subject matter."[3] In the words of Corrado Sofia, another of *18 BL*'s authors, it sought "to reawaken the same enthusiasm expressed by crowds in sports arenas and perhaps to succeed in being more seductive than the cinema, because actual voices and human figures, and the open air surrounding the stage, are all sources of instinctual attraction. The cinema thrusts the spectator into a dark room. On the screen, it presents flat and colorless figures. By its very nature, it is tied to documentary and scientific forms, rather than to an imagination capable of enveloping facts in mystery."[4]

Contrary to a widely held postwar view, fascism's attitude to film had been ambivalent from the start. On the one hand, the fascist state celebrated the medium's power, adopting slogans such as "Cinematography is the strongest weapon" and developing a documentary and propaganda filmmaking industry through the Istituto LUCE.[5] On the other, it was long reluctant to involve itself directly in the business of commercial filmmaking, perhaps because it recognized the relative weakness of the Italian film industry, the overwhelming strength of Hollywood commercial cinema, and the international prestige enjoyed by the Soviet political cinema. As a result, initiatives in the domain of film often aspired to do little more than institute new "ideologically inflected" means of delivery. Telling in this regard was the OND's creation in the mid 1930's of a network of movie theaters and of a fleet of 94 roving film trucks modeled on a *theatrical* precedent: the thespian cars.[6]

But a deeper aversion to film also prompted fascism to single out theater as the privileged fascist art and to place theatrical values at the center of fascist politics. In this regard, Sofia's theorization is exemplary. Film, Sofia suggests, is by its nature a decadent medium: It therefore attenuates the bond between the bodies of spectators and performers, reducing the world to a series of artificial—that is, flat and colorless—projections meant for silent and solitary contemplation. The theater of the masses, on the contrary, restores to the body its central role and in so doing forges a transformative, mutually seductive relationship between representation and reality, art and life. The mass audience and mass performers leave behind the cloistered interiors of the old theater and cinema in order to stand before one another in actual time and space, surrounded by nature and under the grandest of Fortuny domes: the open sky.[7] Within this healthy natural setting, an instinctual attraction between them can break down the barrier between the auditorium and stage, provoking the sort of healthy contagion fostered by athletic events or mass rallies. The spectacle itself is designed to excite such primordial passions. Plot is to be stripped down to its minimal constituent elements: hero versus antihero, black versus red versus white. Actions are simple, readily accessible, and anchored in the historical present. The poetic word is subordinated to the mysterious play of images and rhythms.[8] Physical actions, optical tricks, acrobatics, magic, fireworks . . . in short, *external* effects and affects occupy the place of honor once held in the theater by the values of individuality and interiority.[9] The end result towards which this complex of techniques strives is the forging of a charismatic community (a microcosm of the fascistized Italian nation): "the fusion of thousands and thousands of souls within a single framework of ideas and events."[10]

This, at least, was the theoretical matrix within which the creators of *18 BL* were operating—a matrix bearing traces of a long history, extending back to the French revolutionary festivals and to their dream of tearing down the barrier between stage and auditorium so as to sanctify "the [people's] collective body, or the universal *presence* that had no need to look beyond itself";[11] a matrix informed by Wagnerian fantasies regarding the total work of art, not dissimilar to those that would shape the work of Hanns Johst and Nazi *Thingspiele* from 1933 through 1937.[12] Unlike most of its Nazi analogues and successors, the matrix in question was distinctively modernist, indebted to Bontempelli's writings on magic realism and to contemporary debates on theater and cinema, and theater and sport.[13] Unfortunately, for Blasetti and his collaborators, *18 BL* fell short of fulfilling these ambitions. The new theater of masses was applauded, praised for its audacity and patriotic sentiments, but it was just as often dismissed as a resounding failure. The following sampling of contemporary opinion is indicative:

Yesterday evening we were perhaps subjected more to the *evocation* of the great events occurring around us than were we treated to a *representation* of them. There was less drama than there were intimations of drama.[14]

The *connective tissue* essential to the theater was missing: that sort of harmony that binds together varied actions and ensures that the public is kept in suspense and enthralled during the course of the spectacle."[15]

[This spectacle] has taught us many things, and even if it hasn't made us lose our love for . . . the standard theater with its reliance upon three walls and upon words and gestures, it has demonstrated nonetheless that much can be done in this theater of masses and for masses, a symptomatic dress rehearsal of which was offered in Florence last evening.[16]

The work's principal goal was not attained: that of electrifying, via the mobilization of a mass of 2,000 actors, the mass of over 20,000 audience members. Despite their appreciation of the efforts of those who created and realized the event, the latter remained mostly unconvinced.[17]

When reviewers were not nuanced in their criticism, they were harsh:

It breaks my heart to admit it, but this experiment, whether as a model of the theater or as an exaltation of our national passions, failed nearly 100 percent.[18]

Last Sunday's spectacle was a fiasco, dissipating in little more than two hours so much noble labor, so many intelligent efforts, such high expectations.[19]

The theater of masses was *not* born at the Albereta of the Isolotto. On the contrary, one might say that what was begotten was a certain aversion on the part of the masses towards this sort of spectacle, which was passed off as "theater."[20]

It was a disaster. A foreseeable and foreseen one, inasmuch as this sort of mass spectacle, clumsy from elephantiasis, chaotic because out of proportion, is ill suited to our folk. It may well pass muster in Soviet Russia, where the bulk of sentient beings have developed a taste for the mob's hurly-burly, pushing and shoving, for the din of big blasts, explosions and blazing fireworks, and for the funereal pyre of bloodthirsty capitalism.[21]

This is not to imply that there were not many favorable, even rave, reviews. For instance, Raffaello Franchi, writing in *L'Italia Letteraria*, did not hesitate to affirm that "if one were to offer a totalitarian judgment and to embrace the crowd of 20,000, I would lean towards speaking of a *masterpiece*" (although he was quick to add that "a definitive evaluation will have to await decantation in memory").[22] The anonymous reviewer of *Roma* entitled his commentary "*18 BL*: An Outstanding Success."[23] His counterpart at *Corriere del Lunedì* called the performance a triumph, concluding that "the spectacle at the Albereta constitutes one of the most remarkable artistic expressions of our era."[24] Others, like Enzo Maurri, felt that the first act in particular was "constructed masterfully" (*costruito magistralmente*).[25] Still others, Orio Vergani, for instance, thought "the production machine had moved, on the whole, without stumbling, and often with effects of great beauty and emotion." "Perfection would have been achieved," Vergani added, "if the bad weather had not postponed the rehearsals until Friday."[26]

Despite these favorable evaluations, the volume of criticism was such that the organizers of the experiment were forced to adopt an apologetic stance almost from the start. In his first post-performance statement, Pavolini did his best to limit the harm: "We are not unhappy at having embarked upon the enormous adventure of the first mass theater. Even if we did err in part. . . . But we believe that, now that the experiment is under way, the theater of masses will indeed come into being. We also believe that *18 BL* has proven highly useful in this respect, providing a gold mine of lessons, both positive and negative."[27]

Such valiant efforts at damage control were rendered nearly impossible by the publication in *Quadrivio* of a ferocious attack on Blasetti by a key member of the authorial collective: none other than Corrado Sofia.[28] In the months preceding the performance, there had already been hints of rivalry. Sofia had not hesitated to claim the lion's share of credit for creative input into *18 BL* for himself, nor to publicize his dissatisfaction with

Blasetti's technical and editorial decisions.[29] Now he came out into the open and accused Blasetti of a long list of "treasonous" acts: of having been a poor film director to start with; of having needlessly destroyed the lead 18 BL truck; of developing the spectacle around machines and machine-mediated voices, when contemporary Italians were "staunch enemies of machine-worship";[30] of having rejected a superior stage design proposed by Fulvio Jacchia and Sofia himself; and of having wanted "to revolutionize everything in little more than a month," when, in point of fact, "every revolution must be prepared even in its minute particulars."[31]

Never one to shy away from polemics, Blasetti responded angrily. In an open letter to the editor of *La Tribuna*, he accepted full blame for *18 BL*'s failings but called attention to Sofia's astonishing volte-face: only weeks before, Sofia had been taking full credit for the spectacle; now he pretended to have been disaffected from the start.[32] A counterattack and apologia by Sofia followed several days later, featuring accusations such as that Blasetti's true ambition in *18 BL* had been to earn himself a government sinecure and pension.[33] This in turn provoked yet another furious rejoinder from the film director, as well as intercessions on his behalf by Leo Bomba and Gherardo Gherardi.[34]

As might perhaps have been anticipated, technical problems contributed their share to the mixed reception and controversy that greeted *18 BL*. The vast stage had diminished the audience's ability to participate in every action. Able to hear, but unable to see, many spectators felt no instinctual attraction to the mass of protagonists on stage. Instead

**TRAMONTO AL PINCIO**
Spettacolo per masse

A. Mezio

---

44. Mezio, "Sunset viewed from the Pincio." Cartoon lampooning *18 BL*'s dream of achieving a total realism. From *Quadrivio*, May 6, 1934.

of being transported into an unstable realm where the threshold between reality and the magical/mythical appeared permeable, they were left, like Bontempelli himself, with a lingering "sense of emptiness, depression, and coldness."[35] Perceptions of this kind seem to have been especially frequent among younger members of the audience, at least to judge by eyewitness accounts like the following:

At the time I was a boy. Arriving by bus, I had been assigned a "popular" seat from which one could see the trucks roar by, hear the explosions of paper bombs and music broadcast over loudspeakers, all in a great cloud of dust. Then darkness set in and the military searchlights were illumined. Not much was visible or comprehensible, especially to us youngsters, seated as we were behind a large trench.[36]

Another audience member seated in the "popular section" reports much the same. In Act 1, "The actors—let us refer to them as such—had cried out and we had understood little of what they had said. But who cared? Those voices served as a soundtrack just like the bang-bang of the guns and, besides, it wasn't hard to imagine what a soldier might have said in the trenches' mud or while assaulting an enemy position."[37] But in Acts 2 and 3, "everything appeared uncertain and confused, and the impossibility of understanding what was being said on stage had become irritating."[38] The vision and sound problems were aggravated by the discontinuous, episodic nature of the narrative, and by the often awkward synchronization between the soundtrack and the events on stage. Not least of all, there was the performance's finale, which Blasetti had been unable to rehearse. In a near-disastrous Pirandellian twist, it seems that Mother Cartridge-Pouch changed her mind at the last moment about being buried, and for several tense minutes the combined forces of a dozen actors proved insufficient to roll her over into the swamp. In the end, they succeeded, but only after Blasetti switched off the lights and summoned additional actors and a second truck. When the lights came back on, Mother Cartridge-Pouch was in her grave, but many spectators had already departed and the intended tragic effect had been buried long before the truck.[39] The

**81**

closing whimper is best described by Maurri: "It ended as it had to end: with sparing and awkward applause from the front rows, with a witticism or two muttered under the breath, and with an indulgent grin on people's faces as they exited. The few who had donned black shirts had lost their usual self-assurance. . . . Immolated in a single evening, *18 BL*, about which so much had been said, was soon relegated to silence." [40]

# 6

Technical deficiencies there were, but deficiencies of this kind had also from the start haunted the Soviet and German mass theaters (for instance, Reinhardt's famed Berlin Großes Schauspielhaus, among whose "democratically" arrayed 3,200 seats, fully one-third of the audience could not see or hear what went on behind the stage's central proscenium arch). But at the heart of the controversy surrounding *18 BL* loomed the deeper question of whether a machine was a fitting hero for the fascist theater. Some young members of the crowd thought not, apparently greeting the event's conclusion with cries of, "What the hell do *we* care about a truck?"[1] The objection would be repeated frequently in the ensuing months of debate, always in tandem with criticism of the collective drafting of *18 BL*'s script. (For the fascist imagination, mechanization and collectivization were indissociable.) "The idea of making a machine into a hero, whether that, as some say (but I doubt), of Mussolini, or instead of Marinetti or Pavolini, is a stupid idea," said the novelist and editor Ugo Ojetti. "Art is man. Machines without men are soulless wood and metal; and they are mass-produced as equal, nay, identical."[2]

Ojetti's aversion to mechanical heroes was based on the fear that they summoned up the specter of soulless, deindividualized, mass society: a society founded, not on the values of nationalism, but on those of internationalism. Such a society had a name, and other commentators would prove less reticent about its location and identity: "[Mechanical heroes] . . . are well suited to those peoples for whom the machine has become a religion. . . . to draw near to such mentalities makes it more difficult to uproot the error committed by those who, after a cursory look at our affairs, would assimilate our revolution to the Russian revolution."[3] For these and like-minded viewers, the recourse to a mechanical protagonist and the collec-

Roma... ...Mosca... ...Milano

IL « DUCE » — In piedi, ca-
merati, contro il comunismo !

STALIN — In piedi, compa-
gni, contro il fascismo !

GRANDI — Ed ora, caro Li-
vinof,, sediamoci e brindiamo ai
nostri buoni rapporti.

45. "Rome, Moscow, Mi-
lan": the enemy twins as
viewed by a Paris-based opposition journal. Cartoon
from *Il Becco Giallo* 6.70
(Nov. 20–Dec. 20, 1930). Il
Duce: "Rise up, comrades,
against communism!"
Stalin: "Rise up, comrades,
against fascism!" [Dino]
Grandi: "And now my dear
Litvinof, let us sit down and
drink to our cordial relations." (Grandi was the Italian minister of foreign affairs between 1929 and
1932, and pursued a policy
of entente with the Soviet
Union in order to diminish
the ability of France to
thwart Italian claims to various portions of the African
continent.)

tive authorship of the script raised grave
doubts about fascism's specificity. Like its
enemy twin, fascism was committed to
building an industrial mass society—which
is to say, a society dependent upon the close
interconnection between machines and
human beings. But fascism also claimed to
stand in opposition to Marxist materialism,
utilitarianism, and collectivism, and in favor
of values associated with vague terms such
as soul, spirit, beauty, heroism, individualism, and Latinity. Could such values, however defined, be fully reconciled with mechanization and industrialization? Was the ideal
of a mass society made up of individuals
realizable? Perhaps not for a cultural conservative such as Ojetti; but for committed

modernists like the creators of *18 BL*, the answer was affirmative.

The spectacle's detractors were right in at
least one important respect: *18 BL* was indeed haunted by Soviet antecedents. The
machine as protagonist of mass actions had
long been one of the heroic themes of Soviet
culture, a fact amply documented in numerous divulgative works from the early 1930's,
including Pietro Maria Bardi's *Un fascista al
paese dei Soviet* (A fascist in the land of the
Soviets), which won the Bulgarian Communist Party's Varzraidanie prize; Gaetano
Ciocca's *Giudizio sul bolscevismo* (Judgment
on Bolshevism); Emile Schreiber's *Come si
vive in Russia* (Life in Russia); Waldemar
Gurian's *Il bolscevismo* (Bolshevism); and

René Fülöp-Miller's *Il volto del bolscevismo* (The face of bolshevism).[4] The latter, a contemporary bestseller that devoted two chapters to the Soviet revolutionary theater, claimed that under socialism, "the imitation of machines has been raised to the status of a religious sacrament, comparable to the imitation of Christ," and discussed at length Soviet experiments with collective authorship.[5] The Soviet interest in developing modernist forms of epic founded upon the interaction between machinery and human masses would also have reached Blasetti and his cohorts via the cinema. Eisenstein's theoretical writings were available in translation, and, by the early 1930's, Italian cinema clubs had started to exhibit his silent films, from *Strike* and *Potemkin* to the quasi-documentary *The General Line*, whose triumphal parade of tractors was a possible source for *18 BL*.[6] An even more direct source of inspiration were the Soviet revolutionary festivals: avant-garde experiments in mass pageantry that had stimulated great interest in fascist Italy during the cultural debates of the early 1930's.[7] Among these, the most immediately pertinent is perhaps *The Storming of the Winter Palace*: a collectively authored reenactment of the events of October 1917 cast in the same hyperrealist yet allegorizing mold as *18 BL*. Performed in Petrograd's Palace Square in 1920 before a public of nearly 100,000, this multimedia spectacle surrounded its 8,000 mass protagonists with gunfire, artillery, rockets, and a panoply of lighting effects.[8] As can be seen in contemporary drawings, films, and photographs, its climactic episode featured a white truck carrying the fleeing Kerensky government, with a platoon of Red Army trucks in hot pursuit. Other parallels could be cited from works such as Yuri Annenkov's *The Mystery of Liberated Labor* and Meyerhold's *History of Three Internationals*: the latter involving, in Fülöp-Miller's account, "200 cadets from the cavalry school, 2,300 soldiers, 16 cannons, 5 airplanes with reflectors, 10 mounted reflectors, armored trains, armored cars, motorcycles, field hospitals, etc., etc., not to mention various military bands and choruses."[9] (The proletarian theaters of Erwin Piscator, Ernst Toller, and even Berthold Brecht, which were known and admired in Italy thanks to the writings of Bragaglia and Alvaro, could also be cited in this regard.)[10] However considerable the direct impact of Soviet precedents might have been, it is essential to emphasize that the haunting of *18 BL* was more than a simple question of influence. The drama was built upon a series of binary oppositions that betray similarities between fascism and its bolshevik twin, even as they attempt to institute differences. (Elided by this binarism is fascism's true historical nemesis, liberal democracy.) The red strikers parade, fight, and chant choruses just like their black-shirted counterparts.[11] The metallic howl of their voices echoes the mechanical roar of the fascists' trucks. Both groups are presented as undifferentiated collectives, and both constitute themselves in a choral dialogue with a leader's mechanized voice.

This said, it makes a substantial difference whether the voice in question consists of a wind-up barrel organ playing the tune of Salomé's Dance of the Seven Veils or issues forth from a living equestrian statue in the form of metallic orders and slogans. What I mean is that while the detractors of *18 BL* may have been correct about the work's Soviet resonances, they were blind to the contrast it was attempting to emphasize between fascist and bolshevik attitudes to machinery. For heuristic purposes, I shall formulate this as the distinction between Soviet *mechanization* and fascist *metallization*. A fuller theorization will be offered in due course, but grant for the moment that mechanization and metallization represent two distinct ways of conceptualizing the interface between mass-production technologies and human bodies. "Distinct," but interconnected, so it is hardly surprising that the split became less than absolute as the 1930's unfolded. The assumed name Stalin, after all, means not "mechanical man," but rather "man of steel"; and the growing cultural-political convergence between fascist Italy and Stalinist Russia was just as evident to Trotskyists, who regularly spoke of Stalin's *fascism*, as it was to many Italian intellectuals, who, from the time of the Rome/Moscow debate (1931–32) through Berto Ricci's 1937 call for a "universal revolution . . . with Rome and Moscow alone at the helm" sought to define communism as an imperfect copy of fascism.[12]

No matter how entangled, the distinction captures something essential about the two October revolutions. Mechanization had been one of the driving forces behind the Soviet revolutionary theater. It was identified with an effort to strip the stage bare and disclose its most intimate workings. Instead of a factory of seductive myths and illusions, the proletarian stage would thereby become both an instrument for the demystification of contemporary society and a place where an alternative future could be staged and produced: in short, a factory in which the efficient interaction between mechanized actor/workers, working machines, and a transparent scenic apparatus would exemplify the communist society of the future. Since the actor-worker represented the ideal citizen of this future republic, contemporary dramatists such as Meyerhold sought to transform him or her into a utopian subject identical in every detail to the classless and sexless economic subject the revolution was attempting to forge. Inspired by their economist colleagues, as well as by Emile Jacques-Dalcroze's and Adolph Appia's eurythmic theater experiments, they found in the motion-efficiency studies of Frederick Taylor and others a model for the reduction of the work of acting to a series of biomechanical functions: a machinelike discipline whose objectives were economy, rhythm, and deliberateness. This mechanico-technological reconstruction of man's daily life was viewed, not as dehumanizing or deindividualizing, but, on the contrary, as emancipatory. Mechanization was the means to a utopian end: the creation of a body without fatigue—the robot—and of a society freed from the burden of alienating work—communism.

The creators of *18 BL* were also striving to shape a new society within and outside the confines of the theater, and for them, no less than for the Leninists, the production process was just as integral to the revolutionary spectacle as the final product. Committed to the fascist ideal of an absolute theater that would collapse the boundaries between the real and the ideal, they viewed Soviet-style

46. (left) "Troops defiling before the White government." Scene from *The Storming of the Winter Palace* (1920). From René Fülöp-Miller and Joseph Gregor, *The Russian Theater* (1930).

47. (right) "Victorious military cars." Scene from *The Storming of the Winter Palace* (1920). From René Fülöp-Miller and Joseph Gregor, *The Russian Theater* (1930).

mechanization as the foe of a theatrical "imagination capable of enveloping facts in mystery." The function of mass theater as they conceived of it was at once *ritual* and *inaugural*: "ritual" to the extent that by having actors too young to have participated in the March on Rome reenact the battles of their fathers, it hoped to bridge the gap between the pre- and postrevolutionary generations and thereby to renew the revolution; "inaugural" to the extent that the spectacle was organized and carried out in such a way as to offer a preview of a future fully "fascistized" society.

As regards the latter, the production of *18 BL* was organized along military lines. The 2,000 to 3,000 young actors, mostly male members of the GUF and Fasci Giovanili (although active-duty soldiers, Balilla, and Giovani Italiane, participated) were divided into army-like units, each assigned a number, and

placed under the leadership of an actual war veteran. To judge by contemporary press accounts, their training as thespians was indistinguishable from military training: "The actors were instructed at length in quasi-military fashion";[13] "One is reminded of a large-scale military exercise";[14] "Although they know that it is all make-believe, they sense the faithful resemblance to actual combat";[15] "In this freshly built theater one already breathes the air of war."[16] Functioning as a surrogate Duce, the director oversaw these war games as if he were a field commander. He moved about by motorcycle, barking out orders through a megaphone, and was linked by wiring to the entire expanse of the stage: "In a central cabin containing a network of telephone controls, bells, and variegated signals, the 'director' will, like a commander, have the fate of the spectacle firmly in his grip. From time to time, depending on the unfolding of the

48. Dictators and directors survey the cultural battlefield: *18 BL* control tower. From *BA*.

action, portions of the landscape or details on the stage will be illuminated: a position, a communications trench, a hilltop. The 'vision' will thus be unbroken and synthetic." [17]

The authority, omniscience, and ubiquity granted the director by the network of cables was not limited to the stage. Strictly figurative wires joined him to the city authorities, the military, and the PNF, all of which made a show (however inefficient) of contributing resources, manpower, and technical assistance in order that the vision be realized without impediment. [18] From the start, Blasetti had made clear his demands for absolute authority: "nothing that I have requested can be diminished in scale or granted without full cooperation. . . . the execution of production orders must be absolutely military, which is to say immediate, without hesitation or need for discussion." [19] Heroic acts of the collective will were the order of the day and, whether actual or imagined for propaganda purposes, constituted a spectacle in and of themselves. Rehearsals carried on late into the night (much to the displeasure of the mass of actors). In an ostentatious display of fascism's revolt against the life of ease and comfort, the stage and auditorium were completed after weeks of continuous day and night shifts by a construction crew designed, or so it was claimed, to embody the ideals of discipline, class collaboration, and national mobilization. [20] A majority of its 200 members were unemployed fascists and city employees, although soldiers and student volunteers appear to have worked alongside them. Similar ideals extended to the audience, segments of which were bussed in from the Tuscan countryside or arrived on special trains under the aegis of the fascist youth and afterwork organizations. Even in ticket sales there were to be no "inopportune contradictions or privileges"; *18 BL* would inaugurate a genuine mass art form, so no complimentary tickets were distributed, and even Starace purchased his own ticket. [21] Visibility would be comparable from all sectors of the hierarchically ordered auditorium in order to ensure that one perspective alone would emerge by the spectacle's end: a unified collective vision ordered and organized by a single director/dictator.

Within the setting of this society in a state of perpetual mobilization, machines are not just tools to be used by human protagonists. Their function is a higher one: that of serving as idealized doubles both of the collective and its director/commander. I employ the word "doubles" because, contrary to Soviet practice, two parallel dramatic universes co-exist on stage in *18 BL*: one human and one mechanical; one involving the interplay of men with their leaders; the other that of Mother Cartridge-Pouch with her chorus of 50 trucks. Like their human counterparts, who form a mass of individuals, machines are treated as *irreducible entities* in *18 BL*. They are mechanical individuals that can be organized into larger collective groupings or totalities, or that can be placed in the service of an individual or totality as prosthetic devices. But they cannot be broken down into a series of interchangeable functions or parts. (Within the fascist imaginary, there-

49. *18 BL*: Blasetti and actors during rehearsal. From *BA* (1934).

## AUTOCARRO
## TIPO NORMALE

su chassis Mod. 18 BL (35 HP)

*Cassa* con sponde laterali fisse e sponda posteriore ribaltabile e smontabile. Questo autocarro viene anche costruito con tutte le sponde (la posteriore e le laterali) ribaltabili e smontabili, sì da potersi rapidamente trasformare in semplice piattaforma.

*Dimensioni utili:* lunghezza m. 3,50; larghezza m. 1,73; altezza sponde m. 0,575; altezza dal pavimento al centro dell'arco delle centine, m. 1,60 circa - Tre centine metalliche smontabili, collegate da listelli longitudinali - Copertone impermeabile.

*Sedile anteriore* a 3 posti (compreso quello del conduttore) rivestiti in pelle nera e imbottiti - Capote impermeabile, in tela extra-forte; con grembiale, pure impermeabile, applicato al cruscotto.

Parafanghi alle ruote anteriori - Staffoni per salire, (oppure pedane lunghe in legno) - Due cassette porta-attrezzi.

Un faro autogeneratore (oppure due fari con generatore separato; due fanaletti laterali sul cruscotto, fanalino posteriore alla targa.

Tromba a mano - Borsa utensili d'uso - Crick - Verniciatura, grigio industriale.

fore, it would be inconceivable that Mother Cartridge-Pouch's motor simply be replaced or rebuilt, because it is quite literally her own distinctive mechanical soul or heart.) This principle of irreducibility permits fascist machinery to take on human attributes such as age, gender, nationality, or to exhibit virtues associated with interiority such as willpower and courage. It also ensures that any mingling of man and machine will assume the form of identification and not the exchange of parts or functions. Within this economy of identification, machines stand for an ideal: not that of a body without fatigue or of a society without alienation, but instead the distinctively fascist ideal of *constant exertion and fatigue coldly resisted . . .* in other words, metallization.[22]

Metallization is a paradoxical concept, whose tentacles extend deep into contemporary mass culture, and whose crucial importance to fascism I shall now sketch. Unlike the sexless stage machines of the Russian theater, the mechanical hero of *18 BL* is neither the emblem of an atemporal utopia nor a specimen of advanced engineering. She is simply a mother truck: a plain, utilitarian vehicle destined for obsolescence, a carrier pouch for young soldier-cartridges, which will eventually be used up. The first mass-produced Fiat truck, she embodies the fascist masses, even when singled out with respect to other trucks.[23] Her story, writes Orio Vergani, "is the story of one, of one hundred, of thousands upon thousands of trucks."[24] Two further signs confirm her mass identity: her gender—the masses were always feminized in contemporary propaganda—and her placement under a relay of male governors extending from Ceseri to Blasetti to Mus-

**REDENZIONE**

50. (opposite) (Not) your average revolutionary Mom: brochure for the 18 BL truck. From Archivio Storico Fiat, Turin.

51. (above) "Redemption": the salvific effects of imposing geometry upon the nation's soil. Cartoon from *Il Popolo d'Italia*, June 27, 1934.

solini. If feminized, why, then, should she be a mother? A first-level answer is provided by Pavolini: "The revolution was born in the trucks on which, during the squadrist era, student and worker, field laborer and clerk fraternally sowed [*gettarono*] the characteristic seed [*germe*] of the new state." [25] Mother Cartridge-Pouch is thus marked as a bridge figure between the pre- and postrevolutionary eras. But if her role is to provoke the fruitful spilling of seed that engenders the new state, why should the love that binds her to her boys be maternal rather than hetero- or homoerotic? A clue is pro-

vided by the sole other female presence in *18 BL*: Salomé, evoked via the music of her famously licentious dance. Temptress and bane of John the Baptist in Oscar Wilde's play and Richard Strauss's opera, Salomé is conjured up in order to forge a symbolic link between the menace of decadent sensuality and Marxian materialism. [26] Her scandalous dance involves a double act of seduction: the seduction of her stepfather, Herod, who promises the granting of any wish in return for her performance; and the consummation of her failed seduction of the holy man, whose head she demands (in place of the phallus she has been unable to conquer). Garbled and parodied by a barrel organ in the course of *18 BL*'s socialist oration, Salomé's dance becomes a cheap striptease, akin to the denuding of the Soviet stage, with its false promises of a technico-mechanical utopia. Against such seductive and castratory illusions imported from England, Germany, and Austria—indeed against nonprocreative sexuality as such—*18 BL* elaborates the chaste, metallic countermyth of the Latin mother truck: a normal type of truck (*autocarro tipo normale*) whose norm is heroic service, dedication, and incessant work. To echo the terms of Victoria de Grazia's *How Fascism Ruled Women: Italy, 1922–1945*, whereas Salomé is a sort of "crisis woman . . . a masculinized plaything, a false and alien creature, the product of Paris and Hollywood," Mother Cartridge-Pouch is an "authentic woman": a homegrown "broodmare, mother, and mate," ideally suited to the fascist state's demographic campaigns. [27] In her, on her, through her, the revolution is born. The seed is sown for a

52. Head of state, 1: Thayaht, "Dux." Period postcard of Thayaht's representation in cast steel of Mussolini's head (1929) from the author's collection, reproduced with permission from the Michahelles Archive. In a letter to his brother Ruggero, dated May 12, 1929, Thayaht described it as follows: "The idea of the lictorial axe, of Roman arches, of the warrior's helmet, and of the gaze fixed on a distant future: all these are brought together and interpenetrate to create a whole that *truly resembles* il Duce. This work does not aspire to be a portrait, but rather a symbolic effigy of the dynamic power of the Man in whose hands lies Italy's fate."

coolness, her work of gestation now fully accomplished, she succumbs, only to be transfigured into a symbol of national sacrifice. Like her figurative sons, the soldiers of World War I and the March on Rome, she lays down her body in a final gesture of servitude and self-offering that literally paves the way for Italy's future expansion and glory.

*18 BL* thus ends on something of an elegiac note. The vehicle that had come to personify fascism's resistance to fatigue submits to nature's iron-clad law of degeneration over time via an act of fruitful sacrifice. And she does so at the culminating moment of a work in whose fulgurant high-contrast tableaux the promise of a transfigured national collectivity is always shadowed by the menace of dissolution, loss, and darkness. Fascism never ceased to reflect upon decline, whether in the domain of the body or the history of peoples. Having little faith in the ability of science or technology to alter humankind's temporal predicament decisively, skeptical of incremental metanarratives of progress and enlightenment, it instituted nonlinear myths: myths of catastrophe, redemption, damnation, revolution, reclamation. Secular and anticlerical in its origins, the fascist movement opposed both the idealism it associated with Hegel and post-Hegelian rationalist utopias (despite the Hegelian cast of Gentile's "actual idealism"), just as much as it did Marxian scientific materialism. It tried instead to practice what it called *realism*: an anti-idealist, antimaterialist, and sometimes outright anti-intellectual turn of mind bearing some affinities to Bergsonian phenomenology. Much of the

joyous merging of "men from every social stratum, reconciled among themselves while keeping their necessary and brotherly diversity, all placed in the service of a single civilizing cause, all wearing a single popular uniform of discipline."[28] Able to bear the feverish exploits of 1917, 1922, and 1932 with icy

53. (left) Head of state, 2: Anonymous, "One heart alone, one will alone, a single determination," poster. From Renato Barilli et al., *Gli annitrenta: Arte e cultura in Italia* (1936).

54. (right) Head of state, 3: R. Bertelli, Continuous Profile of Mussolini. From the Paul Sullivan collection (1930).

cultural field of the 1930's shaped itself around the term, whose very slipperiness permitted it to accommodate a wide array of contradictory aesthetic endeavors, extending from later futurist experimentation to *18 BL* to neorealist novelizations of the world of the factory like Carlo Bernard's *Tre operai* (Three workers; 1934) and Romano Bilenchi's *Il capofabbrica* (The factory boss; 1935). "Realism" was variously understood as designating a flight from naturalist description and a return to the elemental forces shaping society and nature; a grappling with

the practical and the actual (as opposed to the ideal); a sober but militant ethos; a transformative, socially grounded concept of art; and the open-eyed acceptance that violence and destruction are necessary if fascism is to achieve its regenerative task.[29]

This said, fascism liked its realism juiced up with magic and myth. It was deeply fearful that too much realism, however the term were understood, could lead back to a sense of sadness and fatigue: in short, back to the ethos of decadentism and materialism that

**93**

the fascist revolution claimed to have overthrown. National skepticism, melancholy, and mourning were symptoms of the liberal-democratic/socialist paralysis that had preceded the March on Rome, and against them fascism preached a gospel of constant activity, cheerful self-creation, and eternal youth, even going so far as to invent secular other worlds for the preservation of its heroes and martyrs. It was in this spirit that an early version of the script for *18 BL* had proposed that Mother Cartridge-Pouch be resurrected after three days of burial. But in the final version of the spectacle, the perils of ending on an elegiac note were evaded by means of a less bathetic or comic device, which preserves the sense of tragedy, but puts forward compensations: a swift shift in focus away from the burial scene towards fascism's present achievements and future promise. The mother truck may have passed away, capitulating to the inexorable reality of aging, but fascism is always already on the move and the ideal of metallization she once embodied has been fully transposed into the human realm by il Duce.

The viewers of *18 BL* did not need to have this final transposition explained to them. The most fleeting allusions would do. A metallic voice heard over loudspeakers, an equestrian profile, and a slogan or two were enough to insinuate that Mussolini was the spectacle's secret protagonist.[30] Such economy of means was possible because by the mid 1930's, fascism had begun to fill its ideological voids with a totalitarian cult. Not a traditional cult of personality, but rather a modernist cult of the dictator's metallized body as missile, as ax, as man of the crowd,

55. Head of state, 4: Anonymous, photomontage of Mussolini. From Umberto Silva, *Ideologia e arte del fascismo* (1936).

as hero with a thousand faces, as helmet, as mask, as head with a 360° gaze and electrical relay. In this vast proliferation of images, fascist artists decomposed and recomposed fascism's most original, though paradoxical, creation: the myth of an individual who could stand at the center of a reconstructed universe; a being, at once hyperphallic and hyperchaste, who might reconcile man with machine, individual with mass, matter with spirit; a deus ex machina for the gigantic theater of modern revolution.[31]

**95**

# 7

Mussolini and Littoria. These, then, are the two proper names *18 BL* puts forward to compensate its audience for the loss of Mother Cartridge-Pouch, the one standing for the first fully fascistized human subject, the other for the first foundation stone of the corporative civilization fascism claimed to have inaugurated. Through the promise they embody, death becomes birth. Tragedy is averted and transformed into comedy. The reversal is confirmed by *18 BL*'s parting gesture: the heroic trumpet call sounded far off in the distance, which fades away only to echo back with redoubled force. Like the mass choral chants that respond to the leader's metallic summons in the course of the drama, this echo that mysteriously amplifies its source enacts the very hope the Lictorial games were founded upon: namely, that by finding a powerful echo among the members of the Lictorial generation, the fascist revolution would not fade away as it moved into its second decade. But a hope is not a guarantee. Even the parting trumpet call is haunted by the possibility that miraculous reversals are themselves reversible. Like its source, the redoubled echo must also fade out. Will it or will it not be reechoed and amplified in turn?

The spectacle attempts to ensure that the crescendo of redoublings will go on indefinitely, thanks to its agitatory effect upon the public. To this degree, *18 BL* functions like a classic work of Soviet-style agitprop (minus the didactic pretenses). Even if it succeeds at this task, the work is haunted by a negative undertone, which rather than being suppressed, is sounded openly. Nothing in *18 BL* suggests that there exist objective transhistorical reasons guaranteeing the triumph of the fascist revolution, any more than the eternal survival of Mother Cartridge-Pouch. Instead, as is typical of fascist culture as a whole, the accent falls on the drama of converting individual willpower into collective effort, expenditure, and sacrifice. The trumpet's metallic voice may continue to be echoed and amplified (both naturally and electronically), but the longer it does, the more emphatically it will underscore the silence with which the series concludes. The loftier the choral crescendo, the heavier the final diminuendo. Hence the urgency of sustaining the sequence and the urgency of the appeal to *18 BL*'s audience. This characteristic double-bind structure or "addiction loop" has the advantage of producing the types of polarization, intensification, and arousal that the fascist movement associated with its overcoming of Western civilization's turn-of-the-century crisis, crystallized in World War I. It pits fascism's endless rallies, its round-the-clock work schedules, its dreams of total mobilization and permanent revolution, its escalating calls for sacrifice, its technological "miracles" and colossal public works projects, its myth of a hyperactive state, and its politics of military expansionism against a backdrop made up of somber certainties: deaths, calamities, and defeats resulting from these collective victories; fatal historical, biological, and telluric laws that constrain human existence and thwart all efforts at resistance, no matter how heroic.[1] It also lends credibility to the claim that there can be no alternative to this dialectic of absolutes. Between these poles there exist only inauthentic or mediocre forms of being: forms founded either on narrow self-interest, on apathy induced by an excess of historical consciousness or asthenic disorders, or on the illusions provided by science, means-end rationality, or technological functionalism.

All of this goes to show that one would do well to take seriously the claim made by organizers and critics alike that *18 BL* was a tragedy and not a work of propaganda in any ordinary sense. A tragedy inasmuch as its three acts amount to a sustained meditation on life as a collective struggle against enemies, against landscapes and natural forces of resistance and disgregation, against the body's losses of energy, against the degenerative effects of time. The work assures its public that these battles have not proven and will continue not to prove futile. Nevertheless, *it cannot envisage a time when such heroic exertions will no longer be required.* Its motto is "Life is war, and the battle has barely begun!" and the brand of realism it promotes, whether on an aesthetic or ethical plane, is not out of line with Joseph Goebbels's steely Romanticism (*stählernde Romantik*), "which does not hide from the hardness of life or try to escape into blue beyonds, a Romanticism which has the courage to confront problems and to stare them straight in the pitiless eye, sternly and unwaveringly."[2] That the first attempt to actualize Mussolini's vision of a "theater for 20,000" should assume the form of a tragedy is not entirely surprising, given the privileged status late-nineteenth-century philology and philosophy accorded this ancient genre (Wilamowitz and Nietzsche come to mind in this regard). Moreover, the uncanny fit between tragic conventions and certain chronotypes and ethical ideals prominent in fascist and philo-fascist modes of thought make the choice seem nearly inevitable. The comic genre, for instance, would have been poorly equipped for the representation of myths of national struggle, destiny, and salvation, or to accommodate a form of theater that was to function as a military training exercise.[3] So for a young critic like Indro Montanelli there was never any question but that tragedy was the dramatic genre appropriate for the consecration of the new fascist hero:

I see the foundations already in place for the advent of a great *tragic* revolutionary Italian art. The new hero is already born and his lineaments are such and so distinctive as to differentiate him with crystal-like clarity from the corpse of the Romantic hero and the aborted Russian one. It is a matter of making him come alive on the stage in his pulsating and full humanity. When the means are available, the great artist will necessarily arise who will endow him with life in a complex and complete *tragic* synthesis.[4]

More difficult to understand (and, therefore, all the more important to an adequate reconstruction of the period's mindset) is how the authors of *18 BL* could have felt such immense confidence—misplaced as it turned out—that a mechanical protagonist could support the tragic structure they had devised or fulfill Montanelli's demand for a "pulsating and full humanity." The tragic genre's emphasis upon impassive suffering, its reliance upon concepts like catharsis and hamartia (the hero's tragic flaw), all seem ill adapted to a truck-protagonist who is at once single and collective, human and inhuman; a truck-protagonist whose dramatic function is to set the stage for the spectacle's true hero: *metallic man*.

Like every hero from antiquity to the present, the fascist hero prefigured by Mother Cartridge-Pouch and fully actualized in Mussolini has a complex genealogy. In reality he is not one, but many, and each of these multiple identities is made up of fragments of preexisting fragments. This said, a lineage can still be drawn up that, if not universally valid, proves revealing as regards certain overall contours of the fascist imagination. First, it should be noted that the dictator who triumphs in *18 BL*'s final act cannot be deemed the descendant of the epic heroes of the premodern or early modern era. Whatever the iconographic features are that he shares with iron-willed commanders like Julius Caesar or with renaissance *condottieri*, they are too superficial to be deeply meaningful. Nor can he truly be identified with the deus ex machina of the ancient stage: a god floated down from outside the scenic apparatus on a cranelike contrivance who provides a closure extraneous to the natural development of a dramatic plot. (If anything, he is closer to the Christian God, given his position of immanence and transcendence vis-à-vis the action on the stage.) Neither classical nor Christian, metallic man is a distinctive product of the high industrial era. He brings together elements from the first industrial revolution—the machine as generative force, the urban crowd—with elements from the second industrial revolution—streamlined design to shield the body from turbulence; new voice, image, print, and transportation technologies to enhance and expand its presence—within the framework of a single myth. He is the god of a scenic apparatus reshaped according to cinematic norms: an apparatus, as already seen, designed to break down all inside/outside, artificial/natural, illusory/real, man/machine dichotomies in pursuit of "a kind of actualized mystical experience of a heroic subject matter"—in the pursuit, that is, of a hallucinatory experience of the real.

The dictator/hero who triumphs in the midst of *18 BL*'s hallucinatory real is defined by his ubiquity. At once protagonist and director, individual and mass, man and machine, producer and produced, he concentrates within him so many individual attributes that he comes to embody a principle of absolute heterogeneity vis-à-vis the homogenized human and mechanical masses of individuals that make up his followers and, for that matter, his radically deindividualized opponents. The "sovereign" (or superior) form of individuality that results cannot be accounted for in preindustrial terms because, as Georges Bataille rightly observes, it would be unthinkable in the setting of an aristocratic institution like the monarchy, founded on a detached relationship between populace and sovereign. The hero of *18 BL* is instead a mass man: a being "who [in the context of fascism's blending of the different social formations from the bottom up] derives his profound meaning from the fact of having shared the dejected and impoverished life of the proletariat. But, as in the case of military organization, the affective value characteristic of impoverished existence is only displaced and transformed into its opposite; and it is its inordinate scope that gives the chief and the whole of the formation the accent of violence without which no army or fascism could be possible."[5] His individuality thus takes shape through acts of mutual mirroring like those that abound in fascist cultural artifacts from *18 BL* to Leni Riefenstahl's *Triumph of the Will* (1935): scenes of anonymous, abstract, geometricized crowds merging with, converging towards, hovering around, and confusing themselves with, a uniformed, abstract leader, in such a way as to suggest that all other emotional bonds (to family, faith, institutions, etc.) have been absorbed into this single totalitarian bond.[6] It is crucial to note that, however departicularized, these crowds are never "just any crowd," any more than the leader is "just any individual." In the words, once again, of Montanelli: "Fascist art does not oppose the mass, but rather *a certain mass*. We do not reject it outright like the early liberal-bourgeois Gide, nor do we permit ourselves to be dazzled by it as do a Demian Bedni and Mayakovsky. The mass as mass, that is, as a brute and blind force, doesn't inspire us Italians. We love it and choose to love it only as a marvelously elastic and dense clay to be modeled by the hand of an able artificer."[7] The sovereign individual requires a *particular* mass—the mass of individuals referred to earlier (in contradistinction to the more fully abstract socialist masses)—in order to constitute himself as the embodiment of a higher collective principle such as the nation. When the camera descends into the masses' midst, what it encounters is thus not a "brute and blind force." Instead, it finds differentiated individuals: individuals like Ugo Ceseri in *18 BL*, who exhibit sharply divergent body types, regional accents, marks of age, class, gender, and character. Within this field of differences, there emerge shared national or racial traits, traits that gain the upper hand thanks to the abstracting effect of common uniforms, choral chants, geometrical choreographs, and ritualized behavior patterns.

The origins of this peculiarly modern model of subject formation take us back to the mid nineteenth century and to early experience of the industrial metropolis as registered in works like Charles Baudelaire's *The Spleen of Paris*. (It is perhaps no accident that Baudelaire's preferred political theorist was

Joseph de Maistre, the great enemy of Enlightenment reason, whom Isaiah Berlin has recently placed at the root of fascism's family tree.)[8] During this formative period, the urban crowd began to be experienced as the perilous site of a release from conventional ego boundaries and as an incubator for new forms of subjectivity. As Elias Canetti has shown in his typological study of human masses, urban crowds were themselves hardly a new phenomenon.[9] What was new was the fact that these multitudes now indiscriminately mixed all segments of society within the setting of an international commodity culture, wherein traditional markers of social class and regional origin had given way to more mutable markers (notably fashion and money). On the one hand, crowds presented themselves as so enormously variegated that individual identity no longer appeared fully legible; on the other, this extreme diversity combined with large scale produced the impression that they had merged into abstract homogeneous masses. Extreme heterogeneity seemed to equal extreme homogeneity. The paradox lies at the heart of Georg Simmel's classic analysis of the metropolis and mental life, which implies an analogy between the city boulevards and the phantasmagoric universe of commodities:

Money, with all its colorlessness and indifference, becomes the common denominator of all values; irreparably it hollows out the core of things, their individuality, their specific value, and their incomparability. All things float with equal specific gravity in the constantly moving stream of money. All things lie on the same level and differ from one another only in the size of the area which they cover.[10]

In the course of the latter half of the nineteenth century, the urban crowd emerged as a site where this loss of quality in the name of quantity could be experienced with special pathos and intensity. "Quality" here refers to a context within which individuality is construed as the equilibrium between a given or secure inner nature (a subjectivity) and a set of traditional outer markers of individual and group difference; "quantity" refers instead to a world of surfaces wherein, having lost its traditional moorings, individuality has been "hollowed out," unbalanced, rendered insecure, and denaturalized and, in the process, both standardized according to the external dicta of economic function and opened up to all sorts of "artificial" manipulations (in the pursuit of "natural" effects). There were divergent reactions to this widely perceived loss of qualitative difference (including attempts to codify new or emerging codes, some facetious, as in the case of Honoré de Balzac's "Concerning the Cravat," some not).[11] They can be grouped into two broad categories. The first has ties to the body/machine complex referred to earlier as "mechanization." It embraced the loss of "quality" in the urban crowd as an emancipatory event, either because it was seen as the natural counterpart to the new political freedoms (liberalism) or because it constituted a first step towards the forging of new economically grounded collective identities (socialism) on the road to a complete "massification" that would abolish individuality altogether (communism). The second either rejected it outright, attempting to preserve prior forms of individuality and social difference (conservatism, monarchism) or embraced it, usually with ambivalence, as an

56. "In the current." From
Mirko Ardemagni, *Supre-
mazia di Mussolini* (1935).

occasion for the (re)forging of quality in radically modern terms. It is in the last of these that fascist metallic man finds his origins (origins that will be transmuted by being brought into direct contact with the worlds of machinery, mass politics, and mass media). His ancestor is the dandy: the hypertrophic individual who is at once man of the crowd and master of the crowd, the sovereign of the boulevard; a creature who is all masks and impenetrable surfaces because he needs to shock in order to shield himself from the shocks administered by the modern metropolis; and, last of all, a being whose glacially cool exterior conceals a raging core of egotism, much "like the crater of a volcano artfully concealed by floral bouquets." [12] I take as my example Baudelaire's prose poem "Crowds," to whose nuances a reading against the grain like the present one cannot adequately attend:

Not all men have the capacity to dip into the multitudes. Luxuriating in the crowd is an art, and its revitalizing effects, obtained at the expense of the rest of humankind, are available only to those whom a fairy endowed, in their crib, with a taste for disguises and masks, hatred of home, and a passion for travel.

Multitude, solitude: equal and interchangeable terms for the active and fertile poet. He who doesn't know how to people his solitude doesn't know how to be alone in a bustling crowd.

The poet is blessed with the incomparable privilege of being both himself and other people at will. Like ghosts that wander about in pursuit of a body to inhabit, he can enter every personality as he pleases. For him alone, everything is vacant; and if certain places seem closed off to him, it is only because he does not consider them worthy of a visit.

The solitary and meditative stroller derives a singular sort of high from this universal communion. He who can readily wed the crowd enjoys feverish raptures that are forever denied the egoist, sealed shut like a coffer, or the idler, hidden like a mollusk inside its shell. Every profession, all those joys and miseries that circumstance may bring, he makes his own.

What men love is petty, meager, and feeble by comparison with the ineffable orgy, the holy prostitution of the soul that offers itself up whole, with poetry and charity, to the chance occurrence, to the unknown passerby.

It is sometimes a good idea to remind the self-satisfied of this world, if only so as momentarily to deflate their doltish pride, that there are forms of happiness far greater than their own, far vaster and more refined. Founders of colonies, shepherds of nations, missionary priests exiled to the antipodes no doubt know something of such mysterious intoxications and, in the heart of the vast family crafted by their genius, must sometimes laugh at those who pity them for their fortunes so unsteady and for their lives so chaste. [13]

There are many reasons why the dandy-poet of "Crowds" cannot be deemed identical to his dictator descendant: his tendency to feel scorn for the oceanic masses, his interest in the most extravagant forms of masquerade, his contemplative and capricious nature, his sense of aloofness from an urban spectacle of which he himself is a symptom, his fussiness and excessive refinement—in other words, an overall tendency to mimic aristocratic tics and traits. Nonetheless, he remains the first modern creature in whom the equation multitude = solitude (or, to return to an earlier formulation, extreme homogeneity = extreme heterogeneity) generates a new type of masculine subjectivity. The hollowed-out, quantitative world of the metropolis is not the site of a loss for him, any more than their exotic locales are for the founder-adventurers, pastors, and missionary priests alluded to in the closing paragraph of the prose poem. On the contrary, it is a land of opportunity: an anonymous feminine space, a dangerously savage nature, to be colonized, explored, seduced, converted, and reshaped in the name of absolute quality: of strictly *un*common denominators like heroism, beauty, empire, ecstasy, truth, individuality, and eternal fame. The shaping process is dynamic, which is to say bidirectional. In the first instance, he is a bather who swims confidently through the urban ocean, a prospector who mines the crowd for its treasures and taps its secret energies, a spirit who freely inhabits every body/shell and then moves on. Once the bath/communion/orgy is fully under way, however, the dandy-poet abandons himself to fevers, pleasures, passions, and intoxications, and the tables seem to be momentarily turned. Now it is he who is feminized, he who is awash in the sea of faces; it is his soul that practices "holy prostitution" and offers itself up to anonymous passerbys.[14] But, in this specific instance (not always the case in Baudelaire), the onrushing vision remains fully under the control of the newly forged visionary subject. By the end of the poem, the bath has become a modernizing baptism. It has cleansed him of the past, raised him to a higher plane of reality beyond bourgeois concepts of happiness and identity, and injected him with a surcharge of vitality. It has replaced all his affective ties to history, family, sexuality, and romantic love with the chaste plenitude of the "vast family" that his genius has fabricated for itself: the urban crowd itself. To invoke the Pauline typology of baptism, if the "old man" was an aspiring aristocrat or monarch, the "new man" who emerges from the waters is a mass man: a total(itarian) individual who, having absorbed all of the crowd's multiplicity within himself, having entered every personage and practiced every profession, has become absolutely heterogeneous vis-à-vis the now absolutely homogenized crowd.

Fascism in general and *18 BL* in particular appropriate this structure and graft it onto an evolving nineteenth- and early-twentieth-century discourse on the machine's interconnections with the human body. "Machine-body complexes"—I borrow this formula from Mark Seltzer—have been a permanent feature of the Western technological imagination.[15] These complexes underwent a decisive transformation during Baudelaire's century in the form of a shift from a static machine/body interlock built on the principle of mechanical analogy to a dynamic one built instead on productivist principles and their obverse: principles of natural decline, dissipation, degeneration, entropy. The classical *machina* was, like the crane of the ancient stage, a trick or artificial device external to nature, able to mime nature but unable either to augment or to diminish nature's treasury of forces. Its ontological status is well illustrated by a device like the mechanical clock, whose spinning wheels replicate the spinning orbs of the cosmos, thereby participating analogically in rhythms thought to be sempiternal; or, at the secular borders of classical machine culture, by the automata and perpetual-motion machines that so occupied seventeenth- and eighteenth-century savants. The thermodynamic studies of Rudolf Clausius, William Thomson, and William Rankine, among others, led to an upending of the classical model and to the foundation of modern energetics. A comprehensive scheme linking machines such as the steam engine and the dynamo to the forces of nature was put in place, differentiating actual from potential forms of energy and concentrating attention on the role played by both mechanical and human work in the conservation, transformation, and dissipation of energy—the machine, that is, came to be viewed as a generative device, just as the human body came to be viewed as a kind of motor. Both were conceived of as sources of output that could be perfected and multiplied through engineering, be it mechanical, human, or social. The enemies of perfection and multiplication were fatigue, stress, and resistance.

Overcoming the resulting limits on output by means of remedial measures became one of the nineteenth century's great passions. These would include the development by materials science of new alloys, metals like aluminum, and, in the early twentieth century, high-speed steels for the construction of machines: lighter, stronger metals, more resistant to corrosion, fatigue, and heat; metals whose extreme ductility made them able to accommodate an infinity of interior or exterior forms. In the domain of human "materials"—the term *Menschenmaterial* is a contemporary coinage—these measures would include regimes of scientific hygiene and physical training of the sort that socialist, fascist, and national socialist regimes would institutionalize: mass and individual bodybuilding designed to promote efficiency, physical and spiritual ductility, and the accelerated recovery of natural (national) reservoirs of strength. Last, but not least, on the industrial front, they would involve what, in Europe, came to be referred to as the "science of work": the engineering of an ideal fit between workers, machines, and factory spaces in the name of expanded productivity. As I have tried to imply in the preceding description, the boundary lines between these three domains had, by the turn of century, become permeable in the extreme, to the point where machine-body complexes had become privileged settings for: (a) dismantling old forms of individuality and proposing new ones; and (b) forging new concepts of the collectivity (family, class, state, nation, world) founded on the link between individuals, machines, and masses. Baudelaire's dandy/urban crowd dialectic was thus (unknowingly) reworked in terms of metallurgical and machinic metaphors, with the result that it moved into the mainstream of the Western sociopolitical imagination.

The following examples show some of the peregrinations these metaphors would embark upon from the outbreak of World War I, by which time they had already been fully codified, through the 1930's, when a recodification took place under the influence of new technologies of communication (cinema, radio, commercial photography, recording, early television) and transportation (automobile, high-speed ocean liners, and aviation), particularly in the latter's links to streamlined design. In his 1916 novel *Young Knights of the Empire: Their Code and Further Scout Yarns*, Robert Baden-Powell could describe a steamship's engine room as follows: "It is indeed an impressive sight to stand below these great monsters of steel and watch them faithfully and untiringly pounding out their work, all in order and ex-

57. "The Old Masses." From Mirko Ardemagni, *Supremazia di Mussolini* (1935).

practice a kind of elite morality, which may also extend to their scout counterparts.

Embedded in the myth of collective duty and productivity is a heroic ethos that is thrust into the foreground in the following two quotations:

There is no sport that, like [boxing], promotes the spirit of aggression in the same measure, demands determination quick as lightning, educates the body for steel-like versatility. . . . Thus the meaning of sports is not only to make the individual strong, versatile and bold, but it has also to harden him and to teach him how to bear inclemencies.[17]

Rising to speak, he bends forward his masterful head, like a squared-off projectile, a package full of good gunpowder, the cubic will of the state. But he lowers it in conclusion, ready to smash the question head on or, better, to gore it like a bull. Futurist eloquence, well masticated by teeth of steel, plastically sculpted by his intelligent hand, which shaves off the useless clay of hostile opinions.[18]

The first is from Adolf Hitler's *Mein Kampf* and occupies a transitional position within the lineage I have been tracing, much as Mother Cartridge-Pouch does with respect to Mussolini in *18 BL*. Hitler's boxer is already a product of the streamlined era. At once a mass man, a monster of steel, and a heroic individual, he possesses an *outside*, made up of a supple but strong metallic skin, and an *inside*, made up of an explosive metallic spirit-motor. The disjunction, however slight (given that inside and outside consist of the same metallic matter), permits his steely body to perform more complex functions than Baden-Powell's boy scout–like engines. No longer a guarantor of productivity, disci-

actly in agreement with each other, taking no notice of night or day, or storm or calm, but slinging along at all times, doing their duty with an energetic goodwill which makes them seem almost human—almost like gigantic Boy Scouts."[16] For the founder of international scouting, steel had become the metal of modernity and the steam engine a role model for contemporary youth. Together they furnished the viewer with a stirring vision of how rationalization, standardization, training, bodily discipline, and tireless work ensured social harmony, moral probity, and the unhindered flow of energy—which is to say, a future of progress and growth for humankind. Baden-Powell's emphasis is on quotidian virtue and moral transparency. His machines are unsurprising. They are not armor-plated. Their surface is their depth, their skin is their soul. But there are intimations that, despite their humble transparency, these "monsters of steel"

58. "The New Masses."
From Mirko Ardemagni,
*Supremazia di Mussolini*
(1935).

pline, regularity, and progress, his body seems to have left behind the private world of the engine room in order to step on stage and to become a potential producer of spectacles for mass consumption and emulation. It has been militarized, transformed into a bullet capable of striking in a flash and a bulletproof shield capable of heroic feats of resistance and endurance. Most important, its ability to shift between aggressive and receptive stances testifies to the fact that it

has been invested with an infinitely malleable *will*, capable of giving and taking form, which is to say, of giving and taking orders. Steel = strength + versatility: this is the equation that Hitler's boxer puts forward.

Similar doublings between inside and outside, receptivity and aggressivity appear in the second quotation: the portrait of Mussolini that serves as a dedicatory preface to *Marinetti e il Futurismo* (1929). The Mari-

**107**

59. Xanti Schawinsky, *1934–XII*, poster for 1934 referendum. From Umberto Silva, *Ideologia e arte del fascismo* (1934).

nettian Duce's unerring instinct for improvisation and surprise, however, transmutes all receptive forms of steel-like versatility into even greater offensive capability. A literal body without holes, the commander is a projectile that penetrates but cannot be penetrated.[19] His surface gives away nothing, much like that "coat of ice" woven and worn by the Baudelairean dandy beneath which lurk the "chaste sensibility and ardent passion," sacred egotism, and the savage urges that feed his art.[20] It both resists and decreases resistance vis-à-vis the exterior world, not because he possesses no depth— only *bourgeois* forms of interiority are alien to him—but rather so as to better shelter his

delicate soul: an anticontemplative core filled with "good gunpowder," always ready to go off. Detonation occurs when, like a sculptor, with knifelike hands, he strips away the "useless" irregularities in the body politic and shapes the fascist mass of individuals into his natural likeness. His every act is one of self-portraiture. This makes his nature, like that of Hitler's boxer, also that of a potential mass mime and performer. His mouth of steel is a press for stamping out metallic slogans for the oceanic mob; slogans whose power derives from the availability of technologies of electronic amplification and diffusion that have the effect of expanding his metallic body.[21] Since he appears to be standing at a podium, the mechanical motions of his head would be invisible were it not for the watchful eye of a movie camera.

My point in assembling this particular sequence of examples is, of course, not to insinuate that a causal chain joins Baudelairean poetics to the Scouting movement to fascism and national socialism. A great many other instances of metallic/machinic imagery could be cited from contexts as ideologically diverse as the Soviet Union, North America, France, Japan, and England; and the dandy-to-dictator genealogy is only one of several lineages that converge in the hero of Pavolini's theater of masses for masses. Rather, my intent has been to show the extent to which conflations of instincts, engines, and metals, strengthened by new possibilities for amplifying and projecting the human voice and body, and redefined by the practice of streamlining, functioned as a medium for envisaging new forms of individuality and collective belonging along the

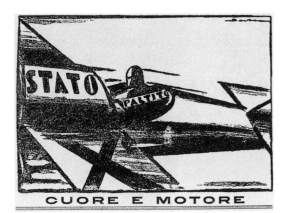

60. "Heart and Motor," cartoon. From *Il Popolo d'Italia* (Oct. 22, 1932).

CUORE E MOTORE

lines prefigured in a text like Baudelaire's "Crowds" and fully actualized in products of the fascist era like Asvero Gravelli's newspaper *Ottobre*, whose sports section was futuristically entitled HEARTS MOTORS MUSCLES STEEL. The forms in question vary measurably, responding as they do to differing constraints, interests, and narrative or metanarrative pressures. They can be usefully classified, however, according to their lesser or greater affinity with what, by the end of World War I, had emerged as the two predominant ways of conceptualizing the interface between human bodies and mass-production artifacts and technologies: the *mechanical* and the *metallic*, or *mechanization* and *metallization*.

The opposition between mechanization and metallization can be traced back to Romantic art theory. More specifically, it replays and modifies the influential dichotomy proposed in August Wilhelm von Schlegel's *Lectures on Dramatic Art and Literature* between mechanical and organic form: the latter, in Schlegel's account, being associated with the formal fluidity of Shakespearean tragedy;

the former with the rigorous formal constraints characteristic of neoclassical art.[22] Such oppositions are easy enough to deconstruct. As seen in the quotation above from Baden-Powell, where one finds metallic ideals embedded within a rhetoric of mechanization, there can be little doubt that, on some level, the metallic always already involves some notion of the mechanical and vice versa. A similar deconstructive strategy might be worth pursuing if this inquiry were tracking transversal links between simultaneous semiotic chains, technologies, and institutions in the nonlinear, rhyzomatic mode that has been proposed by Gilles Deleuze and Félix Guattari.[23] But, since its aim is to contribute to a differentiated history of modern culture, it necessarily operates on a more linear interpretive-descriptive plane, where surface markers of distinction are to be taken seriously, despite (or indeed because of) the overlapping fields within which they function. It therefore defines mechanization and metallization as *two distinctive ways of punctuating what is essentially the same body/machine copula*.

I have already hinted that the second term, *metallization*, has a special relationship to the era of streamlined design, requiring as it does a complex relationship between metallic skin and metallic motor-heart. As for the first term, *mechanization*, it has roots that extend back to the Enlightenment. In its turn-of-the-century form, it underwrites, to one degree or another, a wide range of modernist cultural and intellectual stances, from the constructivist epistemologies of the Viennese logical positivist circle, to Bauhaus experiments with function as form, to Fordist and Taylorist-inspired forms of social engi-

61. Benito Mussolini as pilot; press photograph from the author's collection (1934).

neering in America, to Soviet ideas regarding collectivization and culture. However diverse, all of these envisage the reduction of human qualities to the quantities and logical/physical laws that define the machine world and nature as an emancipatory event: emancipatory inasmuch as such a reduction entails the stripping away of the mystifying and falsifying veils imposed by tradition, superstition, prejudice, and habit. To this negative task corresponds a positive one: that of the utopian reconstruction ("engineer-ing") of the real and/or society upon a fresh foundation made up of elementary principles and truths—concepts such as structure, functionality, labor, synergy, science, equilibrium. Within this setting, man and machine are both envisioned as essentially transparent apparatuses, whose exterior skins reflect their interior souls, apparatuses made up of value-neutral, interchangeable functions. The totality they form is analyzable and precisely equal to the sum of its parts.

62. "Keeping trim." From Mirko Ardemagni, *Supremazia di Mussolini* (1935).

**111**

This stands in stark contrast to the metallic ideal's qualitative concept of totality: qualitative because the whole composed of bodies and machines, often visualized in organic or vitalistic terms, is never reducible to the sum of its functions and parts. The metallic whole—be it the nation, the heroic individual, or the hallucinatory spectacle—always embodies a higher/lower/deeper principle that is extrarational, and this suggests a correlation with what Georges Sorel referred to as "myth" (as opposed to "utopia"). "Myths are not descriptions of things," Sorel writes, "but expressions of a determination to act"; a myth cannot be refuted, since it is, at bottom, identical with the convictions of the group, being the expression of these convictions in the language of movement; and it is, in consequence, unanalyzable into parts

which could be placed on the plane of historical descriptions."[24] The forging of modern myths in the Sorelian sense, particularly myths of quotidian heroism and national redemption, was a pervasive preoccupation of 1920's and 1930's Italian culture just about everywhere on the cultural/ideological map, from the writings of Giovanni Papini to post–World War I futurism (Marinetti, Carli) to the metaphysical movement in painting (de Chirico, Carrà) to the Novecento (Bontempelli, Sironi) to the PNF (concerned, you may recall, with the need for "a myth" that could be believed by university youth). Metallization inserts itself comfortably into this context as a response to a question I earlier traced back to the mid nineteenth century: how can industrialization and modernization be achieved without a loss of qualitative difference? The answer initially resembles that provided by mechanization. The hollowing out of the human and its reduction to the quantities that define the machine world and nature reconnect the subject to elemental principles that bourgeois-liberal society had either denied or sublimated. But these principles are imagined differently: not as the building blocks that would permit a rational reconstruction of society or the real, but rather as explosive subterranean currents to be tapped and channeled into monumental new forms. *The metallic arises as the site of reconciliation between these "hot" fluid forces and a will to "cool" clear-cut forms.*[25] Hence, for example, in the Hitler and Marinetti quotations, the steel-like subject is never characterized by a simple relationship between exterior and interior, shell and soul, even if both are cast of the same metal. This enables him to blend malleability, improvisatory skill, speed, torrential energy, and the ability to shock, with strength, constancy, coolness, and rock-hard solidity. Likewise, in *18 BL*, the surface of Mother Cartridge-Pouch's body is simultaneously impenetrable and yielding. Although armor-plated only in part—the mark of her transitional function—she is largely bullet-, mob-, and fatigue-resistant, ubiquitous on every battlefield, and given to unexpected eruptions (as when she over-turns the table of parliament). Yet she is also infinitely accommodating, serving as supply vehicle, troop carrier, bearer of fascist squadrons, hearse, and, finally, construction truck. What is ruled out by this duality is metallization's principal nemesis: formless-ness. Flab, muck, murk, mud, indiscipline, in-distinctness, egalitarianism, apathy, confu-sion, disengagement: these are just a few of the demons metallic body/machine com-plexes exorcise by speedily erecting mas-sive, hierarchically ordered structures—such as the fascist new town of Littoria, where these once were only swamps; by rapidly or-ganizing human bodies into mass forma-tions, where once there was a headless mob; or by streaking across the world's oceans and continents in rigid aerial formations (like Italo Balbo in his Atlantic crossings). These geometrical volumes or *monuments in motion* are the redeemed mirror image of the world's soft and slow morasses. They present themselves, not as artificial, but as a kind of intensified prolongation of nature, in the same way that *18 BL*'s hard-edged "realism" is achieved by fortifying the real—represented by actual bodies, landscapes, trucks, explosions, guns—by means of tech-nical, mechanical, and electronic enhance-ments. In neither case is there the sort of foregrounding of device, artifice, or function that one might expect in a strictly mechani-cal context. The vision must be real, solid, immediate, overwhelming in its impact. Always on the move, it refuses to disclose the divisions that would render it analyzable into parts. The guarantor of this seamless whole, whether envisaged in terms of the production process or product, is the giver of form, the mass artificer and geometer: the director-dictator.

# 8

Fascism would continue to labor at the task of shaping metallic subjects and a distinctive fascist culture long after the spectacular failure of the first theater of masses for masses. The decade that followed saw imperial conquests, but also increasing repression, the imposition of racial laws, and a general cultural narrowing under the growing influence of Nazi Germany. As for the dream of *18 BL* and the total theater it had hoped to inaugurate, the faithful continued to insist that it was still the only solution to the epochal crisis of the theater, even in the turbulent aftermath of April 29.[1] Vigorous discussion and debate carried on through the summer of 1934, much of it hinging on the interpretation of Mussolini's April 1933 SIAE speech. Nicola Manzari, fresh from his victory in the drama criticism contest at the 1934 Littoriali, spearheaded the attack from within the GUF, arguing in *Il Messaggero* (as he had done successfully during the competition) that Mussolini had never intended the formula "theater of masses" to imply anything more

than communion with the crowd—a communion best achieved with individual protagonists; denouncing *18 BL*'s preference for machine values over human values; and accusing Blasetti of having mimicked the worst attributes of the talking cinema: in particular, its use of electronic amplification ("the metallic, inhuman, cosmic voice surging forth between the stage and the audience").[2] These ideas, already familiar from the postperformance reviews, had gelled into commonplaces by mid-May 1934, at which time one begins to encounter cartoons and mocking one-liners like the following one from *Corriere Padano*'s "Orchestrina" column: "We think it evident that 'theater for masses' means that the masses should stay put in their seats and off the stage."[3] Similar polemics were kept alive at least into early 1935, when Balbo's newspaper still judged the topic timely enough to merit publication of an item by Edoardo Anton faulting the proponents of mass theater for their treatment of Mussolini's phrase as "the formula of a religious rite, operating on a metaphysical plane such that it surpasses all human understanding." Anton reserved his sharpest words for Venturini and company: they constitute a self-appointed priesthood of intellectual prodigals, capable of indiscriminately heaping together the formulas "theater of masses" and "for masses" and then "heading home happy to have bewildered everyone." In the critic's view, theorists of mass theater were at best juvenile pranksters who brought to mind Nietzsche's aphorism "Beneath the skin of every real man there is a child who wants to play." [4]

That such fierce reproaches were still being vented fully a year after *18 BL* first entered the Italian public's imagination testifies to the raw nerves that Pavolini's spectacle had struck in traditionalist circles, whether because of its equation between populism and avant-gardism or its emphasis on fascist collectivism, machine/body links, and electronic enhancements of the human voice. But they also must be viewed as attempts to forestall an ongoing effort within influential sectors of the arts community to relaunch the enterprise begun so inauspiciously on the night of April 29, 1934. These commenced in earnest some two months after the performance with the publication of a pair of important theoretical statements in *L'Italia Vivente* (and of an additional article in *Il Mattino*) by Blasetti.[5] The director had been mostly silent since the end of his polemic with Corrado Sofia, and in these essays, reproduced in Appendix A, he responded to his critics in even more eloquent and forceful terms, defending the plausibility of his interpretation of the formula "theater

of masses," debunking contrary views, and justifying his use of cinematographic realism and of new voice/image technologies. One of Blasetti's principal purposes in this regard may have been to regain the favor of two of his most respected critics, d'Amico and Bontempelli. The operation may have been successful, at least in part, although a letter to Bontempelli dated August 7 still indicates a high level of tension, if not uncertainty:

Dear Massimo,

A girl who came to see me told me that she had renounced being introduced by you because you supposedly said that you "didn't want to do her harm" given your criticism of *18 BL*. So be it. This means that Bontempelli doesn't think I'm worth a dime anymore. Now they tell me, on the contrary, that you and Forzano have nominated *18 BL* for the Viareggio Prize. Which of these two "testimonies" am I to believe?[6]

The nomination seemed improbable even to Blasetti. But his fears that he had lost Bontempelli's esteem may not have been entirely unfounded to judge by the omission of any mention of *18 BL* in Bontempelli's Volta Congress presentation later that same year (on which subject see below). As for Silvio d'Amico, although he never seems to have returned to the subject of *18 BL* in subsequent writings or to have recanted his earlier views, he did include a chapter on the "theater of tomorrow" by Corrado Pavolini (Alessandro's brother) in his *Storia del teatro italiano* (History of the Italian theater; 1936).[7] Highly critical and devoid of any trace of fraternal indulgence, this chapter represents the last major public acknowledgment of *18 BL*'s inaugural role vis-à-vis Mussolini's "grand call [of April 1933], unanswered until the present." Corrado Pavolini asserted in it that

*18 BL* was a courageous attempt; but not more than a mistaken one; nor has a successor been born as of yet. It would be too easy at this point to list *18 BL*'s errors . . . [a list follows]. There is no reason to bury these truths; and I can aver that, much to their credit, those who promoted the initiative acknowledge them. Nevertheless, it is always meritorious to have dared. It will prove useful in the future to know that one ought *not* to proceed down this path. Because in some matters only practical experience is or can be valuable; only putting oneself personally on the line. But however one judges it, *18 BL* remains a revolutionary experiment.[8]

This negative assessment may seem more like an epitaph than a summons to renewed action. It did not, however, preclude a wholesale endorsement of the project undertaken at the 1934 Littoriali:

A fascist theater can only be—on this we are all in agreement—a theater of masses. But the definition is still too generic; so much so that the Russians and Germans have adopted it and are going about, with differing concepts and results, translating it into practice. For us the mass cannot be either shapeless or undifferentiated, as in the Russian case, or ideological and numeric, as in the German one. The Italian mass of today (and forever into the future) is "corporative."[9]

Pavolini's views resonate with those of other informed observers of the contemporary theatrical scene who, motivated by conviction and a need to save face, continued to advocate the cause of fascist mass theater during the summer and fall of 1934. Among these one would have to count Indro Montanelli, whose incisive musings on the new mass hero and the fascist theater I have al-

ready had occasion to cite.[10] The most august was perhaps Anton Giulio Bragaglia, whose support for Blasetti's project had always been carefully nuanced and framed in the futurist designer/director's own longstanding campaign in favor of a small-scale experimental "theatrical theater" (*teatro teatrale*) meant to continue the work of his Teatro degli Indipendenti.[11] Bragaglia had read deeply and widely in theater history and was acquainted with an extraordinary range of contemporary cultural forms, from African-American music to Southeast Asian dance to Argentine *sainetes* (one-act farces) to the political theater of Piscator, Brecht, and Meyerhold. This erudition may explain in part why Bragaglia was the sole contemporary interpreter to have recognized that one of the spectacle's key weaknesses lay not so much in its confusion of realist and nonrealist elements—a favorite target of critics—as in its simpleminded pursuit of total realism: a blind spot shared with significant other sectors of a cultural field dominated by the "documentarist" aesthetic (which would in turn beget postwar neorealism).

In a critical essay published in *La Vita Italiana* and later republished in *Ottobre*, Bragaglia noted that, despite itself, the *18 BL* authorial collective had tried to stage counterfeit battles much like the ancients with their mock sea-fights (*naumachiae*) and stadium combats. "These sorts of spectacular reconstructions, reevocations of the real," he declared, "are artistic in large measure, but within them practical action and 'real life,' which is to say politics and propaganda, can have the effect of killing art as if it were mere artifice. A minimum of artifice (technical, thus poetical) must be retained in some form, so that one not simply repeat life as it actually is."[12] Indeed, as seen earlier, a panoply of techniques and technologies usually associated with nonmimetic or antimimetic forms of representation were deployed in *18 BL* to redouble mimetic effects under the presumption that the portrayal of "life as it is"—or, at least, "life as it is" on the intensified, and for fascism, *normative*, plane of reality that is the battlefield—would be sufficient to enrapture the audience. The procedure may have seemed familiar to Bragaglia, inasmuch as it is prefigured in Marinetti's early experiments with words-in-freedom poetry, where avantgarde experimentation was placed in the service of an aesthetics of reportage so as to achieve what I have referred to elsewhere as *absolute mimesis*.[13] To Bragaglia, a solution of this kind appeared naive. A "political *theater/spectacle* of the fascist era" required far more awareness of ancient, medieval, and modern popular nonrealist precedents: for example, gymnastic performances, ritualized forms of combat, jousting, circuses, mystery plays, commedia dell'arte, vaudeville, and music hall shows. This wide horizon of historical models might be incorporated into contemporary cultural forms by a sustained attempt to "extract from [modern] sport, and from the passions it inspires, the aesthetic elements of an art spectacle."[14]

Mussolini's theater of masses was very much at the center of debate during the next major event in the history of the Italian theater (and one of the foremost drama symposia of the decade): the Italian Royal Academy's October 1934 congress on the dramatic theater. Attended by such world-renowned figures as Edward Gordon Craig, William Butler Yeats, Walter Gropius, Walter Unruh, Ashley Dukes, Maurice Maeterlinck, Jacques Copeau, Gerhardt Hauptmann, Jules Romains, and Alexander Tairoff (an early collaborator of the Peredvizhnoi Teatr and founder of Moscow's Kamerny Theater), to name only a few of the foreign dignitaries, the Volta congress—so referred to because of the sponsorship of the Alessandro Volta foundation—was presided over by Luigi Pirandello and largely organized by D'Amico.[15] Pirandello, who would receive the Nobel Prize a month later, had never been very enthusiastic about the theater revolution launched (however abortively) by Mussolini's SIAE speech. Indeed, despite a long-standing bond based upon his conversion to fascism in the wake of the Matteotti assassination, the playwright's relations with il Duce had long been fraught with tensions: tensions attributable to Mussolini's populist revolutionism and Pirandello's tragic pessimism, to a contrast in styles and temperaments (famously evident in their attitudes towards women), to Pirandello's conviction that his drama was deeply (which is to say, not just superficially) revolutionary and anti-bourgeois, and to his resulting frustration at the Italian state's refusal officially to consecrate his role in some sort of national state theater. So it was surely out of deference to the supreme leader that he opened the Volta congress with a sidelong and only mildly critical allusion to special events like *18 BL* and the open-air theater festivals:

Still today, during the summer months or in springtime under the open sky, the people are summoned to attend exceptional and magnificent spectacles in ancient amphitheaters or, in the context of annual or biennial celebrations, in this or that city, square, or specially prepared site. These spectacles do not, however, provide an answer to the "theater problem" as it has presented itself in every civilized nation (a problem of civilization): under the guise, that is, of the nightly enclosed theater. You will have to determine whether the so-called "theater of masses" offers a solution, or whether the latter is necessarily imaginable only as a recurrent celebration and grand but temporary spectacle, like, for that matter, the sports events that draw, yes, great masses of spectators, an overflowing crowd; but retain, all the same, an "exceptional" character and are not, nor are capable of becoming, quotidian in nature.[16]

A brief excursus into the cinema's encroachment upon drama's traditional functions in everyday life followed the above remark, after which Pirandello returned to the theme of mass theater, but this time in terms of the need to enhance theater's competitiveness by building stadiumlike facilities: "It is to be hoped that this conference's proposals and discussions will show that the most effective and practical way to bring the people back into theaters will be constructing these new locales: and, perhaps, in this manner the hoped-for theater of masses will come about in spirit."[17] Hard at work on a series of oneiric "myths" for the stage, Pirandello felt no aversion to rehearsing the standard critical and ideological themes of the moment, even if without any special sense of conviction. His principal allusion here was to the second of the five thematic clusters established by d'Amico to structure the congress's debates. They were (in chronological order):

1. The present state of the theater vis-à-vis other forms of spectacle (film, radio, opera, sports competitions)
2. The architecture of theaters; theaters of masses and small theaters
3. Contemporary developments in set design and technique
4. The place of spectacle in the "moral life" of peoples
5. State theaters; their current conditions and differing modes of organization in various nations

The speakers selected to intervene on the second topic were Joseph Gregor, Bontempelli, Gropius, Ciocca, and Hendrick Theodor Wijdeveld. Gregor, a prominent Austrian writer and theater historian, was the broadest in his scope, providing a sweeping overview of theater architecture from antiquity through the present, punctuated by brief excursuses into contemporary Soviet experiments, thespian cars, and American university theaters. He was followed by someone who, unlike Pirandello, was a true enthusiast: Bontempelli, whose talk was introduced as "a commentary upon a single phrase of Mussolini's." Into the "extremely profound" spiritual content of this phrase—"theater of masses"—Bontempelli now delved.[18] (Ciocca, Gropius, and Wijdeveld would consider its material and technical dimensions.) What ensued was a patchwork of commonplaces drawn from Bontempelli's prior writings. Among the themes touched upon were the primordial nature of man's yearning for poetry, art, and spectacle; the imperative that theater maintain its popular roots; the active role played by the public in all authentic forms of spectacle; the dawn of the "Third Era of humankind" in the wake of World War I, and the need for an apposite body of myths; and, finally, the inaugural role mass sporting events would necessarily play in bringing about an authentic theater for 20,000—a theater that, Bontempelli concluded, "we must favor with all of our forces." [19]

A good number of these motifs were echoed by the star speaker of the second portion of the congress: Walter Gropius, the legendary founder and director of the Dessau Bauhaus.[20] Unbeknownst to his Italian hosts, Gropius's appearance in Rome marked the first phase of his flight from Nazi Germany. His contribution on theater architecture assumed the form of a presentation—indeed, his final presentation—of the Total Theater project he had developed with Erwin Piscator back in 1927 (the very reason for his being invited to the Volta congress).[21] Although inspired by strictly nonfascist aesthetic and ideological criteria, this stadiumlike mass theater must have seemed eminently "fascist" to his Italian audience. And not just for reasons of design. With his talk of "rousing the masses" (die Massen aufzurütteln), of rebuilding the spirit through rebuilt buildings and bodies, and of "mobilizing all spatial means so as to shake, storm, and surprise the public out of its studied apathy and force involvement in the play" ("Mobilisierung aller räumlichen Mittel, um das Publikum in seiner intellektbetonten Apathie aufzurütteln, zu bestürmen, zu überrumpeln und zum Miterleben des Spiels zu nötigen"), Gropius's rhetoric was largely consonant with that of a Pavolini, Blasetti, or, for that matter, Mussolini.[22] Like the "theater of totality" proposed by his colleagues László Moholy-Nagy in the mid 1920's, Gropius's theater was to be total on a number of levels.[23] It would fuse together all three classical theater stage-types (proscenium stage, arena, court), accommodate a wide diversity of spectacle forms (film, theater, sports, instrumental and choral music, parades, exhibitions, etc.), and provide a "magnificent demonstration of what our age has produced out of iron, glass, concrete, and metal, ordered according to the laws of proportion, rhythm, color, and the structure of materials!" [24]

Most of all, the totality Gropius sought, much like that sought by Blasetti's theater of the Albereta, was one of effect. Thanks to mechanical/technological wizardry, the Total Theater would be an instrument for representation so infinitely flexible, variable, and strong that it would overpower spectators, wake them from their apathetic sleep, place them under the spell of the spectacle and under the absolute control of the director-demiurge. The goal was a reengineering of society and the real:

The spectator is caught under a cloudy or a starry sky, surrounded by ocean waves or masses of people running towards him, while he is entranced by the dramatic actions of the central round arena. The division between acting and the audience no longer exists ["Die Trennung zwischen Spiel und Publikum ist überwunden"]. Words, light and music no longer have a set place. The director becomes sovereign and dictates the course of the audience's interest according to the changing needs of the play. He alters position and spatial forms and mercilessly subjects the audience to the dynamics of his imaginations.[25]

Total Theater thus equals total power equals total community within the framework of the technologically intensified reality the Total Theater makes available. Winfried Nerdinger's gloss seems apposite in this context and helps to explain the favorable reactions of congress participants such as Marinetti and Salvini and the unfavorable ones of Edward Gordon Craig and Wijdeveld: "Here

63. Walter Gropius and Stefan Sebök, the Total Theater, model (1928). From RAI, *Atti—Convegno di lettere* (1935).

one is struck by the problematic nature of total design, the Bauhaus's foundational principle: it is but a small step from total to totalitarian domination of humankind! Piscator's overturning of the absolutist court theater with a democratic theater form turns—at least in Gropius's interpretation—into its contrary."[26]

Stepping up to the podium right after Gropius's elegant lyrico-technical meditations could not have been an easy task for the plump and homely Gaetano Ciocca. A relative unknown in this company of world-famous architects and dramaturges, Ciocca had been refining his mass theater designs for over a year now, and would continue to do so into the late 1930's, well after Mussolini's "grand but unanswered call" had been answered to the satisfaction of nearly everyone. His training, moreover, was limited to the domain of industrial engineering, and he had no real track record as either an

architect or theater designer. But, at times, it was Ciocca who sounded like the true *Bauhäusler*, presenting a sober and factual analysis of stadium acoustics, geometry, and crowd flow; praising the machine for freeing workers from brute fatigue; and envisaging a theater of "optimism and initiative" within which the titanic protagonist of tomorrow would be "the enlightened will of mankind and the creative power of labor."[27] Following Ciocca, whose presentation was criticized by some (d'Amico, Gregor, and Virgilio Marchi) but well received on the whole, came the final speaker in this portion of the Volta congress: the noted Dutch theater architect and director Wijdeveld. Wijdeveld's remarks concerned the fashioning of a new individual, a new community, and a new theater under the aegis of modern states: "Russia, Italy, Germany, Turkey, and America have begun to organize their forces, which are to build up this new *will*, this great unit."[28] Special attention was devoted to the first two nations, the first being found wanting for its spiritually inadequate, propagandistic notion of theater, the second being praised for its "young spirit" and renewed pursuit of "order, discipline, health" and "new harmony."[29] Eager to please his hosts, Wijdeveld would go on to recommend that Italy develop a series of "study theaters" (much like the GUF theater described below) under the aegis of Edward Gordon Craig, out of which "plays as noble as the ecclesiastic mystery in the Churches" would be sure to grow, as well as "festivals that earthbound, healthy people will hold."[30] By the time of the final day of the congress, however, his attention was riveted on the thespian cars, whose structure he so admired that he exhibited a series of slides and called for the "throwing overboard of all the superfluous scenery and stage machinery" so as to give birth to the aforementioned study theater of people's festivals.[31]

I have lingered over the debates of the Volta congress not only because of their importance to the history of theater in the 1930's but also because they illustrate just how permeable were the borderlines between "fascist," "socialist," and even sometimes "liberal" modes of envisaging a theatrical revolution. In October 1934, phrases such as "theater of masses" or "theater for 20,000" did not appear to the non-Italian discussants as irredeemably fascist (or, for that matter, socialist) in nature, nor did the notion of linking together mass theaters, political rallies, and sporting events. (The fact is striking given the emphatically fascist character of presentations like Bontempelli's.) Within the setting of a universally acknowledged crisis of the theater and in large part independent of ideological inflections, the effort to place the masses on the stage or to bring them into open-air stadiums, to reenergize traditional drama via new voice and image technologies, to experiment with large-scale, visually driven or body-based models of spectacle that could promote activist modes of reception and forge new body/machine conjunctions, seemed part of a common continuum, at whose opposite pole were the avant-garde laboratory-theaters of the preceding decades.

My second purpose in retracing the Volta congress debates has been to demonstrate how, despite the emergence of a common discourse on mass theater, 18 BL had already been dropped from the frame of reference. Over the six days of the meeting, there was much discussion of thespian cars (evoked by Wijdeveld, Gregor, Marchi, and Romagnoli), of stadium-style facilities and open-air performances, and of the need to assimilate elements from other forms of spectacle into the domain of the theater. However, the path blazed by Blasetti and his cohorts was never once alluded to by those in the know. This would seem especially significant given that in addition to Bontempelli and d'Amico, the Volta congress participants included Luigi Bonelli, a member of the authorial collective (who twice referred to the Littoriali in the course of discussions), and the director Guido Salvini (who had published a remarkable comparative study of 18 BL and the Soviet mass theater). Even the following speech by Wijdeveld attacking the Gropius/Piscator Total Theater project did not provoke any reaction on the part of the Italian participants:

Away with all these projects for the theater of masses, as long as we have no *plays* to perform in them! We are starting at the wrong end! We must begin with actors, not with buildings. We must look for something plain and simple, something that comes from our innermost senses: a new mystery perhaps and therefore a new play for the people. Humanity is new born and prefers to play on the grass and in the fields to entering the new playhouse architects would build for them. Italy might set an example by beginning on a simple stage, finding new forms for the expression of the coming new life. Italy might imbue the actor with new life, for it is he that has the play of the future in his hands. Actors have now lost their position on the stage, in the theater and . . . in life![32]

Its technological complexities aside, 18 BL surely fulfilled most of Wijdeveld's criteria. In the genesis of 18 BL, the play had come first and had assumed the form of a revolutionary mystery play. Staged under the open sky and in the fields before a reborn people, it portrayed the "coming of life" and drew its actors directly from life. But there was silence. The explanation is by now rather self-evident: 18 BL had become too much of an embarrassment even for staunch defenders like Salvini. The uncontroversial and highly successful thespian cars and outdoor festivals were rapidly taking over as the principal response to Mussolini's April 1933 summons.

This is not to suggest that the battle for an avant-garde mass theater of youth had come to an end by October 1934. Debates continued to rage within circles close to Alessandro Pavolini and the Littoriali through the summer and well into 1935. In the immediate wake of the 1934 edition of the games, the PNF national secretary, Starace, had ordered a study to evaluate their effectiveness in promoting the development of a future fascist vanguard. The verdict arrived at was mixed. It was felt that the level of student enthusiasm and participation had been more than adequate, that a new collectivist spirit had successfully supplanted bourgeois individualism in Italy's university elite, and that the overall intellectual quality of the competitions had been excellent (hardly surprising, given that the participants included the best minds of the fascist/antifascist generation). The report noted some signs of indiscipline and political recalcitrance—particularly so among young Catholics, whom it found wanting in their knowledge of fascism's syndicalist and socialist roots, and therefore given to imagining that fascist corporativism was a Church-inspired doctrine! [33] It also observed with some surprise that "every refer-

ence to Rome and *romanità* [Roman spirit] provoked quasi-ironic interjections. At the root of such attitudes was the wish and the conviction that youth ought to *make* history and not to take their place in it as if settling upon a throne." [34] This vein of antitraditionalism seems to have coexisted with more than a modicum of political disengagement, inasmuch as a significant proportion of competition entries had neither interpreted nor reflected the "revolutionary spirit of their times." For example, not one of the six comedies that made it to the finalist stage in the drama contest contained a single reference to fascism, or, for that matter, to the contemporary scene. The report's recommendation was, therefore, that the competition guidelines remain as liberal as possible as regards matters of form, but that political themes be rendered obligatory in order to accelerate the creation of an art of fascist times. Proclaimed as official policy in September 1934 (along with several other reforms), this sharpened thematic focus might well have appeared as a renewed affirmation of the kind of political theater essayed in *18 BL*. Certainly, the themes announced for the 1935 Lictorial games create an impression of continuity. Mass photography was to be the topic of the photography contest. The architecture competition was devoted to designing stadiums for the masses. The drama criticism sessions were again dedicated to discussing Mussolini's theater of 20,000. Entries in the playwriting competition had to be comedies performable "either in an enclosed or an open-air theater" that, like acts 2 and 3 of *18 BL*, were "inspired by an episode from the fascist revolution." [35] Even the games themselves would now become something of a mass event. Through an easing of restrictions, the number of student participants would be doubled.

These surface signs were to prove misleading. Any real hope that an avant-garde mass theater might arise out of the Lictorial games was fading fast, perhaps owing less to ideological pressures than to a desire to bury all the controversy. The 1935 games were well attended: so well attended, in fact, that some complained that debate was impossible and repetition of the prior year's work inevitable.[36] The theater-criticism competition was singled out for special censure in this regard, dealing as it did with mass theater, when, as *Il Cantiere*'s Roberto Ducci put it, "mass theater had been damned last year both in word and in fact."[37] The tide had irrevocably shifted. A year later, the playwriting competition substituted the call for "inspiration from episodes from the revolution" with the celebration of "the unity and integrity of the Italian family." Young architects were asked to design barracks for an artillery division instead of mass stadia. Only the drama criticism contest, concerned with the use of theater as a propaganda tool, bore the remotest trace of Blasetti's experiment.

The war both for the survival of the theater of the Albereta and for the kind of theater that it had championed had actually been lost sometime during the summer of 1934. Lost when the contest for future spectacles, first announced on April 14, was proclaimed anew, only to be quashed both from within the GUF and from above (or so it would appear on the basis of fragmentary archival sources).[38] Important testimony to this effect comes from a memorandum written in early July by Francesco Rossi, an engineer who

had been on the organizing committee of the Lictorial games and was close to Blasetti, Pavolini, and the Florentine GUF. Addressed to Giovanni Poli, it seeks his approval to send out a press release, because "only three months remain before the submissions deadline and it's time to refresh people's memory."[39] The accompanying press release boasted that the confirmation of the contest "brings to an end the lengthy polemics that have cluttered the pages of daily newspapers and begins a new chapter in the history of this young theater."[40] It continues, adopting a more aggressive stance:

Given the first result [*18 BL*], everyone has wanted to get in a critical word. Many have felt the urge to plunge the dagger in anew and to play the dastard, hoping to administer the coup de grace; many have laughed scornfully; many have joyously dusted off old scenes printed on onionskin paper and sought refuge in the wings of old-style theaters, hoping that this insanity, this fraud for 20,000 people, had forever killed off this type of theater in order to give birth to *little theaters* [*teatrini*], lovely in Goldoni's time, and now alleged to be our sole hope of salvation.[41]

The mention of little theaters is crucial here, pointing as it does beyond *18 BL*'s "external" enemies to forces within the GUF, led by Manzari and the future communist leader Pietro Ingrao, that had argued at the 1934 Littoriali and were continuing to argue, much like Wijdeveld at the Volta congress (and, long before him, most of the participants in *La Fiera Letteraria*'s 1929 referendum on small versus large theaters), for a different approach to the fascist theater: one founded on small-scale experimental study theaters. To this position, which dovetailed closely with that of the defenders of the Bragaglia and Bontempelli/Pirandello art theaters, corresponded a revised understanding of the "theater of masses" formula. In the words of Bonelli (again at the Volta congress): "Those youth held that 'theater of masses' did not necessarily mean theater to be performed before a public of 20,000 or, even less so, to be performed by thousands of actors; rather, the phrase refers to a theater no longer addressed to a small and select audience, but to the people, the great mass of people; a theater able to move the mob and to interpret its feelings, directing them towards the pursuit of the highest ideals." [42]

The growing success of this small-theater formula led the defenders of *18 BL* to view the failure of the spectacle itself as yet another tragedy to be overcome through the heroic actions and indomitable spirit of the elite they imagined themselves to be. In his aforementioned memorandum, Rossi therefore argued that "the new theater willed by the DUCE, and for which we all feel the need, must defy all risks because it is the daring and warlike fascist theater that knows not difficulty and overcomes all obstacles, no matter how insuperable. The courageous must engage in combat and lay bare their ideas." [43] He concluded:

The generation that arises in the midst of mountain dangers, that defies the tempest, that puts itself on the line in order to conquer ever greater heights, tolerates the old theater filled with smoke and with paper. It tolerates it and tries to ignore the shaky castles and rumpled canvas sets, especially when listening to beautiful music that can stand alone without the accompaniment of choreography. The new theater will have great means and great resources, but most of all it will make possible the realization of spectacles hitherto unthinkable in terms of realism, the verisimilitude of optical and acoustical effects, and the contemporaneity of action.

To our first performance maybe only twelve people will come, greatly afraid of having wasted money on their tickets. Be patient! If this dozen audacious souls is enthused by what it sees and recounts to others what they would not have believed before, even the sheep [*pecoroni*] who were awaiting the outcome before deciding to stick out their necks will show up. [44]

Rossi's fantasy is the by-now-familiar one of an avant-garde mass theater that breaks through the tawdry illusionism of the bourgeois theater in order to plunge the spectator into a transfiguring real. Such heroic dreams soon came into conflict with the political and fiscal realities of planning for the 1935 Littoriali, because, despite Pavolini's sympathy, the proponents of a Blasettian theater of masses no longer had a firm base of support. A consensus had emerged within the GUF that the theater of masses "does not require gigantic material means as much as it does gigantic artistic ones" and that the best means to achieve this end were small "experimental mass student theaters" designed to furnish "the regular mass theater with works and dramatic concepts" worthy of Mussolini's "amphitheatrical/theatrical era." [45] The emergence of this consensus notwithstanding, *18 BL* would long remain a topic of discussion in *I Littoriali*, the games' monthly magazine, where it was inevitably cited as a collectivist misreading of il Duce's individualist formula. [46] It was also sometimes invoked during the theater criticism competition of the second edition of the youth Olympics of the spirit. But the contest for future mass spectacles, and with it the dream of transforming the theater of the Isolotto into a permanent academy where

**123**

a fascist Aristophanes might someday emerge, vanished almost without leaving a trace. (Although its possible impact upon the Nazi mass theater movement may be worthy of further investigation.)

In the place of both the contest and imagined academy, there arose instead a new institution—a little theater—genetically tied to the first theater for 20,000 but distinct: the Experimental Theater of the GUF (Teatro Sperimentale dei Gruppi Universitari Fascisti), later redubbed the GUF National Theater. Conceived by Ingrao at the 1934 Littoriali and directed by *18 BL* collaborator Giorgio Venturini, this Florence-based entity would administer the Lictorial theater competitions from 1935 on and serve as a drama school, with acting, directing, set design, and costume divisions. Not unlike an American collegiate theater, it also functioned as a "theater-laboratory, experimental workshop, [and] testing bench" for young dramatists to perfect their craft before small audiences, and a site of lecture series like those that gave rise to d'Amico's earlier-alluded-to *Storia del teatro italiano*.[47] Despite initial claims that it would promote revolutionary forms of theater committed to overcoming the isolation and elitism of avant-garde theater studios, the GUF theater's actual practice was fairly conventional, even if its history and contributions to the Italian stage deserve further study.[48] On the whole, it institutionalized a middlebrow theatrical modernism and, even on those rare occasions when it attempted a foray into the domain of experimental political theater, it did little more than pay lip service to the Mussolinian ideal of a mass theater capable of "stirring up the great collective passions" and "bringing to the stage that which truly counts in the life of the spirit and in human affairs."

This turn towards small-scale theater for the university-educated few would amount to a modest victory for those cultural forces that had been struggling for a revival of Bragaglia's experimental theater and of the Bontempelli/Pirandello art theater. It would also amount to an indefinite postponement of the once-urgent task of developing an original fascist theater. (Propagandistic plays did continue to be written, but they would remain a marginal phenomenon.)[49] The delay was a matter of some embarrassment but was smoothed over by defining fascist theater in the broadest possible terms. In the words of Dino Alfieri, minister of press and propaganda and, after 1937, minister of popular culture: "Let it be said once and for all that fascist theater is not a theater that places the daily events of the regime on stage, but a theater, altogether free in its subject matter, that draws its inspiration from the conception of life that is proper to fascism—it is inspired by the fascist ethos."[50] Just what Alfieri understood by "inspiration" is unclear (and probably deliberately so). But if one is to judge by his actions as a government official, fascist theater, for Alfieri, consisted of little more than non-antifascist theater produced under fascist rule. So, just as the label "Augustan literature" refers to works composed during the reign of Augustus, the first Roman emperor, the label "fascist theater" denotes nearly every work of theater written in Italy after the March on Rome.

Alfieri's expansive definition bears important consequences as regards the formula "theater of masses," which now comes to refer to a less singular notion than Pavolini and his peers had believed. In the years subsequent to *18 BL*, the phrase was ever more exclusively interpreted in a culturally mainstream, populist key: not as calling for a Soviet-like theater of abstract multitudes and machines animated by a ubiquitous metallic hero; nor as denoting an experimental epic theater that might bring acting masses face to face with masses of spectators. The fascist mass theater would instead become "a theater for the people," harkening back to the nineteenth-century stage, massified, and democratized by the use of large-scale facilities, electronic amplification, flood-lighting, radio broadcasting, and state-initiated incentive and reward systems. The concept did not exclude (even if it was never typified by) the sort of mass choreographies being experimented with in Germany during this very period, whether in the form of cultic *Thingspiele* ("Thing" plays), *Arbeiterweihespiele* (Worker "consecration" plays), or political festivals like the Bückeberg National Socialist Harvest Festival held in October 1935.[51] It remained sufficiently elastic to accommodate national treasures such as the works of Pirandello (whose reputation grew considerably after his death), and the production practices it allowed for were sometimes just as "modern" and inventive as those put forward by experimentalists. But this theater's characteristic heroes would be the great men of ancient and modern Italian history, as featured, for instance, in the operas of Mascagni or the historical dramas of Forzano. The preferred stage settings, reflecting the same backward-looking tendency, would be Italy's ancient theaters and monuments. The point is taken for granted in Mario Corsi's authoritative *Il teatro all'aperto in Italia* (The open-air theater in Italy; 1939):

The mass theater has found its perfect home in the arena . . . a home where it is possible, as nowhere else, to gather together (and prodigiously so) all of the elements that make up a great spectacle, so as to fuse them into a wonderful architectural figure, thereby yielding a unique poetry. With its countless seductions, with the picturesqueness of its ruins, with its extraordinarily imposing scale, with the heartbeat of its crowds, the Verona arena not only doesn't diminish the substance and value of that which is performed, but rather burns away, strips off, eliminates the slough. Here what is ephemeral in works vanishes, and what is essential, transcending time, fashion, the corruption or correction of culture and taste, acquires a new consistency and radiates unexpected and ever more persuasive charms.[52]

Definitively consecrated as the material solution called for in Mussolini's SIAE speech, ancient arenas now took the place of athletic stadia or artificial battlefields as the key production sites for fascism's "unique poetry." And where a worthy architectural figure was not readily available, it could be manufactured, as at Sabratha, the last ancient theater placed in service, and therefore an appropriate symbol of the regime's post–*18 BL* politics of spectacle. Unlike most of its counterparts on Italian soil, the arena in question, located in the northwestern corner of Libya near Tripoli, was a true Roman amphitheater. Built on the periphery of the colonial city of Sabratha Vulpia, it lay in ruins beneath the desert sand until 1922, when an archeological survey first discovered its existence. Several years of subsequent excavations revealed that the theater's remains were vast but incomplete: so incomplete that only a speculative reconstruction would be

64. The Roman theater at Sabratha during a performance of Sophocles' *Oedipus Rex* (1937). From Mario Corsi, *Il teatro all'aperto in Italia* (1939).

possible. To this end, Giacomo Guidi, the superintendent of excavations and monuments in Tripolitania, developed a plaster model loosely "inspired by other monuments of the epoch of Septimus Severus," mostly from nearby Leptis Magna.[53] Presented to the provincial governor, Italo Balbo, at the 1933 Tripoli trade fair, the project received his immediate approval "for cultural as well as for touristic reasons."[54] The theater was speedily rebuilt so that its inauguration could be woven into the fabric of events—mass choreographies, air shows, ribbon-cutting ceremonies for new highways and triumphal archways—that would accompany Mussolini's 1937 tour of the Libyan colonies.[55] For

the occasion, Romagnoli's translation of *Oedipus Rex* was presented by Renato Simoni and Guido Salvini, in a staging that "stripped away . . . every archeological incrustation and imbued it with an air of modernity, so as to render the work more accessible to an audience of our era."[56] The production's highlight was its musical score by Andrea Gabrielli, borrowed from the updating of Sophocles that had marked the 1585 opening of Palladio's Olympic Theater in Vicenza. The Sabratha performance was designed so that it might take on comparable importance: "When, right before sunset on March 19, 1937, il Duce entered the glorious monument and took his seat above the orchestra where, twenty centuries earlier, Roman senators would have been seated, the audience had the impression that three great epochs in world history were simultaneously present in the theater of Sabratha: the Greek era, through the play about to be performed; the Roman, whose ancient might and incomparable spiritual prestige were attested to in the great edifice; and that of the new Italian empire, embodied in the Man the empire had needed and known how to create."[57] Three eras, at once inside and outside of time, with another—the Renaissance—discreetly interwoven: all brought to life before the eyes of thousands of soldiers, colonists, and colonized in the service of an "eternal empire." If only the smells of fresh paint and plaster had not reminded the audience that substantial portions of the architectural complex were still visibly "too new and too luminous"![58]

In conclusion, as the contrast between the GUF National Theater and Sabratha demonstrates, the partition separating elite and

126

65. Mussolini seated at the center of the Roman theater at Sabratha during a performance of Sophocles' *Oedipus Rex* (1937). From Mario Corsi, *Il teatro all'aperto in Italia* (1939).

mass forms of dramatic art was strengthened during the second half of the 1930's, both in the policy realm and in the domain of aesthetic production. The former—the elite or small-scale theater—was entrusted with the task of cultural experimentation, however obliquely related to national tradition or fascist ideology, the ever-vaguer understanding being that the long-term payoff for the regime's relative tolerance would be the advent of an original fascist repertory. In contrast, the "popular" theater was assigned the task of presenting modern, but recognizably tradition-bound, national models of high culture on an ever-vaster scale, the values of fascist modernity and *romanità* being expressed less by the content of the spectacles themselves than by the means of delivery, the setting, the interclass character of the mass audience, and the use of recent communications technologies. (The com-

mercial theater continued, mostly unhindered, along its prior course.) One important effect of this disjunction was the closing down of the cultural-political space *18 BL* had striven to fill. Squeezed off of the cultural map, recalled to memory only as a negative lesson and misinterpretation of il Duce's farsighted mass theater formula, the self-designated "theater of the future" soon found itself deprived of all future prospects, perhaps much to the relief of the parties most directly concerned. Blasetti's amphitheater on the Isolotto was dismantled and the site left fallow until the mid 1950's, when the artificial hillocks were reshaped into a suburban development (although a few traces of Blasetti's landscaping are still apparent to well-informed eyes). As for Blasetti himself, in the wake of his two theoretical statements on mass theater in *L'Italia Vivente*, he plunged anew into the cinema (never to return to the theater until the conclusion of World War II).[59] His first post–*18 BL* cinematic effort was *Vecchia guardia* (Old guard): his most resolutely fascist work and one very much indebted to *18 BL*, whether on the thematic, the formal, or the technical plane. A "polemical film against foreign technicians and machinery," its paean to squadrism assumed the form also of an *18 BL*–like celebration of Italian machines, men, and soundtracks: "The cameramen are all Italian. . . . The trucks are all Italian. For the first time ever the soundtrack was made with Italian machinery."[60] *Vecchia guardia* gave rise to difficulties with Luigi Freddi, the director of cinematography in the Ministry of Press and Propaganda, who objected to its underhanded call for a reconciliation between the nation's political forces: difficulties that would escalate over subsequent years as Blasetti grew disenchanted with the regime. With his usual bluntness, he recalled the shift in a postwar interview: "I remained a committed fascist so long as Mussolini, surrounded by plows, new farm machinery, and new factories, declared: 'This is the war that we want to fight.' I believed him. When I later understood that there was another kind of war that he preferred, or at least was prone to taking on, then my support for the regime ceased. The moment of decision for me came with the invasion of Ethiopia."[61] Indeed, in 1940, he refused to direct the war film *Quelli di Bir-el-Gobi* (The men of Bir-el-Gobi), choosing instead to invest his energies in a series of films, including *La corona di ferro* (The iron crown; 1941) and *Nessuno torna indietro* (No turning back; 1943), in which gloom triumphs over hope.

The path followed by members of the authorial collective was not entirely dissimilar. Many remained faithful to the regime; few, if any, passed into open opposition until the wartime period. But *18 BL* proved a disillusioning experience all the same. Sofia and Lisi each plunged anew into their writing: the former mostly as a journalist and correspondent for the Stefani wire service, the latter as a novelist of deeply Catholic inspiration. Bonelli and Gherardi each churned out several dozen more comedies apiece and continued to enjoy success both in the repertory of thespian cars and on the traditional stage. Venturini, as already noted, assumed the directorship of GUF Experimental Theater, a position he held through the early 1940's, even as he contributed regularly to the Maggio Musicale festival. In 1938 he was selected to oversee the transformation of Florence into a massive stage set for the ceremony marking the completion of Hitler's visit to Italy.[62] (Bonelli cohosted the radio broadcast of this event, known as "the celebration of the salute" [*la festa del saluto*].) Several years later, under the Salò Republic, Venturini was elevated to the post of director general of spectacle in the Ministry of Popular Culture. For Pavolini, the failure of *18 BL* proved a minor setback. It may have encouraged his turn away from the theater over subsequent years: years during which he remained in intimate contact with the Roman film world. (He was instrumental, for instance, in rescuing *Vecchia guardia* from the opprobrium of Freddi.) The mid 1930's found him in Ethiopia reporting on the military exploits of Galeazzo Ciano for the *Corriere della Sera* (reports he would later rework into a travelogue entitled *Disperata*). Ciano returned the favor by having him named president of the International Trade Institute in 1938; eighteen months later, he succeeded Dino Alfieri as minister of popular culture. His rise through the fascist ranks reached its inglorious apogee under the Republic of Salò, where he served as national secretary of the Fascist Republican Party (Partito Fascita Repubblicano) and distinguished himself by his virulent anti-Semitism (in an effort to overcompensate, perhaps, for a lifelong association with Jewish cultural milieux).

The understandable desire of many participants to leave behind a painful disappointment is far less telling than *18 BL*'s elimination from the official memory of the regime (and, perhaps, as a collateral result, from postwar cultural history). Five years after the fateful performance of April 29, Dino Alfieri would apply the definitive seal and condemn *18 BL* to perpetual oblivion. Writing in his capacity as head of the Ministry of Popular Culture, he had occasion to recount the story of "The First Theater of Masses" in the program notes of the Estate Musicale Milanese (Milan's summer music and opera festival):

"It is necessary to create a theater of 15,000 or 20,000 persons," concluded il Duce. The good seed was sown. To the classical theater of Siracusa and the opera of Verona—the two cities to whom the title of pioneers in the open-air theater necessarily goes—are now added the special moral and cultural value of the OND's thespian cars, theaters in Florence, Venice, and this and that city. . . . [But] the honor goes to Milan for having been the first of Italy's major cities to leave behind academic discussions and to move out, with the alacrity characteristic of fascist initiatives, into the realm of grand accomplishments.[63]

With the staging of the first Estate Musicale at the Castello Sforzesco in 1937, "the first 'theater of masses' in fascist Italy was founded," Alfieri concluded.[64] While Alfieri's love for his adoptive Milan may help explain the lavish tribute, the fact remains that the Florentine open-air theater to which he alludes was not that of the Albereta but rather that of the Boboli gardens: a traditional open-air theater and counterpart of the classical open-air theaters of Siracusa and Verona. This new foundation story did not slip by unnoticed. A sharp rejoinder appeared on the pages of *Meridiano di Roma*, surely encouraged by the indefatigable Bardi:

What does any of this have to do with the theater for masses? . . . [the thespian cars, theatrical Saturdays, radiophonic theater, and open-air spectacles at sites like the Castello Sforzesco and the Boboli Gardens] are forms of spectacle that are original, occasional in nature, and more or less well suited to a mass audience. But they do not constitute a true theater of masses, because a true theater of masses must possess distinctive features, an autonomous life of its own, a unique structure.

We must begin construction of a theater for masses. All half-measures are ridiculous in an era like our own, an era that should have to borrow *nothing* from the past.[65]

While borrowings from the past continued to proliferate, the epic of Mother Cartridge-Pouch left behind no progeny. It had vanished into the darkness much like the figures in *18 BL*'s intricate chiaroscuro tableaux. With it disappeared the hopes of a generation of young intellectuals—no matter how innocent or misguided they may appear from the perspective of our own fin de siècle—for the advent of a revolutionary fascist theater.

The following reproduces Blasetti's "Theater of Masses, Theater for 20,000," a two-part essay published in *L'Italia Vivente* in the immediate wake of the polemics unleashed by the performance of *18 BL*. Part 1 was originally published in *L'Italia Vivente* 4.7 (May 10–24, 1934): 6; part 2 was published in *L'Italia Vivente* 4.8 (June 10, 1934): 9. It rehearses Blasetti's views on the theater of masses, his dispute with rival interpretations of Mussolini's phrase, and his notion that mass theatrical spectacles ought to be built around a series of spatio-temporal condensations and displacements.

## ■ I

"It is necessary to prepare a theater of masses, a theater able to accommodate 20,000."

The statement seems precise enough. First: theater of masses. Second: theater for 20,000. Two concepts are involved, not a single one repeated twice.

Accustomed to stating and resolving [things] in totalitarian fashion, always essential and concise in self-expression—all the more so when addressing intellectual milieux where mental quickness is a given—the Chief could neither state the matter incompletely nor repeat himself.

He could not, that is, look only to the spectator's pit and focus upon it alone.

The entire question of a new performance site presented itself to him according to logical sequence: first, in terms of the place of action; next, in terms of the place of the audience.

Besides experience, reckoning and reason confirm his logic.

———

The sequence is as follows:

What does the phrase "theater of masses" mean? A theater where "the spiritual nucleus, the event around which spectators are gathered—to cite Silvio d'Amico's felicitous words—is the exclusive responsibility of the masses?

Surely not. A chorus without a chorus-leader is a heart without blood. And a chorus-leader without an antagonist is a heart that beats in vain.

A theater, then, in which the masses, human or mechanical, are transformed into an overpowering scenoplastic whole or into a wondrous array of special effects and tricks? A theater where the masses occupy the central place and exact their revenge upon many decades of works like *The Dawn, The Day, The Night* and *The Human Voice*?

Certainly. This is the meaning of "theater of masses" as I see it.

Spectacle needs to recover that breadth of compass characteristic of a poetry capable of interpreting, marking, and exalting the lives of entire peoples and not the laundry of individuals. It needs to recover a vast and imposing physical organism, wondrous as one penetrates within. A return to the (formally) ingenuous, to the elementary, to the mass of 20,000 as it shall be for all eternity.

Besides, let's put a third interpretation to the test:

Theater for masses without masses.

Enter the seating area of this theater and look around. However the audience is arrayed—you can dream up any seating arrangement you would like—imagine the proportions of a single actor from the perspective of the vast majority of the 20,000 spectators.

Almost microscopic. One could strengthen the actor's presence by inverting the theater's design. The public could be seated below and the spectacle placed above in such a way that, instead of appearing flattened into the ground, figures are cut out against the sky. But all physiognomic play would still be completely lost.

The result? Masses of words will be thrown into the balance of theatrical values. (Bragaglia estimates 20,000 words per average play.) And

with masses of words will come philosophical excurses, psychological introspection, sentimentaloid serenades. A fine vindication this, because for many centuries philosophy and psychology, two sciences for the chosen few, have had a home of their own: the book. Worse still, they can also take full advantage of their country villa, still in a state of good repair: which is to say, of the elite theater. What a conquest for sentimentaloid serenades (which, the sooner they are forgotten, the better it will be)!

Once the individual actor has lost the possibility of making use of masses of words (as seems highly appropriate in our century of revolt against parliamentary democracy), this legitimate heir of the spirit of the revolution will have to express himself through movement, space, the evidence of gesture (not melodramatic, but perhaps clownlike), and essential words. And only *truly essential words* that express, by means of poetic creation, "that which truly counts in a people's life."

———————

(Will this limit the means of expression? No, they will simply be displaced. From the mass of words to the word of the masses, from physiognomic play to movements that express and determine a work's defining moments, from stasis to action. Mussolini did not suppress the word; he suppressed idle chitchat. Nor did he mandate action; rather he mandated useful and necessary action, action that is timely and essential.

Will this limit the variety of subject matters? Once again, no: the means of expression will be displaced. The advantage of working on a large scale and the resulting verbal constraints are sure to create obstacles that the mediocre will be unable to overcome and sure to set traps that will ensnare the merchants of facile scenic trickery. Such difficulties and the certainty that derives from rigorous selectivity will provoke and stimulate. They may well give rise to new poets by forcing them to look upwards and far beyond.)

---

Summing up: the reading of a funereal letter, the blowing of noses, slow drags on cigarettes are all excluded, as are introspection, philosophical treatises, serenades.

Only essential words and actions.

Can an entire spectacle of this sort be sustained if limited to only two, four, even ten actors?

Silvio d'Amico thinks so. And I can only hesitate when faced with the prospect of contradicting someone who, in the domain of the theater, can readily silence me whenever he so desires.

But I am encouraged, nonetheless, by my belief that Silvio d'Amico wanted only to react to the danger that the theater of masses would be interpreted as a theater of mass actors alone, which is to say, as a choreography stripped of all dramatic content, deprived of that which must exist in order to concentrate and hold the attention of 20,000 persons: namely, a *fatto*— an event, an action, a story line. Now the spectacle that was supposed to be performed on April 29 was intended otherwise; it did not coincide with the spectacle that, owing to categorical imperatives under no one's control, was actually performed. And, if my guesswork is correct, the Roman critic's reaction is right on the money.

Accordingly, I don't think that it will seem presumptuous for me to hope that Silvio d'Amico would concur with the following:

No theater of mass actors only.

Nor a theater without masses.

No theater without individual heroes.

Nor a theater of individual heroes only.

■ II

In short: "It is necessary to prepare a theater of masses."

First question:

Would it be best to imitate Greek, Roman, or medieval models? Or, forgoing them entirely so as to evade their influence, would it be better to try to create an entirely new model, however rudimentary in nature?

If Aeschylus could be polled across the twenty-five centuries that separate him from the present, I feel certain that, before uttering a single word, he would oblige us to look from every possible angle at the *machina* with which he portrayed the nymphs' wingèd chariot in *Prometheus*. He would then point to an internal combustion engine, to a high-power electrical substation, and to a radio station. He would conclude by telling us that the response lay right before our eyes: in the varying mechanical, as well as social and religious lives of people. Therein resides our dignity.

And it consists in the following:

That the mass theater for 20,000 spectators, the new theater, the theater just now being born must spring forth from the sensibilities, instincts, and creative impulses of today. It cannot seek its sources in culture or tradition.

In other words, it cannot exhume old formulas, bring the dead back to life, breathe the dust of libraries, because to do so would be equivalent to going into the battlefields of tomorrow with the military regulations, formations, shields, and daggers of Caesar's decuman soldiers.

(In answer to a partisan rhetorical objection: the fighting spirit of the Roman legionaries is besides the point. I am unconcerned here with the passions and human ambitions that today's Aeschylus would have to exalt. Rather, to put it bluntly, I am talking about devices like electrical searchlights. And what I rule out is that Roman tripods and torches should either take their place as a means of illumination or limit their use.)

———————

Second question:

Can the emerging theater forms of today neglect the fact that they must appeal to an audience that has been crowding into movie theaters for the past thirty years? An audience, in other words, that for thirty years has become used to seeing "true," used to seeing without spatial or temporal limits, used to seeing different locations simultaneously, while years and decades are reduced to minutes?

Obviously not. It goes without saying that it would be useless for the theater of masses to try to encroach upon others' prerogatives. In order for it to exist at all, it must be just as distant from the new cinema as it is from the old theater. I hasten to add that the theater of masses cannot appear more like a ghost of times past than as an image of present times. It cannot be backward, slow, spatially and temporarily bounded by the stage's standard assemblage of wings, curtains, and variously chewed-up walls; which is to say, *it cannot be bounded by the unity of place that governs all stage actions in a traditional theater.* (As for the rotating stage, we are convinced that it is only the latest avatar of Aeschylus' *machina*: a sign of progress along the well-trodden road, but hardly a radical new departure.)

So is Massimo Bontempelli mistaken when, in his frank and affectionate review of the first mass spectacle, he defines the theater as "concentration, synthesis, life molded into intensity and speed through the 100 walls that are placed around it"?

All true.

As a matter of fact, we are in total agreement (as confirmed by his use of the word *speed*). My only quibble being that I would hope that

his hyperbolic reference to "100 walls" is meant only to buttress the central concept.

We are in agreement because he is calling for "concentration." And concentration hardly depends upon the existence of walls. All that it requires is a concentrated light beam separating off one part of the stage from the circumambient shadow or darkness. The eye goes right to the spot.

Moving pictures have conditioned today's audiences to expect rapid shifts, so it is of crucial importance that this focal point on stage multiply and alternate from one instant to another in order to accelerate the temporal and spatial flow.

This was the reason for spreading out the performance site over a 200-meter front. Two hundred meters that can become only twenty whenever and wherever it is desirable.

This was the reason for extending the play's action out into the middle of the auditorium and for abandoning all limiting backdrops, walls, and wings. Which is to say, not out of glaring ignorance concerning the dangers of dispersion and the virtues of concentration, but rather:

*To escape the unity of place that determines where all actions can unfold* (whose fetters will forever hobble the nineteenth-century theater), and, once the plot line has been developed by means of successive phases of concentration,

*to grant breadth of compass and a field of action to the choreographies, catastrophes, and spiraling crescendos* that are available and, in my view, essential to the mass theater.

Among *18 BL*'s reviewers, Salvini alone, thanks to finely attuned directorial sensibility, was able to grasp the "concentration" accomplished by means of light beams equivalent at once to 100,000 walls and to no walls at all. (He displayed a courage, generosity, and critical acumen on this occasion that fill me no less with gratitude than with admiration.) If the overall impression, however, was indeed one of scattering, I am ready to acknowledge a serious production flaw: a flaw that calls into question *only* that evening's performance and the individual who was responsible (and who today asserts his full responsibility) for that performance.

But the aesthetic and technical criteria that governed the first attempt at a mass theatrical experiment must be preserved in spite of the storm of controversy unleashed by the first full-scale dress rehearsal.

I make this point not to apologize for myself. A director must be judged by his results and the fact that he feels the need to explain himself in words is always already a sign of insufficiency.

Nor do I wish to defend the careful preparations, the seriousness of intent, the rigorous vision of those who, before the director and alongside the director, undertook this difficult endeavor.

Rather I write out of conviction that the theater of masses represents the revolution's first battle to carry out its first revolutionary conquest in the domain of spectacle.

Let it be stated, then, with precision:

A performance failed.

A director failed.

But a new form of spectacle was born.

It was born not mute but speaking; not deformed but well proportioned; endowed with a new and distinctive system of organic forces capable of achieving what would have been unthinkable within the confines of prior forms of spectacle. A child of the times and not of the libraries, it was engendered out of enthusiasm, faith, and tenacity, but also out of knowledge, sensibility, and aesthetic skill.

And it was christened, and properly so, the "theater of masses."

# APPENDIX B

■ *18 BL*

Performed April 29, 1934

*Organized by*: Alessandro Pavolini

*Conceived by*: Luigi Bonelli, Sandro de Feo, Gherardo Gherardi, Nicola Lisi, Raffaello Melani, Alessandro Pavolini, Corrado Sofia, and Giorgio Venturini

*Script developed by*: Sandro de Feo, Nicola Lisi, Raffaello Melani, Corrado Sofia, and Giorgio Venturini

*Final script redacted and written by*: Alessandro Blasetti

*Director*: Alessandro Blasetti

*Assistant to the Director*: Flavio Calzavara

*Liaison to local and national authorities*: Giovanni Poli (consul and vice-secretary of the GUF)

*Theater designed by*: Alessandro Blasetti

*Set designs by*: Giorgio Venturini

*Theater decor and props designed by*: Ferdinando Gatteschi

*Theater entrance designed by*: Giannetto Mannucci and Maurizio Tempestini

*Music*: Renzo Massarani

*Choreography*: Angela Sartorio and the Bonora Company

*Lead actor*: Ugo Ceseri

*Actors*: Giovani Fascisti, Balilla, Giovani Italiane, Arditi, and Squadristi

*Pilot of lead airplane*: Vasco Magrini

*Music*:

| | |
|---|---|
| Orchestra | "Trumpet Calls and Dances for *18 BL*" by Renzo Massarani |
| Barrel Organ | "Dance of the Seven Veils" from *Salomé* by Richard Strauss |
| Band | Processional drumming (performed live in the closing scene) |
| Chorus | "The Captain's Testament" |

"Mother, Weep Not over the
Assault"

"Sleep Well, Berta"

*Recorded Soundtrack*

Act 1 "Trumpet Calls" (Massarani)

"The Captain's Testament"

War sounds (machine guns,
artillery, bombs, sirens, etc.)

Act 2 Mob sounds

Factory sirens

Dance of the Seven Veils (from
Strauss's *Salomé*)

Act 3 "Mother Weep Not over the
Assault"

  "  "  "  "  "  "  "  "

"Sleep Well, Berta"

"Dances" (Massarani)

Factory whistle

"The Captain's Testament"

  "  "  "  "

  "  "  "  "

"Trumpet Calls" (Massarani)

### ■ ALESSANDRO BLASETTI (1900–1987)

Blasetti first appeared on the cinematic scene as a film critic for Carli and Settimelli's *L'Impero* during the early 1920's. This early journalistic activity led him to found a series of film journals that would prove instrumental in reviving the mostly dormant Italian film industry: *Il Mondo allo Schermo* (1926), *Lo Schermo* (1926), *Lo Spettacolo d'Italia* (1927–28), and, most important of all, *Cinematografo* (1927–31). In December 1928, he established the pivotal, but short-lived, production cooperative Augustus and set about directing his first film, *Sole*. Concerned with the draining of the Pontine marshes—a theme Blasetti would return to again in *18 BL*—*Sole* earned praise from Mussolini and many critics for its fascist populism and for its blend of stark realism and heroic idealism. The film was not a box-office success, but it marked the beginning of a prolific career that would extend well into the 1980's. Only Mario Camerini would enjoy comparable success as a film director during the fascist decades. Blasetti's prominence is attested to by the fact that, at the age of 32, he was chosen to direct the first Italian film school at Rome's Academy of Santa Cecilia (a position he held between 1932 and 1934). Blasetti also taught scriptwriting, acting, and cinematography at the Experimental Film Center at Cinecittà through 1942, which led to his designation as "everyone's teacher" in postwar film circles.

In addition to his teaching activities, Blasetti directed more than a dozen feature films over the decade subsequent to *Sole*: among them *Resurrectio* (the first Italian sound film) and *1860*, probably his most accomplished early film. Still admired for its formal inventiveness, *1860* anticipated numerous techniques that would later become standard features of the neorealist cinema. But its patriotic topic and masterfully choreographed crowd scenes were doubtless what led Pavolini to invite him to direct *18 BL*. It is also worth noting that 1934 was the year Blasetti directed the feature film *Vecchia guardia*: a paean to fascist squadrism of such intensity in its evocation of the "outlaw phase" of fascism that it barely escaped censorship. In his subsequent work, Blasetti experimented with a wide diversity of genres, including the "white telephone" film, literary adaptations, and comedies. Among these films, critics have singled out *Quattro passi tra le nuvole* (1942) as a work that deserves inclusion within the neorealist canon.

In the postwar era, Blasetti returned briefly to the theater, directing *Il tempo e la famiglia Conway* (1945), *Ma non è una cosa seria* (1945), *La foresta pietrificata* (1947), and *La regina e gli insorti* (1951). But the cinema remained his primary concern. He directed many more feature films and documentaries, was one of the inventors of the episodic film, is credited with discovering Marcello Mastroianni, and received numerous awards for his cinematography. The degree to which he had come to personify the Italian film industry can perhaps best be measured by Luchino Visconti's casting of Blasetti as himself in the 1951 feature *Bellissima*.

Principal writings: *Come nasce un film* (1932); *Cinema italiano oggi* (1950); *Il cinema che ho vissuto* (1982); *Scritti sul cinema* (1982).

Films: *Sole* (1929), *Resurrectio* (1930), *Terra madre* (1930), *Nerone* (1930), *Palio* (1931), *Assisi* (1932), *La tavola dei poveri* (1932), *1860* (1933), *Il caso Haller* (1933), *L'impiegata di papà* (1934), *Vecchia guardia* (1934), *Aldèbaran* (1935), *La contessa di Parma* (1937), *Ettore Fieramosca* (1938), *Retroscena* (1939), *Un'avventura di Salvator Rosa* (1940), *La corona di ferro* (1941), *La cena delle beffe* (1941), *Quattro passi tra le nuvole* (1942), *Nessuno torna indietro* (1943), *Un giorno nella vita* (1947), *Fabiola* (1948), *Prima comunione* (1950), *La fiammata* (1952), *Peccato che sia una canaglia* (1954), *La fortuna di essere donna* (1955), *Amore e chiacchiere* (1957), *Europe by Night*

(1959), *Io amo, tu ami . . .* (1961), *Liola* (1963), *Io, io, io . . . e gli altri* (1966), *La ragazza del bersagliere* (1967), *Simon Bolivar* (1969).

For further information, see Adriano Aprà's introduction to Alessandro Blasetti, *Scritti sul cinema* (Venice: Marsilio, 1982); Gianfranco Gori, *Alessandro Blasetti* (Florence: La Nuova Italia, 1984); Elaine Mancini, *Struggles of the Italian Film Industry During Fascism, 1930–1935* (Ann Arbor, Mich.: UMI Research Press, 1985); Paola Micheli, *Il cinema di Blasetti, parlò così* (Rome: Bulzoni, 1990); Luca Verdone, *I film di Alessandro Blasetti* (Rome: Gremese, 1989).

### ■ LUIGI BONELLI (1893–1954)

World War I veteran and member of the Arditi (assault troops). First worked as a journalist in the postwar period (1919–25). Starting in 1922, he began his career in the theater collaborating with Ferdinando Paolieri on a series of farcical operettas, beginning with *Bacco in Toscana*.

In 1926 Bonelli began writing under the Russian pseudonym Wassili Cëtoff-Sternberg, a device meant to tweak the noses of Italy's drama critics, whom he faulted for the speed with which they decried the poverty of the contemporary Italian theater and praised theatrical imports. By the late 1920's, Bonelli/Cëtoff had become a celebrated author of comedies in the grotesque vein (among them *Il topo, L'imperatore,* and *Cicero*). He began writing screenplays in the early 1930's, and among his early credits were *Palio*, a collaboration with Blasetti, which probably led to their joint involvement in *18 BL.* In subsequent years, Bonelli would go on to write screenplays to such films as *L'incantesimo tragico*, directed by Mario Sequi. At the time of the 1934 Littoriali, Bonelli was national secretary of the playwrights' union (the Gruppo Sindacale Italiano Autori Drammatici), one of several such positions that he would hold during the second fascist decade. A good number of Bonelli's early plays are collected in his two-volume *Le commedie a letto*.

Plays: *Storienko* (1924), *Dramma di sogni* (1926), *Il medico della signora malata* (1926), *Il topo* (1927), *Il mio cuoco e la mia amante* (1927), *L'imperatore* (1929), *La barca dei comici* (1930), *Il Gigli e la sua commedia nuova* (1933), *Cicero* (1934), *L'uomo che sorride* (with A. de Benedetti; 1935), *Fra diavolo* (with G. Romualdi; 1936), *Il mestiere del galantuomo* (with G. Romualdi; 1936), *Mazarino* (with L. d'Ambra; 1937), *La quarta parete* (with L. d'Ambra; 1937), *Boccaperta in furberia* (1942), *Avventura ad Aix-les-Bains* (with A. de Benedetti; 1951), *L'imperatrice in vacanza* (1953).

Operettas: *Bacco in Toscana* (with F. Paolieri; 1922), *La maschera nuda* (with F. Paolieri; 1923), *Stenterello e il granduca* (with F. Paolieri; 1925), *Rompicollo* (1925), *Calandrino* (1926), *Isola verde* (with C. Lombardo; 1927), *I monelli fiorentini* (1928), *Operetta* (1928), *Piccola Salambò* (1931), *La fiera* (1935).

Screenplays: *Palio* (1932), *Paradiso* (1932), *O la borsa o la vita* (1933), *L'uomo che sorride* (1937), *Anime in tumulto* (1941), *Elisir d'amore* (1941), *Una notte dopo l'opera* (1942), *La guardia del corpo* (1942), *Trent'anni di servizio* (1944), *Capitan Demonio* (1951), *L'incantesimo tragico* (1952), *Gli angeli del quartiere* (1952).

For further information, see the collective volume *Scritti in onore di Luigi Bonelli* (Rome: Edizioni Universitarie, 1940).

## ■ FLAVIO CALZAVARA (1900–1981)

Calzavara was a director best known for adventure films, literary adaptations, and period dramas. Although he had worked as a director's assistant on numerous earlier projects (including *18 BL*), his real debut as an assistant director took place with the filming of Romolo Marcellini's *Sentinelle di bronzo* (1937), a mythic representation of Italy's conquest of Ethiopia. In the wake of this film, Calzavara undertook his first and most successful directorial effort: *Piccoli naufraghi*. Blending documentary and fictional materials, *Piccoli naufraghi* narrated the story of Italy's invasion from the perspective of a group of youths. In his subsequent films, Calzavara left behind colonial themes, although he remained faithful to the regime through the Republic of Salò. In the immediate postwar period, he moved briefly to Spain, where he completed *El curioso impertinente* in 1948. By the early 1950's, however, he was back in Italy, where, among other things, he directed several detective thrillers.

Films: *I piccoli naufraghi* (1938), *Don Buonaparte* (1941), *Il ladro sono io!* (1941), *Il signore a doppio petto* (1941), *Contessa Castiglione* (1942), *Carmela* (1942), *Confessione* (1942), *Calafuria* (1943), *Dagli Appennini alle Ande* (1943), *Resurrezione* (1944), *Peccatori* (1944), *El curioso impertinente* (1948), *Contro la legge* (1951), *Sigillo rosso* (1951), *I due derelitti* (1952), *Dieci canzoni d'amore da salvare* (1953), *La pattuglia dell'Amba Alagi* (1953), *Napoli piange e ride* (1954).

For further information, see Gian Piero Brunetta, *Storia del cinema italiano, 1895–1945* (Rome: Editori Riuniti, 1979), 341–59, and Marcia Landy, *Fascism in Film: The Italian Commercial Cinema, 1931–1943* (Princeton: Princeton Univ. Press, 1986), 44–46.

**143**

## ■ UGO CESERI (1893–1941)

During the 1920's, Ceseri established himself in the theater with the companies of Novelli, Ruggeri, Picasso, Almirante, and Falconi, as well as working briefly, under Forzano's direction, with the Compagnia Dannunziana. In the early 1930's, he turned to the cinema, where he was frequently cast in roles in which he embodied the simple virtues of the rural populace. His principal films during the decade were Blasetti's *Vecchia guardia* and *Un'avventura di Salvator Rosa*, as well as Mario Camerini's *Figaro e la sua gran giornata*, Guido Brignone's *Passaporto rosso*, and Goffredo Alessandrini's *Seconda B*. His work for Blasetti in the film *Palio* (1932) probably led to his selection for the starring role in *18 BL*.

---

Films: *Figaro e la sua gran giornata* (1931), *Palio* (1932), *La cantante dell'opera* (1932), *Una notte con te* (1932), *Oggi sposi* (1933), *Cercasi modella* (1933), *Seconda B* (1934), *Tenebre* (1934), *Frutto acerbo* (1934), *Vecchia guardia* (1935), *Aldebaran* (1935), *Passaporto rosso* (1935), *Maestro Landi* (1935), *Nozze vagabonde* (1936), *Ginevra degli Almieri* (1936), *Musica in piazza* (1936), *Non è una cosa seria* (1936), *I due sergenti* (1936), *I fratelli Castiglioni* (1937), *Contessa di Parma* (1937), *L'orologio a cucù* (1938), *Crispino e la comare* (1938), *La mia canzone al vento* (1939), *Papà per una notte* (1939), *Retroscena* (1939), *Un'avventura di Salvator Rosa* (1940), *Mare* (1940), *Fortuna* (1940), *Cantate con me!* (1940), *La canzone rubata* (1941), *Mutter* (1941).

## ■ SANDRO DE FEO (1905–1968)

Initially a journalist for *L'Ora* (Palermo) and co-editor of *L'Italia Vivente*, de Feo joined the editorial staff of *Il Messaggero* in 1933, where he served for a full decade as a film and theater critic. During this period, he contributed to a wide range of journals, including *Il Selvaggio* (on the Rome/Moscow debate), *Critica Fascista*, *Omnibus*, *Tutto*, *Oggi*, *Legioni e Falangi*, and *Il Mediterraneo*. *18 BL* was for him, as for Sofia, a disillusioning experience that would very gradually lead him away from the fascist fold. By the wartime years, he had emerged as a prominent figure within liberal Resistance circles, and in the war's wake, he became a founding editor of *Il Risorgimento Liberale* and *Corriere Lombardo*. His most enduring contribution to postwar culture was made as theater critic for *Corriere della Sera*, but he worked as well for *Il Tempo*, *La Stampa*, and *L'Europeo*. His writings on theater have been collected in the two-volume *In cerca di teatro*, edited by Luciano Lucignani (Milan: Longanesi, 1972).

Although primarily a journalist, de Feo was also an active scriptwriter from the mid 1930's through the mid 1950's and counted as his first screenplay a collaboration with Nino d'Aroma entitled *Ragazzo*. This (now lost) film is remembered as the first feature-length sound film produced in Italy.

---

Screenplays: *Ragazzo* (with Nino d'Aroma; 1933), *Re dei denari* (1936), *Lo smemorato* (1936), *Pensaci Giacomino!* (1937), *È caduta una donna* (1941), *La morte civile* (1942), *Documento Z 3* (1942), *Una piccola moglie* (1944), *Accidenti alla guerra* (1949), *Marechiaro* (1949), *Europa '51* (1952), *La provinciale* (1953), *Vestire gli ignudi* (1954), *Tre storie proibite* (1954).

## ■ FERDINANDO GATTESCHI

Along with Tempestini, Gatteschi was one of the designers of the façade of the Palazzo delle Esposizioni at the parterre of San Gallo (the space where the artworks from the Lictorial games were exhibited and where the competitions transpired). He also contributed (with

Mannucci, Tempestini, and Venturini) to the design of the art exhibition of the Littoriali, designed and built the canvas and wood bayonet-crowned books that were used to light Blasetti's stadium, and executed the poster announcing the performance of *18 BL*.

## ■ GHERARDO GHERARDI (1891–1949)

Gherardi began his career as a journalist with *L'Avvenire d'Italia* and *Il Resto di Carlino*, and was a frequent contributor to reviews such as *Comoedia, Augustea, Cinema, Circoli, Costruire, Scenario, L'Orto,* and *Meridiani.* Along with Dario Niccodemi, he was co-founder of the Experimental Theater of Bologna. During the 1930's, he emerged as Italy's most popular and prolific writer of comedies. Among his more than fifty plays are *Vertigine* (1923), *Don Chisciotte* (1926), *Tragedia contro luce* (1927), *Ombre cinesi* (1932), *Il focolare* (1934), *Truccature* (1934), *Questi ragazzi!* (1934), *I figli del marchese Lucera* (1935), *L'arcidiavolo* (1935), *L'ippogrifo* (1936), *Partire* (1936), *Passabò vita perduta* (1937), *Le stelle ridono* (1938), *Il burattino* (1938), *Autunno* (1939), *Lettere d'amore* (1940), *Tumulto* (1940), *Cappuccetto rosso, arcifiaba* (1941), *Oro puro* (1941), *Fuga dal castello in aria* (1942), *Il nostro viaggio* (1948), *Non fare come me* (1950), and *Un tale che passa* (1952). Gherardi was also the author of several plays in Bolognese dialect, including *Spanezz* (1927), and of *Balilla attraverso i tempi*, a propagandistic comedy written for the Opera Nazionale Balilla and performed in September 1934.

Gherardi wrote screenplays for films such as *Questi ragazzi!* (Maria Mattoli, director; 1937), *Dottor Antonio* (Enrico Guazzon, director; 1937), and *Return, Most Beloved* (Guido Brignone, director; 1947).

Selected writings: *I passeggeri di Caronte* (1920); *Nè mosche nè zanzare* (1922), *Cartoni animati* (1932), *Opere scelte: Sei commedie* (1953).

For further information see chapter 12 of Enzo Maurri's *Rose scarlatte e telefoni bianchi: Appunti sulla commedia italiana dall'impero al 25 luglio 1943* (Rome: Abete, 1981); Baldo Curato, *Sessant'anni di teatro in Italia da Giovanni Verga a Ugo Betti* (Milan: Denti, 1947), 274–84; and Mario Bonetti, "Gherardo Gherardi," *Portici* 2 (1951): 31–35.

## ■ NICOLA LISI (1893–1975)

An antibourgeois Catholic intellectual and contributor to reviews such as *Il Frontespizio, Meridiani, L'Orto,* and *Primato,* Lisi belonged to the group of young Florentine writers known as the "calendarists" (which included men such as Betocchi and Bargellini). With the latter, he co-edited and authored his first publication, an almanac entitled *Il calendario dei pensieri e delle pratiche solari* (1923). Later, there followed the plays *L'acqua: Rappresentazione umana* (1928), *La via della croce* (1953), and *Aspettare in pace* (1957); and the narrative works *Favole* (1933), *Paese dell'anima* (1934), *L'arca dei semplici* (1938), *Concerto domenicale* (1941), *Diario di un parroco di campagna* (1942), *Amore e desolazione* (1946), *La nuova tebaide* (1950), *Mistici medievali* (1956), *La faccia della terra* (1959), *I racconti* (1961), *La mano del tempo* (1965), *Il seme della saggezza* (1967), *Parlata dalla finestra di casa* (1973), *I caratteri* (1981), and *Diario dalle opere* (1983). Lisi also produced an edition of Giulio Cesare Croce's *Bertoldo, Bertoldino e Cacasenno* (1929), co-edited (with Augusto Hermet) the volume *Scrittori cattolici dei nostri giorni* (1930) and translated the Gospel According to Matthew, as well as several catechistic works.

For further information, see Carlo Bo, *Diario aperto e chiuso, 1932–1944* (Milan: Edizioni di Uomo, 1945), *Nuovi studi* (Florence: Vallecchi, 1946); Emilio Cecchi, *Di giorno in giorno* (Milan: Garzanti, 1954); E. N. Girardi, *Il mito di Pavese e altri saggi* (Milan: Vita e Pensiero, 1960); Giovanni Getto, *Letteratura religiosa dal due al novecento* (Florence: Vallecchi, 1967); Luisa Mangoni, *L'interventismo della cultura: Intellettuali e riviste del fascismo* (Bari: Laterza, 1974), 167–72; and F. Mazzariol, *Nicola Lisi, viaggiatore incantato* (Forlì: Forum, 1977).

## ■ GIANNETTO MANNUCCI (1911–1980)

Mannucci was a young sculptor and painter connected with the Florentine GUF at the time of *18 BL*. He designed a medallion and the Mussolini Trophy for the Lictorial games, as well as collaborating on the design of the art exhibition of the 1934 Littoriali. During subsequent years, he wrote for the review *Costruire* and contributed works to the 1937 Paris International Exposition, the Venice Biennial (1934, 1936, 1938, 1954, 1956), Milan Triennial (1940), and Rome Quadrennial exhibitions (1939, 1951), as well as receiving a number of regional commissions, including one for the train station of Santa Maria Novella in Florence. By the time of the war, Mannucci had moved outside the fascist fold and joined the Action Party (Partito d'azione). He continued his artistic career into the postwar period, although his reputation remained a regional one.

For an overview of his work, see Enrico Crispolti's *Giannetto Mannucci: Anni trenta-ottanta* (Rome: Edizioni Latium, 1991), which elides his political work from the 1930's, and Umberto Badini et al., *Giannetto Mannucci, 1911–1980* (Pisa: Pacini, 1987).

## ■ RENZO MASSARANI (1898–1975)

A student of Ottorino Respighi's, Massarani was a promising young composer whose career was interrupted by the imposition of racial laws in 1938. During the 1920's, Massarani was affiliated with Mario Labroca and Vittorio Rieti, and wrote for *L'Impero*. His operatic and puppet theater compositions include *Bianco e nero* (1921), *Guerrin detto il meschino* (1928), *I dolori della principessa Susina* (1929), *La donna del pozzo* (1930), and *È nata una bambina* (1933), in addition to which he composed a ballet entitled *Boè* (1937). Among his orchestral, chamber, and instrumental works are: *Dal lago di Mantova* (1922), *Pastorale* (1923), *Sinfonietta* (1924), *Introduzione, tema e sette variazioni* (1934), and *Il molinaro* (1935), as well as a number of madrigals and songs. In 1930 he participated in the first International Music Festival held in Rome, which included performances of the work of avant-garde composers such as Honegger, Prokofiev, and Stravinsky. (In a post-festival review, Massarani defended Stravinsky against vulgar nationalist attacks.) In 1933, with Giuseppe Mulè, he organized the national exhibition of the fascist musicians' union, and in 1936 he participated in the Olympic musical competition in Berlin, with *Squilli e danze atletiche*: a composition closely related to his *Squilli e danze per il 18 BL*. Despite ardent pro-fascist convictions, Massarani, a Jew and "fascist of the first hour," found his works banned in 1938. After that time he ceased his activities as a composer, eventually emigrating to Brazil, where he continued on as a music critic but prohibited performances and/or publication of his music.

For further information, see John C. G. Waterhouse, "The Emergence of Modern Italian Music (up to 1940)," (Ph.D. diss., Oxford Univ., 1968), 674–79; Harvey Sachs, *Music in Fascist Italy* (New York: Norton, 1988), 89, 96, 185–88;

and Fiamma Nicolodi, *Musica e musicisti nel ventennio fascista* (Fiesole: Discanto, 1984), 264, 287.

### ■ RAFFAELLO MELANI (1897–1960)

A Catholic intellectual who began his involvement in Florentine drama circles during the late 1920's, Melani translated Lope de Vega, collaborated closely with Venturini's GUF Experimental Theater, directed works like Tullio Pinelli's *Il padre nudo*, and, most of all, was author of works such as *Santa Celestina: Sacra rappresentazione in due parti* (Quaderni di Proscenio [Florence: Giannini, 1935]). The latter, composed in 1928 and staged in 1933 at the San Remo outdoor festival (with Cele Abba, Nando Tamberlani, Amedeo Nazari, and Fulvio Testa among the cast members) was most likely responsible for his inclusion in the *18 BL* authorial collective. He subsequently described this modern mystery play as the first attempt to revive this genre in Italy and as a predecessor of the "Representation of Saint Uliva" directed by Jacques Copeau for the 1933 Maggio Musicale Fiorentino (on which subject, see Melani's preface to the 1935 edition). After the *18 BL* debacle, in which he played a very minor role, he continued to assert the validity of the sacred theater as a fascist theater:

Who knows whether this timid and imperfect attempt to recover the theater's religious function in the remembrance and celebration of great spiritual trials points to the resurgence of a more vibrant dramatic subject matter and reason in keeping with our unquenchable thirst for goodness and nobility, for high and universal things, for actions nourished by a sense of the divine? Will it not ultimately lead theater back to a popular audience that (quite properly) is today ever increasingly absenting itself, whether owing to boredom or to disgust? Does it not respond to Benito Mussolini's admonition in a memorable speech that urged authors to turn once again to the people with grand theatrical works in which the great collective passions find dramatic expression? Because too often today the theater, with all its oddities and abstractions, with all its disenchantment and skepticism, is nothing more than an obfuscating and deforming mirror of human life, a cynical debunker of supreme spiritual values. ("Preface," *Santa Celestina: Sacra rappresentazione in due parti*, xii)

### ■ ALESSANDRO PAVOLINI (1903–1945)

A member of an influential Florentine family (his brother Corrado being a noted dramaturge and his father a well-known academic), Pavolini joined the fascist movement in 1920 and participated in the March on Rome. He was from early on associated with the fascist youth organizations and during this first phase contributed to such intransigent journals as *Battaglie Fasciste, Rivoluzione Fascista*, and *La Montagna*. This early militancy coexisted with a strong interest in cultural and artistic matters, which led him to intervene in the *Critica Fascista* debate on fascist culture (1926) and in defense of Pirandello's *italianità*, as well as to publish short stories (in *Solaria*), a play (in *Comoedia*), and a *romanzo sportivo* (*Giro d'Italia*). In 1929 he was named to the rank of federal secretary and became founding editor of *Il Bargello*, whose feverish advocacy of the PNF party line did not preclude a cultural page open to some of the period's leading young intellectuals, including Bilenchi, Rosai, Vittorini, and Pratolini. Appointed in 1932 to the directorate of the PNF, Pavolini entered parliament in 1934 and assumed the presidency of the Confederation of Professionals and Artists in the month preceding the staging of *18 BL*. The mixed success of the Littoriali of Culture and Art did not slow down Pavolini's ascent through the party ranks, nor did it end his career as a journalist (he continued to write for newspapers such as *Il Bargello* and *Corriere della Sera* and even directed *Il Messaggero* during the regime's final years). After a succession of lesser charges (which included membership in the National Council of Corporations) and

**147**

thanks to the protection of Mussolini's son-in-law Galeazzo Ciano (in whose later trial and execution he played a role), he was chosen to succeed Dino Alfieri as minister of popular culture, a position he held between October 1939 and February 1943. By this time closely affiliated with Nazism and with the regime's racial policies, Pavolini fled to Germany after Mussolini's defeat in July 1943, where he joined the core group that would play a leading role in the Italian Social Republic (the so-called "Republic of Salò"): Renato Ricci, Roberto Farinacci, and Giovanni Preziosi. Pavolini was named by Mussolini as secretary of the Fascist Republican party at the time of the foundation of the republic (September 1943), a role that he took on with the intention of promoting intransigence and a social politics founded on anticapitalism, collectivization, workers' control of the economy, land reform, imperialism, pan-Europeanism, and anti-Semitism. As the republic slipped into chaos in the following year, Pavolini assumed military powers. He conscripted all party members into the so-called Black Brigades and launched a fierce campaign of antipartisan raids. The accelerating allied advance up the Italian peninsula during 1944 and early 1945 led Pavolini to argue that the republic's forces ought to make one final heroic stand, but events overtook him. In April 1945, he accompanied Mussolini on his flight to the republic's sole remaining foothold, Milan. Both were captured and executed by partisans.

---

Selected "literary" writings: *Le fatalone: Un atto tropicale* (1929); *Giro d'Italia-Romanzo sportivo* (1928); *Disperata* (1937); *Scomparsa d'Angela* (1940); *Nuovo Baltico, viaggio* (1935).

---

For further information, see Arrigo Petacco, *Pavolini: L'ultima raffica di Salò* (Milan: A. Mondadori, 1982); Marco Palla, *Firenze nel regime fascista*, 1929–1934 (Florence: Olschki, 1978), 171–230; and Silvio Bertoldi, *Salò: Vita e morte della Repubblica Sociale Italiana*, 3d ed. (Milan: Rizzoli, 1976).

### ■ CORRADO SOFIA (1906– )

Journalist, writer, scriptwriter, and later, director of documentary films. Sofia began his career as an occasional contributor to Interlandi's *Il Tevere* during the late 1920's. By the turn of the decade, he had shifted over to *La Stampa*, to which, among other things, he contributed a reportage on a journey to the Soviet Union (whose impact would subsequently be felt in his theater writings and polemics). In 1932 he undertook another journey, this time to China for *Gazzetta del Popolo*. By the mid 1930's, Sofia was writing fiction for *Quadrivio* and film scripts for *Il Selvaggio*, and he had become a member of the editorial board of *Critica Fascista* (1933–40) by the time he was called upon to participate in *18 BL*. During the period that followed, Sofia continued to publish in journals such as *Comoedia, L'Italia Vivente*, and *Primato*, while serving as the Agenzia Stefani's correspondent in Belgrade and Athens, as well as working for the Italian embassy in Yugoslavia's cultural office. Sofia's support for the regime began to drift during the later 1930's, and by 1943 he had joined the Resistance. This earned him a place alongside Leo Longanesi, Vasco Pratolini, and Enrico Falqui in the list of "traitors" denounced by Mussolini in "Canguri giganti" (*Corrispondenza repubblicana* [Nov. 11, 1943]; *OO* 32.266) who, although now affirming antifascist convictions, had received gifts and subventions from the fascist state. In the postwar era, Sofia pursued an active journalistic career and would contribute to *La Stampa, L'Espresso, Gazzetta del Popolo, Il Mondo, L'Illustrazione Italiana*, and *Corriere della Sera*. He also authored numerous books, including *Noto, città barocca* (1986) concerned with the city of his birth (whose vice-mayor and cultural councilor [*assessore*] he briefly became), *Belkis ci salverà* (1993), *Avventure in Cina* (1987), which contrasts his 1932 trip to China with a later one to Maoist China, and *Pirandello: Storia di un amore* (1992), which concerns Pirandello's love for Marta Abba. His later years were, however, devoted principally to the cinema, and he wrote, produced and/or directed more than a dozen documentaries (most made for RAI television) on topics as diverse as Egyptian archeology, Southern Italy, Verga, Guttuso, Maccari, and Pirandello. He currently resides in Rome and Noto and is at work on a book entitled *Genti di Sicilia*.

For further information, see my interview with Sofia in Appendix E.

### ■ MAURIZIO TEMPESTINI

Collaborated with Mannucci on the design of the boat bridge that served as the principal entrance to the theater of the Albereta. Also involved in designing the art exhibition of the 1934 Littoriali, Tempestini designed and built two special ticket booths for *18 BL*.

### ■ GIORGIO VENTURINI (1908–1981)

Venturini began his distinguished career in the theater with the writing and production of *La storia del soldatino piccino-picciò* (1931), *Le nozze di Rosetta* (1932), and *La principessa senza cuore* (1933). A close associate of Corrado and Alessandro Pavolini, he served as vice-secretary of the Florentine GUF between 1934 and 1936 and as the director of *Il Bargello* after Alessandro Pavolini's departure. During that period, he contributed to the design of the art exhibition at the 1934 Littoriali, as well as participating in the set design, playwriting, and directing competitions. In the wake of the Littoriali, he founded the GUF Experimental Theater in Florence, which he directed until 1943. Ven-

turini was frequently involved both in the organization of the Maggio Musicale Fiorentino and in directing works for the festival. Among these productions, he is remembered for two performances in the Boboli Gardens—his staging of Michelangelo's *Tancia* (1936) and co-direction, with Corrado Pavolini, of Monteverdi's *L'incoronazione di Poppea* (1937)—and for a remarkable 1938 staging of Vecchi's *Amfiparnaso*, with sets and costumes by the painter Gino Severini. In that same year, he was responsible for the elaborate mass choreographies, open-air set designs, and lighting and pyrotechnic effects that were devised to welcome Hitler to Florence. Venturini's fascist faith remained unaltered through the end of the war, and between September 1943 and April 1945, he served as general director of the theater in the Ministry of Popular Culture of the Republic of Salò.

In the postwar period, Venturini rarely dabbled in the theater, instead pursuing a vigorous career as a producer of documentary and feature films. He collaborated with directors such as Antonioni, de Robertis, and Damiani. Among his productions were *Fantasmi del mare* (F. de Robertis, director; 1948); *La mano della morte* (Carlo Campogaltiani, director; 1949); *Le roi cruel* and *I cosacchi* (V. Touryansky, director; 1959 and 1960); *Il sesso degli angeli* (Ugo Liberatore, director; 1968); *A Black Veil for Lisa* (M. Dallamano, director; 1969); *Ondata di calore* (Nelo Risi, director; 1970). It would appear that Venturini was still active through the late 1970's, when he and Alessandro Orlandini published *Padrone, arrivedello a battitura* (1980).

For further information, see Alessandro Sardelli, "Decorazione murale, architettura e coreografia nelle parate del regime fascista: Il caso di Firenze durante la visita di Hilter," *Biblioteca Teatrale* 19–20 (1990): 189–204.

# APPENDIX D

The following is a tentative reconstruction based on published materials, archival sources, and the fragmentary records preserved in the BA and ACS. In numerous cases the dates provided are approximations.

## ■ 1933

*April 28*   Mussolini gives a speech summoning Italian dramatists to "prepare a theater of masses, a theater able to accommodate 15,000 or 20,000 persons" at the 50-year anniversary celebration of the Italian Society of Authors and Editors (SIAE) in Rome.

*Late April*   Pavolini is involved in polemics regarding the "eclectic" and "cosmopolitan" character of the first Maggio Musicale Fiorentino, for whose organization he was partially responsible. He defends the festival in the pages of *Il Bargello* and argues for the forging of a new popular but experimental theater.

*June 15*   Sofia publishes "Necessità di un teatro" (The need for a theater [*CF* 11.12: 239–40]) criticizing both the traditional theater and Bra-

gaglia's art theater and calling for the creation of a "revolutionary" youth theater in Rome.

*August 25*   *L'Italia Vivente* devotes an entire issue to the need for an experimental state theater under Bragaglia's directorship. The issue includes essays by de Feo ("Appunti per un teatro di masse" [3.14: 9]) and Bonelli ("Fare un teatro di propaganda" [3.14: 6–7]).

*September 15*   A follow-up piece by Sofia appears in *Critica Fascista* ("Per un teatro d'arte a Roma" [11.18: 357–60]) gathering together responses to his June 15 article by Ardengo Soffici, Corrado Alvaro, Corrado Pavolini, de Feo, Eurialo de Michelis, and Mario Mafai.

*October*   In his capacity as organizer of the 1934 Littoriali, Pavolini envisages an inaugural spectacle that will realize Mussolini's "theater of 15,000 to 20,000 persons."

*October 28*   Bomba publishes "Il vecchio camion" ("The Old Truck") in *L'Italia Vivente* (3.18: 6–7), a nostalgic musing on the intimate connection between fascist squadrism and 18 BL trucks. Sometime earlier, Bomba had made a series of paintings of 15 TER and 18 BL trucks, one of which was reproduced in *Bianco e Rosso*, the journal of the Fiat afterwork organization.

**November 1**   Sofia publishes a final follow-up to his June 15 article in *Critica Fascista* (11.21: 414–17), including responses from d'Amico and Bragaglia.

Bardi publishes a proposal for a "fascist mystery play" in *Quadrante*, unaware of Pavolini's intentions. The text reads as follows:

Three visions in a large stadium.

To represent fascism in scenic terms in keeping with the spirit of the "theater of masses" and by means of a synthesis of the fundamental and determining episodes of its history.

The aim is to create an enduring form of spectacle, for which reason it is essential that the present plotline be submitted to il Duce, who will have to determine its definitive physiognomy.

A nocturnal spectacle.

Three visions:

*The Great War*

*The Revolution*

*The Peace and Power of Fascism*

**First Act**   (The stage: a canal running east to west, with a bridge extending across it; a hovel on the southern side; railroad tracks encircling the stage, branching out from the northern side; an assemblage of floodlights along the stadium roof-line.)

War scenes with infantrymen, *Arditi*, artillery batteries, aviation, etc. The bridge is fought over. It is crossed. The troops set out towards the southern side of the stage. A soldier embellishes the hovel with Mussolini's phrase: "Better to live a lion's life for a single day, than to endure 100 years as a sheep." The troop trains appear and unload soldiers. The floodlights cast light on the episodes, one after another. The soldiers triumphant.

**Second Act**   The veterans return to this side of the bridge. On the opposite side, noise and indiscipline. The hovel is painted red by subversives. "Action teams" [*squadre d'azione*] are organized. Clashes.

Portrayal of the Berta incident on the disputed bridge. Victory to the action teams. The subversives are dispersed. The fascist masses set out to march on Rome. Trains brimming over with squadrists.

**Third Act**   After victory, the return to order. Scenes of disciplined masses; episodes of work and faith. The bridge rebuilt as a sign of peace and concord. Worker trains. Country dances. Flags. The raising of the flag over the stadium's tower. The masses set out through the southern portals to parade across the city.

**Components**   Powerful masses. The masses as protagonist of the spectacle. Music and choruses from the war, the revolution, the countryside. The lighting of fires.

**Techniques**   No professional actors or dramaturges, Giovacchino Forzano included. The masses selected from among the associations and, first and foremost, from the OND, Fasci for youth, and GUF.

**Conviction**   Stadiums will be the birthplace of the theater of masses.

**Quoted from "(Proposte) Sacra rappresentazione del fascismo" ("[Proposals] A fascist mystery play") *Quadrante* 7 (Nov. 1933): 4.**

**Early November**   Several meetings take place at the Casa del Fascio of Florence to discuss the structure, planning, and organization of the Littoriali of Culture and Art under the supervision of Pavolini. After lengthy debates, a draft of the program for 1934 and of the regulations for future Littoriali is redacted and submitted to Starace. The former includes plans for a mass theatrical experiment.

**Mid-November**   Word has begun to spread about the intended mass spectacle, and Giovanni Poli receives various inquiries, including one from Paolo Sella, who proposes a spectacle built around Menenius Agrippa's famous speech, reported in Livy's history of Rome (2.32), about the human body and the need for its organs to work together to ensure its health, just as society's social classes must collaborate in order to ensure the health of the body politic. The letter reads as follows:

In the first part, the incident is to be reenacted much as it occurred during the Roman period by means of rhythmic movements performed by masses of youths and through the displacement of actors.

In the second part, the same fable will be reenacted but introduced into the modern era. Various tableaux representing the vertiginous activities of our time will be placed before the spectators' eyes. The forces of fragmentation that work within the confines of the state will also be symbolized.

In the third part, by way of a conclusion, a series of alternating scenes will demonstrate the efforts to coordinate and organize all these dispersed energies so as to create the foundations of a new order.

As concerns the mode of staging, it will be necessary to create a platform at the stadium's center so that masked actors, much as in an ancient Roman theater, can perform there. On all four sides of the platform, there will be two masses of youths (male and female) who will perform the same function as a Greek chorus. They will narrate the story for the audience in the form of a recitative, interpreting it and unveiling its hidden meaning.

**(Sella to Poli, dated "Genoa, Nov. 9, 1933," in ACS-PNF-DN-GUF, b. 44, f. 604)**

Poli responds on November 14: "While I have no objection to the idea of Menenius Agrippa's apology, it won't be possible to put it into practice. From 30,000 to 40,000 people will be attending the mass theater spectacle, and the notion of restricting the size of the stage strikes me as neither desirable nor easy" (Poli to Sella, PNF stationery, dated Nov. 14, 1933, in ACS-PNF-DN-GUF, b. 44, f. 604).

Sella replies some time thereafter:

I had a brief conversation with comrade Marcelli [presumably the film director Romolo Marcellini] concerning the possibility of staging the spectacle in Florence for the Littoriali of Culture.

In your letter you indicate that you like the idea, but that the show ought not be restricted to a single stage. This wasn't my intention. The spectacle is made up of *masses in movement*. The central platform is occupied by only a few masked actors, whose role it is to embody the *passions that animate the crowd*, which is to say, to stand in for *the leaders*.

The apology of Menenius Agrippa depicts Roman society in its disintegrative phase. Groups of workers from the fields, workshops, cities, army, head off in different directions from one another as indicated through mass rhythmical gymnastic movements.

At the center of the stadium, a few characters must serve as the *fulcrum* of the action. They are the *leaders*, and it is to them that the mass movements refer.

**(Sella to Poli, from Rome, undated, in ACS-PNF-DN-GUF, b. 44, f. 604)**

Poli seems to have remained unconvinced.

***Second Half of November*** Starace approves the plans as submitted. An executive committee made up of members of the Florentine GUF is set up under Pavolini's guidance to oversee the organization of the games. The committee includes Ginnasi, Venturini, Mannucci, Tempestini, Rossi, and Gatteschi.

To organize the planned mass spectacle, Pavolini begins to assemble an editorial collective from among the most prominent younger fascist playwrights, critics, set designers, and directors. Bonelli, de Feo, Gherardi, Lisi, Melani, Sofia, and Venturini all agree to participate in this endeavor. Bonelli and Gherardi had come to Pavolini's attention as well-established figures who had authored numerous successful comedies and been active in debates concerning the crisis of the traditional theater, youth theaters, and the need to develop specifically fascist dramatic forms. (Bonelli was national secretary of the Italian Union of Playwrights in 1933–34.) Sofia and de Feo were emerging writers who had gained notoriety during the *Critica Fascista* debate on the desirability of an "art theater" for youth. Lisi and Melani were young Catholic writers known to Pavolini through Florentine literary circles and because the latter's *Santa Celestina* had been performed at the San Remo outdoor theater festival in July 1933. Venturini was a young playwright/director based in Florence who had been actively involved with GUF theater groups and,

**153**

from the start, assumed the key leadership role alongside Pavolini.

*December*   A first meeting is held at the Casa del Fascio in Florence attended by all members of the collective, as well as by Giovanni Poli. A variety of possible approaches and plot structures are considered, until unanimous agreement emerges that a Fiat 18 BL truck should be designated the protagonist of the spectacle. Ginnasi, secretary of the Florentine GUF, describes the meeting as follows: "Sitting around a table one night discussing the theater of masses, they threw around ideas and names . . . the Rubicon . . . the Legionary . . . Caesar Augustus . . . the Victory. . . . Instead they gave birth to a simple truck: a subject that won everyone's support right away" ("Dietro le quinte dei Littoriali di cultura ed arte," *Il Bargello* [March 25, 1934]: 2).

At subsequent meetings, various narrative structures are proposed and discussed, and on the basis of these deliberations, a rough plot is agreed to by all. Individual scenes are assigned to each of the authors, with Sofia assuming the principal script-writing responsibilities.

Venturini alludes to the coming spectacle in his essay "Teatro d'oggi" (Theater Today) published in the inaugural issue of *I Littoriali della Cultura e dell'Arte: Rivista Mensile* (1: 36–40), a journal that was also to serve as the official guidebook to the 1934 Lictorial games.

■ **1934**

*Early January*   The drafting process continues. Sofia publishes an essay entitled "Cultura e sport nella rivoluzione fascista" (Culture and sport in the fascist revolution) (*CF* 12.2 [Jan. 15, 1934]: 21–23).

*Late January*   Pavolini selects Blasetti as the director of *18 BL*.

*Beginning of February*   Venturini writes to Corrado Pavolini: "On behalf of your brother Alessandro, I am writing to ask you to remind Blasetti not to miss the meeting of the organizing committee of the mass spectacle scheduled for Thursday 8th at our Federation headquarters. I have already notified Sofia and de Feo, but if you see either of them, I would appreciate it if you could remind them as well" (Venturini to Corrado Pavolini, misdated "Jan. 5" [actually Feb. 5], 1934, BA).

Corrado Pavolini writes a reminder note to Blasetti.

Bardi has by now become aware of the planning efforts. He writes the following brief column ("Corsivo 100," *Quadrante* 10 [Feb. 1934]: 23):

Our readers will recall that I put forward the following idea in the eighth issue of *Quadrante*: a portrayal of fascism by means of a "mass theater" in three acts (war, revolution, peace) to be staged at Florence's Berta Stadium.

It has recently come to my attention that something similar is being done (as a matter of fact, in Florence) under the direction of Alessandro Blasetti.

It is always pleasing to note the ease with which ideas travel. And no less pleasing that *Quadrante* is such an effective generator of ideas. The spectacle of our endeavors coming to fruition is, for us, a joyous one.

*February 8–10*   Meetings of the authorial collective with Blasetti take place at Casa del Fascio in Florence. For several days they discuss various aspects of the performance: the narrative, the design of the theater, the production, the stage, and the performance site. The authors read out loud the acts and scenes they have composed. Revisions are suggested before submission of a final draft to Blasetti. A project for the stage, designed by Fulvio Jacchia (in collaboration with Sofia) and involving two large fixed walls and a conveyor-belt backdrop, is presented to Blasetti. Blasetti rejects it, finding it too conventional. More radical design possibilities are also considered, including Blasetti's own notion of an inverted Greco-Roman amphitheater, but are judged unfeasible given the available sites.

The February 10 meeting is reported as follows (*Il Bargello*, Feb. 11, 1934, 3):

The authors and director met again yesterday evening to discuss the great mass spectacle that will inaugurate the Lictorial games.

The meeting was chaired by Dr. Alessandro Pavolini, secretary of the Florentine Federation of the Fasci di Combattimento, with Consul Poli, vice-secretary of the GUF in attendance. In its course, the basic plot contours of the spectacle were discussed: contours that were the result of the collaborative efforts of a group of young authors from all parts of Italy.

The staging of the plot was also discussed in considerable detail. Likewise a performance site was selected. A truly imposing array of resources will be mobilized for the occasion so as to permit highly original scenic and choreographic effects, which are sure to have a deep and enduring impact on the development of the Italian theater.

**February 11–14**   The final drafting process begins. Following Pavolini's instructions, the completed drafts are provided to Blasetti as soon as completed.

**February 15**   Poli sends Sofia to Cortina d'Ampezzo, where the winter Littoriali of Sports are being held, and hence where all the GUF regional secretaries are gathered. Dispatched as a representative of the organizing committee, he remains there for a week and presents plans for the inaugural spectacle of the cultural-artistic Lictorial games.

**February 18**   After a series of site visits made with Rossi, Blasetti, Venturini, and city officials, the Albereta of the Isolotto is confirmed as the definitive performance site for *18 BL*.

**February 21**   Sofia publishes "Verso i Littoriali della Cultura: Teatro di masse—*18 BL*" (Towards the Littoriali of Culture: *18 BL* mass the-

ater), a lengthy essay describing the development of the spectacle and its site, in *La Stampa*.

**February 22**   A first evening of tests are performed in the Albereta using a rented truck, with Blasetti and Venturini present.

**February 24**   Blasetti begins planning for the spectacle, designing the theater, and assembling a final script.

Blasetti contacts Ceseri by express letter and requests an informal commitment to participate in the experimental work.

**February 25**   Ceseri responds in the affirmative to Blasetti's request: "For the moment I have no other obligations and, as always, would look forward to working with you. I can also assure you that I have absolute confidence in you. Whatever you ask me to do, I will obey, within the bounds of art. I don't know anything [about the work itself]. As for the other conditions you mention: most likely" (dated "Rome, Feb. 25, 1934," BA).

A second evening of tests are performed in the Albereta with a rented truck, with Blasetti present.

**February 26**   Blasetti and Sofia return together by train to Rome.

**March 1**   Initial construction work begins at the Albereta.

Blasetti returns to Florence with Calzavara. With the help of some actors and his assistants Venturini and Calzavara (accompanied in turn by Gatteschi and Mannucci), he begins blocking out portions of the opening two acts of the spectacle. In the process he draws up a series of notes (*Prime considerazioni e proposte*). The document, preserved in BA, foresees the following rehearsal schedule.

1. General rehearsals and definitive ordering of screenplay, dialogues, and choruses (up until March 15)

2. Lighting and sound rehearsals, check (from March 15 to March 20)

3. Testing of key production elements (actors, leaders of masses, a few trucks; from March 20 to 30)

4. Simultaneous dance rehearsals (beginning March 20; of half of masses and essential elements, from April 1 to 14)

5. [Rehearsals] of the whole (from [April] 15 to 20)

Logistical problems, as well as heavy rainfall during the middle of April, would make it impossible to stick to the schedule as outlined.

**March 2**   The *podestà* of the Comune of Florence allocates 35,000 lire for work on the access roads to the theater of the Isolotto.

**March 4**   A first announcement appears in *Il Bargello*, describing the site and structure of the theater, as well as the character of the spectacle to be presented.

**March 7**   Blasetti sends an official letter of engagement to Ceseri from Florence, asking him to state his conditions.

**March 8**   Pavolini meets with Blasetti and, after a discussion regarding various particulars, requests a detailed budget.

**March 9**   In Rome, a proposal for the seating area of the mass theater is submitted to the GUF secretariat by Fratelli Innocenti, a firm specializing in tubular steel constructions. The proposal, covering only 9,000 places at a cost of 10 lire a spectator, will be judged too costly by Blasetti.

Blasetti submits a formal budget to Pavolini listing the materials and personnel he will need, and detailing the services and equipment promised by the city, military engineering corps, and army. He estimates the total cost of the spectacle at 175,000 lire. Annotations in Blasetti's hand suggest that the document was discussed in person with Pavolini, who suggested lowering the pay of the artists and elim-

inating any payment to members of the authorial collective.

**March 11**   The pace of construction begins to increase at the Albereta. During the week of March 11–17, the number of hours worked will double with respect to the prior ten days.

**March 13**   Blasetti telephones Poli and notifies him of the Florentine Comune's inability to supply the light projectors they had promised.

**March 14**   Blasetti writes a follow-up letter to Poli (dated Florence, Mar. 14, 1934, BA):

After our telephone call and per your instructions, I am writing to confirm the fact that the Comune of Florence cannot under any circumstance provide the projectors that we had anticipated.

As we agreed upon, thus, I am awaiting the arrival of the needed projectors from Rome and expect you to request them from the Cines film company.

*It would be highly prejudicial to the spectacle's success if they were to arrive after the twentieth of the current month.*

**March 15**   In the morning, Blasetti meets with Pavolini to discuss, among other things: problems regarding the cooperation of the Giovani Italiane; a synopsis of the spectacle; two press articles; the arrival of several machinists from Rome; the testing of explosives; and the administrative censure of certain of his measures.

In the afternoon, Blasetti meets with Gatteschi (to discuss the set designs and props); with Mannucci and Tempestini (to discuss the design of the entryways to the theater); and with Venturini. He also checks with Massarani, Sartorio, and apparently, Poli (regarding the missing projectors).

In the evening, a pyrotechnics rehearsal is held.

**March 16**   Pavolini writes again to Ceseri (who had apparently not yet given his formal approval to Blasetti's March 7 letter of engagement).

**March 17**  Ceseri responds to Blasetti, officially committing himself to star in *18 BL*, and requesting several perquisites.

Blasetti travels to Rome.

**March 18**  In Florence, Massarani and Sartorio meet to work on the dance portion of the musical score.

In Rome, Blasetti submits a copy of a synopsis of *18 BL* to Poli, asking for his feedback and approval; he avers that the third act remains incomplete.

The construction schedule begins to accelerate, with 4,482 lire expended on workers' salaries between March 18 and 24.

**March 20**  Having returned to Florence, Blasetti submits a copy of the same incomplete synopsis of *18 BL* to Pavolini, once again asking for feedback and approval (dated Florence, Mar. 20, 1933, BA):

I am enclosing less a brief synopsis than a general sketch that attempts to coordinate and integrate the various notes that the authors passed along to me (in a form that was still disorganized and disconnected).

I found it necessary, that is, to start by elaborating an overall diagram of the spectacle, without attending to all the details. Afterwards, once I have your approval, I shall prepare the full-fledged three-page synopsis that will be submitted for approval by superiors.

. . . the third moment still isn't fully drawn up and imagined. I think that the death of the truck is well depicted, but am having trouble finding an appropriate tableau [*quadro*] with which to conclude the spectacle: a tableau that will be even more powerful and grander than the already strong and grand finales of the prior acts.

I can't yet envisage this . . . but I have been able to envisage many other key moments taken from the material I received. I'm sure that something will come to mind as soon as the heat of preparations will have stimulated my imagination.

**March 22**  In the morning, Blasetti meets with Pavolini regarding needed assistance from the military. Given difficulties in gathering a sufficient number of boats to build the planned double boat bridge, they discuss possible alternatives (viz., having the entire public accede to the theater via the Oltrarno entrance). Blasetti rejects these options, insisting that a boat bridge is essential. The meeting is followed up by a letter in which he reaffirms this conviction and lists all the material urgently needed from the military for the spectacle to be able to go forward even on April 28 or 29.

Blasetti recapitulates the overall situation in a letter to Poli dated March 22, 1934 (BA):

The site has been studied carefully, a logistical framework developed, and a detailed work plan drawn up so as to ensure that the stage and auditorium will be completed on time. (I have had to depart from the original budget by substituting some of our own extra workers for the 30 men promised [but not delivered] by the Army.

Next I reread, completed, and pulled together the fragmentary plot materials that were handed over to me.

Finally, I took the following up on the various requests that were made to the armed forces, the Comune, and the PNF's Florentine organizations: requests for men and resources that will be essential to the spectacle.

The result of this is that only today do I feel capable of making a precise inventory of the [spectacle's] potential value, of its demands, and of the resources available to carry it out.

This experiment could prove truly imposing and important from the standpoint of its political and aesthetic consequences. It may well give rise to a new theater, to a Mussolinian theater.

But, precisely because of this importance and certainty of success, I could never forgive myself (nor, for that matter, should I be forgiven) if the opportunity were to be wasted because of neglect on my part or a laxness in pointing out gaps and deficiencies in the resources available.

The letter proceeds to detail six problem areas: (1) the lack of middle-range spotlights; (2) the availability of only two out of the needed six long-range military reflectors; (3) a shortage of some 160 meters' worth of boats out of the 200 required to build a double boat bridge; (4) the need for 700 infantry uniforms; (5) the need for another 20 trucks; and (6) delays in the city's construction of a gravel-covered access roadway. Blasetti then adds:

To this list of worries you need to add that of the distinctive lack of enthusiasm clearly demonstrated (despite Attorney Ginnasi's best efforts) by the university students who were to form the core of the spectacle—there would be no point in forcing them, because the results would be counterproductive—and by [the] female contingent in general. The latter seem to be refusing to take part in the mass actions and in the dance. I hope that now you will understand why I can't possibly be expected to continue to assume full responsibility for the production of the spectacle planned for April 22. (p. 2)

In closing, he returns to this matter: "As for the female contingent, my hope is that Dr. Pavolini will succeed in unblocking and clarifying the situation by the end of the week. As for the university students, I shall try to do without."

**March 25**  Massarani completes the musical score in collaboration with the choreographer, Sartorio.

The final and by far the most intensive week of construction work on the theater begins, with 12,606 lire expended on workers' pay, covering continuous day and night work shifts.

**March 28**  Calzavara reports to Blasetti on, among other things, the still-missing projectors, ongoing problems with the Giovani Italiane, the city's completion of the main access road, the landfill operation, and additional budget expenses deriving from leveling of the site and the construction of a rear access road.

**March 29**  Blasetti writes a note to Pavolini asking for a meeting to establish the price of tickets and to set in motion their distribution.

**March 30**  The first major press campaign begins with articles appearing one after another in *Gazzetta del Popolo* (anon.), *La Nazione* (anon.), *Il Bargello* (Pavolini), *Il Telegrafo* (Sergio Codeluppi), *L'Ambrosiano* (Agenzia Stefani).

**April 1**  Construction work continues, in particular on the hills to be carved into the landscape, as does installation of a network of electrical cables. The sound and lighting systems undergo their first tests. The barbed-wire barricades (built under the supervision of Gatteschi) are put into place.

At the Casa del Fascio in Florence, Pavolini gathers together 2,000 young actors selected from the various fascist groups and explains the political and cultural importance of the spectacle. It appears that the use of some professional dancers from the Bonora Company has been decided by this time, in order to address the difficulties encountered with the Giovani Italiane.

**April 4**  Total expenditures to this point for the remuneration of workers are 22,187 lire, according to a statement issued by the administrative office of the Littoriali.

**April 5**  Blasetti sends Pavolini a supplemental budget covering the 37,700 lire that will be required to cover services promised by the Comune and military engineers but not provided. The request is approved and supplemental construction begins during the following week.

**April 11**  Pavolini sends a brief response (dated Apr. 11, 1934, BA) to yet another request by Blasetti for a one-week delay:

The weather seems to be improving. We simply *have to make it* by the 22nd. Tomorrow the full-scale publicity campaign begins, and it is essential to provide an exact date. On the other hand, and this is the reason for my writing, the human material (young fascists) could not be so *well* employed if there were a delay and news of a postponement would be demoralizing. I am fully aware of what I am demanding of you, but I know that our efforts will not be in vain.

Despite frequent rainfall, large-scale rehearsals for the spectacle begin.

**April 12**  The order for a custom-designed public address system is placed with the Philips Company, at a cost of 7,750 lire.

**April 13**  Pavolini again reassures Blasetti by postcard (dated Apr. 14, 1934, BA) that the weather will improve: "Tomorrow brings a new moon. The weather is improving, you'll see."

**April 14**  The contest for future mass spectacles is announced.

**April 15**  Pavolini publishes a front-page article in *Il Bargello* announcing—somewhat prematurely—the completion of the theater and that rehearsals are proceeding apace.

Ticket sales begin.

A plot synopsis of *18 BL* is sent out via the Agenzia Stefani to newspapers throughout the country. In the ensuing days, many will publish the text. The full "screenplay" is published by *Gioventù Fascista* (4.8 [Apr. 15]: 12–14) and prefaced as follows:

In preparation for April 22, a spectacle is being put together in Florence with accelerated labor and incandescent passion: a spectacle that is destined to establish a new first [*un primato*—i.e., a world record] for fascist Italy and to contribute to a renewed people's theater in Europe and throughout the world.

The Littoriali of Culture and Art—expression of our university youth, the flower of our race—provide the appropriate setting for this bold, revolutionary, and novel undertaking.

Against the backdrop of the Tuscan hills, a powerful and synthetic adventure is brought alive for thousands of spectators by marshaling all the technical-artistic means that light, sound, and movement can provide.

The possibilities made available by film, radio, theater and the most daring choreographies are all blended together into a simultaneous harmony, so as to communicate deep emotions to the mass of spectators.

The work's subject matter is meant to affect the entire people.

A new tradition is thus founded that links up to the glorious tradition of celebrations and shows held in ancient Rome, the Renaissance, and in so many other periods of the history of our civilization.

**April 16**  Massarani writes to Blasetti asking whether the spectacle will still go forward on the 22nd; how the dance portion of the program is proceeding; whether the records have arrived; whether the required double-platter player has been procured. He says he will be in Florence on the 21st for the scheduled dance rehearsal and to help set up the speaker system.

**April 18**  Pavolini sends a postcard to Blasetti notifying him that Galeazzo Ciano and his wife, Edda, will be in the audience on April 22.

Pavolini sends out personal invitations to local and national political officials.

The ticket office announces that one-third of the tickets for *18 BL* have already been sold.

Construction of the bench seating in the stadium begins.

**April 19**  Despite continuing rainfall, final touches on the theater are put in place; work on the seating areas and on the two means of access to the theater continues (the boat bridge and roadway). Blasetti proceeds with final tests on the lighting and sound systems.

The planned full-dress rehearsal is postponed owing to inclement weather.

**April 20**  Another full-dress rehearsal has to be canceled.

The organizing committee of the Littoriali meets and decides that it has no choice but to postpone the spectacle until April 29.

**April 21** The one-week postponement is announced in *La Nazione*, but reaches *Il Bargello* too late. The latter paper runs a front-page notice announcing that *18 BL* will go forward as scheduled.

The Lictorial art exhibits at the Parterre San Gallo of the Great Exhibition Hall open.

**April 22** The Lictorial games are inaugurated by Achille Starace, national secretary of the PNF.

The rain continues intermittently.

In the evening, a full-dress rehearsal of *18 BL* is staged with Starace and the press corps present.

**April 23** At the Littoriali: the competitions in theater criticism, cinematography, and music take place. The theater criticism competition is judged by Bonelli, d'Amico, Enrico Rocca, Giambattista Vicari, and Giachetti. Concerned with Mussolini's "theater for 20,000," it gives rise to much anticipatory criticism of *18 BL*. In the view of many participants, rather than implying the involvement of a mass of actors, the Mussolinian formula refers exclusively to a mass audience. Pietro Ingrao, who would be awarded third place by the jury, argues for the creation of a revolutionary youth theater "to reach the crowd and to permit young playwrights to gain experience and see their works performed. But neither a theater or theaterlet for mere initiates, nor a philodramatic theater or a theater of snobbish authors and spectators. An animating and vivifying theater, with stage and auditorium open to all: a theater that takes on a vast artistic and social role" (quoted in E. Ferdinando Palmieri, "Necessità di un teatro fascista affermata ai convegni dei Littoriali," *Il Resto di Carlino* [Apr. 24, 1934]: 3).

**April 24** The science competition is held at the Littoriali.

**April 25** The competitions in literary and art criticism are held at the Littoriali.

**April 26** The fascist doctrine competition takes place at the Littoriali.

**April 27** The political science competition is held at the Littoriali.

The rains have ceased, and Massarani writes to Blasetti from Rome asking whether the performance is on for the 29th, clarifying his travel plans in that event, and asking Blasetti to set up a rehearsal involving the drummers and the Philips technicians.

Final rehearsals begin.

**April 28** The colonial studies competition is held at the Littoriali.

The announcement that *18 BL* will indeed be performed on April 29 is made.

Construction of the boat bridge over the Arno begins.

**April 29** The boat bridge is completed by midday.

Sofia and the other non-Florentine members of the authorial collective come to Florence by train to attend the performance.

*18 BL* is performed at 9:30 P.M. before an estimated audience of 20,000 spectators. Spectators include Ciano (head of Mussolini's Press Office), Edda Mussolini, Paolo Pesciolini (the Florentine *podestà*), Arturo Marpicati (vice-secretary of the PNF), Renato Ricci (president of the Opera Nazionale Balilla and under-secretary for physical education), and Giacomo Paulucci di Calboli (president of the LUCE Institute).

**May 1** The spectacle receives a mixed though predominantly negative critical reception in the Italian press.

**May 6** Sofia publishes "Il parere di uno degli autori: TRADIMENTO!" (The opinion of one of the authors: TREASON!) his first open attack on Blasetti in *Quadrivio* (2.28: 3–4), flanked by unfavorable articles on *18 BL* by Luigi Chiarini ("*18 BL*") and Marcello Gallian ("Una notte d'aprile"), under the banner headline: "Mass Criticism of a Mass Spectacle." Sofia writes:

We were musing about Mussolini during the entire performance: musing about how his ideas have never been more frivolously interpreted. For there could have been no greater act of treason vis-à-vis his statements regarding the creation of a mass theater. [What Mussolini had in mind] was neither an enclosed theater nor a conventional one. And every mannerism, every technique was to be left behind at the instant that one makes contact with the actual grass and stands under the moon, surrounded by actual clouds. His would be a theater in which verism, intimism, bourgeois mediocrity, and the petty ideals of individuals are all dismantled. All this in the name of a higher spirituality that must impose itself such that the audience finds itself immersed in a deeply poetic atmosphere. (p. 3)

The essay closes with an evocation of the Greek theater of Siracusa:

The fact of the matter is that a theater of masses, a theater of heroes, great passions, masks, and choruses—the theater willed by Mussolini—did once exist. And now that the bourgeoisie's mediocre civilization has collapsed and heroes have once again reappeared on the world stage, the theater of Siracusa again becomes modern just as, along with it, ancient Rome is renewed. All that we are awaiting is the advent of a poet capable of singing the glory of the Black Shirts. (p. 4)

***May 9*** Blasetti counters Sofia with a lengthy letter published in *La Tribuna*:

In the last issue of *Quadrivio* there appeared an outburst by Corrado Sofia directed against me and whoever it was that was so frivolous as to entrust me with the task of directing *18 BL*.

The reader can decide for himself whether this ink was spilled out of sentiment or resentment, out of devotion to a collective enterprise or out of personal hatred. . . .

The letter closes:

Corrado Sofia's excess exuberance seems to me to have brought him well enough into focus. I only wish to comfort him regarding the "brutally sacrificed" truck. The truck in question was rescued from the Fiat wrecking yard. It lived an extra fifteen days so that it could die a death that, if the performance had fully succeeded, would have been glorious as well as inventive. . . .

***May 10*** Blasetti publishes the first installment of a post-performance theoretical essay on mass theater in *L'Italia Vivente* (4.7: 6) under the title "Teatro di masse, teatro per ventimila" (Theater of masses, theater for 20,000), accompanied by a sharp attack on Sofia by Bomba entitled "Tradimento! . . . Tradimento!" ("Treason! . . . treason!") (4.7: 7). Bomba counters Sofia's attempt to distance himself from the fiasco by affirming sarcastically that:

We . . . of course knew (since he himself had underscored the point) that *he* was the true author, that the others had *barely* contributed to the discussions in Florence, that he had felt it necessary to retire to Cortina in order to draft his script. Later we could not help but observe his holy indifference when the first news stories referred not only to his name but also to that of the others.

Since it was supposedly he who reworked the story of *18 BL*, we feel obliged to ask him whether, in the course of his earthly existence, he has ever set foot on one of these trucks?

Since Sofia was too young to have fought in World War I and was not a fascist of the first hour, Bomba notes, the answer is "never." The article concludes with insinuations that Sofia is either an opportunist or an antifascist:

It is true that an act of *treason* did occur, Corrado Sofia: that of your pen, which went astray while your brain was off wandering somewhere around Siracusa . . . . You come from a region that abounds in miracles. So who knows? Maybe amidst the legion of beautiful things that you seem to know about far better than the story of an 18 BL truck, you will become the poet that you yourself dreamed up. The poet whose arrival we old blackshirts, with our bodies scarred (and not by prickly pears), await—oh, so, so impatiently!—so long as he will make the effort to narrate that which, to your credit, you refer to as our glory.

But confidentially speaking, my dear author, fascism will get along just fine without you, just as it has since 1919.

The Lictorial art exhibition at the Parterre San Gallo closes, having had over 30,000 visitors during the three weeks it was open.

**May 11**  Standing alongside Giovanni Gentile, Bontempelli gives a public speech in Rome for the opening of the 1934 session of culture courses for foreigners. He recognizes the failure of *18 BL* and suggests that Mussolini's phrase "theater for 20,000" was "perhaps meant less as a material or achitectonic program for builders than as a spiritual summons to artists: return to the soul of the crowd!" ("Bontempelli sul 'Teatro per 20.000,'" *La Tribuna* [May 11, 1934]: 4)

**May 13**  The polemic rages anew as Sofia counterattacks at great length in "Il corago immaginario" (The imaginary chorus leader) (*Quadrivio* 2.29: 1–2):

Everything was made available to him: power, money, troops, young fascists, aircraft, set designers, engineers, writers, workers, trucks, cannons, bombs, telephones, fireworks, musicians, spectators. It sufficed for him to express the slightest wish and it was granted right away. Only one thing was lacking from the beginning: any sensitivity whatsoever towards art and poetry. Now, in order to distract, he launches a personal attack, as if the question of the theater of 20,000 could be reduced to two insignificant individuals. I could refuse to respond to him tit for tat, given that I could hardly care less about either myself or about him, and given that what I had wanted to say was something principled. But when a man tries to save his hide by drawing a mustache on the queen of hearts such that in the eyes of the public she becomes the king of spades, a character study could prove use-

ful. And if he didn't succeed in bringing the much-awaited *18 BL* to us, our hope is that at least someone can attend his performance of the *Imaginary Chorus Leader*.

**May 15**  Blasetti publishes a second letter of rebuttal in *La Tribuna*, flanked by a brief critical article by Claudio Massenti ("L'esperimento fiorentino dello spettacolo di massa"), calling for a continuation of experiments with mass theater. Blasetti closes his letter with a call for an end to the polemic:

That's enough.

Dragged into this unsavory episode, I have had to remove all the dirt that Corrado Sofia intended to bury me with.

Sterile dirt, as is inevitable when the question at hand involves two young collaborators working on a single fascist work. Dirt that now tumbles back on top of him.

It is my sincere hope that he can shake it off his clothes by means of a bold and honest self-examination. If not, let him continue. Let him spout adjectives and engage in self-contradiction so as to cultivate the illusion that he has gotten in the last word. As for myself, I am putting a stop to this unwarranted form of publicity.

**May 20**  Sofia fires a brief final salvo entitled "Ultimi bagliori" (Last flares) in *Quadrivio* 2.30: 4.

**May 26**  Gherardo Gherardi intervenes in the Sofia-Blasetti dispute, engaging in a self-critique ("Difendo Blasetti," *Il Resto di Carlino* [May 26, 1934]: 3):

Eight authors each of whom is presenting a project of an entirely disparate nature—all founded upon an *a priori* error—possess one virtue: that when you get them together, they won't fight, because they believe neither in the projects of others nor in their own. We all struggled to understand what was expected of us. We groped in the dark, relying upon guesswork as regards the intentions of comrades who, although hardly poets, deserved the highest respect, the calmest consideration, because of their high intelligence. No single force or will drew us together; only the desire to do something new and good that, beyond the particularity of our characters . . . could serve as a revolutionary celebration and hymn in praise of il Duce, sung for the first time in a theatrical mode by thousands of hearts filled with a single inspiration and fused together in a single artistic rite. . . .

It goes without saying that this was no way to proceed. One doesn't compose a front-page article, not to mention a masterpiece, on the basis of today's marching orders. What was needed was the *one*. This is the point. So much effort went into depersonalizing the spectacle that, in the end, it was necessary to appoint a dictator: Blasetti.

A defense of Blasetti's errors follows, after which Gherardi returns to faulting the authorial collective for not opposing the selection of a film director:

While it is true that the novelty of the enterprise and its beauty left each of us hesitant and uncertain as regards our artistic judgments, the fact remains that this does not authorize us to try to evade responsibilities that were very largely our own. What did Blasetti do? His job: the job of a cinematographer. He encountered scenes that were too wordy; he made them mute. He saw masses in motion; he added a soundtrack. He received four, five, six scripts; he merged them. He had no choice in the matter. He drew his inspiration as best he could, which is to say from his own filmic imagination. A director is a director. One cannot fault him for not being a poet. He grabs the poetry that he can get his hands on. Blasetti committed treason against no one.

The essay concludes:

Let us hope that certain mistakes will not be repeated, and that it will not be forgotten that a theater without words is a mutilated giant, that the masses are "one," and that poetry prefers the simplest of devices in order to reach into the heart of the multitudes. It has no overriding need for high-powered beams.

***June 3*** Blasetti republishes his May 10 *L'Italia Vivente* essay accompanied by its second and conclusive part. Both appear, however, under the new title "È nato il teatro di masse" (The theater of masses is born) in *Il Mattino di Napoli*, selected, it would appear, in order to respond to the severe critical thrashing that had been administered by Giuseppe Longo's "*18 BL* a Firenze: NON è nato il teatro di masse" (*18 BL* in Florence: The theater of masses was NOT born) (*Gazzetta di Messina* [May 4, 1934]: 3).

***June 10*** Part two of Blasetti's "Teatro di masse, teatro per ventimila" is reprinted in *L'Italia Vivente* (4.8: 9).

***July*** Bragaglia publishes "Lo spettacolo per masse" (The spectacle for masses) in *La Vita Italiana* 22.251.

Riccardo Ricciardi, the secretary of the Florentine GUF, writes to Poli (dated July 6, 1934, PNF letterhead, in ACS-PNF-DN-GUF, b. 12, f. 120):

After long negotiations with the Royal Academy of the Fidenti in Florence, I have finally succeeded in obtaining the transfer of both the theater and the attached facilities.

The Florentine GUF Experimental Theater has thus come into being, and, once it has completed the appropriate trial period, expects to become national.

We will undertake a vigorous cultural program in preparation for the Littoriali and we will attempt to make our own modest contribution to the Italian theater (within the limits of the possible).

Our program will include productions of new plays written by fascist university students from all parts of Italy, concerts, conferences, educational films as well as politically interesting ones.

***August 19*** Sofia pursues his polemic with Blasetti (but now in veiled form), publishing an essay entitled "Esperimenti del teatro russo" (Experiments in the Russian theater; *Quadrivio* 2.43: 9) which seems largely based upon his 1930 journey to Russia and whose central point is that Soviet models ought to be known in order that they *not* be imitated.

***October 8–14*** The Volta congress on the dramatic theater takes place at the Royal Academy in Rome. Participants include Pirandello, Maeterlinck, Gropius, Craig, Dukes, d'Ambra, Alfieri, Tairoff, Marinetti, Wijdeveld, Pierantoni, Politis, Maurice, Ciocca, Bontempelli, and Bonelli. The last three all intervene on the subject of "theaters of masses." Sofia, present as reporter for *Quadrivio*, notes that Tairoff "among all of the Soviet directors, is he who makes greatest use of mechanical means" (*Quadrivio* [Oct. 21, 1934]: 1–2).

**November** The GUF Experimental Theater is officially inaugurated in the former seat of the Royal Academy of the Fidenti in Florence, under the directorship of Venturini. It would subsequently become the *National* Experimental Theater of the GUF.

# APPENDIX E

## ■ MUSSOLINI AND THE THEATER

*Schnapp*: I have come to you, the last witness of a theatrical endeavor dating back more than half a century, because there still remain certain gray zones in my reconstruction of the event and of its broader cultural-historical horizons. My first question concerns the origin of the call for a fascist "theater of masses for masses." Whose idea was this?

*Sofia*: Mussolini's in the first instance. Then Alessandro Pavolini and Giorgio Venturini decided that they would try to put it into practice. I became involved in the project thanks to Venturini, an acquaintance of mine, who harbored hopes that I would become one of the principal directors of the new Italian theater. This was my great ambition at the time.

*Schnapp*: As a matter of fact, you had published several screenplays before becoming involved with *18 BL*.

*Sofia*: Yes. One had appeared in Mino Maccari's influential review *Il Selvaggio*. My intent had been to get one of these screenplays into production. But the theater was my true passion: a field, however, in which I was fated never to achieve any real success. One of my plays, entitled *Qualcuno nel palazzo* [Someone in the palace] did win the 1946 Rosso di San Secondo prize. Based on my experiences during the German occupation of Rome, it is set in the Palazzo Venezia, Mussolini's former headquarters, where a number of fellow resistance fighters and I sought refuge. By that time I had left fascism behind and taken up the antifascist cause. [When I was] faced with a death sentence as a result of refusing to follow the government in its flight to Salò, several friends convinced me to hide inside the Palazzo Venezia. We uncovered a sewer line that led from the palace courtyard all the way to the Trevi fountain. We wanted to incite a revolt, to free Rome after the king's escape. This is the story that the play recounts through the private struggles of Antonello Trombadori, the revolutionary who organized the bombing of Via Rasella with the goal of starting an uprising among the political prisoners being held by the Germans at Regina Coeli. Instead, the bomb led to their execution, a punitive measure. Such was the tragedy of Antonello, who nevertheless received a silver medal for his courage.

*Schnapp*: Was this work composed immediately after the events that it describes?

*Sofia*: Yes, but it never reached the stage, owing in large part to the turbulent character of the times.

*Schnapp*: I would like to return now to Mussolini: to be precise, to his readings and to his friends in the theater world.

*Sofia*: His closest associate was Giovacchino Forzano. Forzano's advice was sought and followed with some frequency.

*Schnapp*: But wasn't Forzano's theater too convention-bound to fulfill the call of Mussolini, Bottai, and others for an authentic "art of fascist times"?

*Sofia*: Certainly. As young intellectuals, we wanted nothing to do with it. We dreamed of forging a new culture, a revolutionary culture. We felt deep scorn for Forzano, a scorn that was both literary and generational. Mussolini knew our views. An intelligent man, despite the tragic errors he would commit during the latter half of the 1930's, he was keenly aware of Forzano's limits. Telesio Interlandi, who had occasion to see him often, regularly proposed other contacts in the theater world, among them Vitaliano Brancati. I doubt that many people today will recall Brancati's play *Everest*, which concludes with the illumination of Mussolini's head sculpted into the mountain (much like Mount Rushmore). On opening night, the public buried this colossus in boos. It was strictly forbidden to criticize Mussolini at the time. Someone said that Brancati was a moron, but the poet Trilussa averred that he was a genius: "He finally succeeded in getting Mussolini booed!" Soon thereafter Brancati repented for his fascist enthusiasms. He crossed swords with Interlandi and wrote a work that

dismantles *Everest* entitled *Il vecchio con gli stivali* [The old man in boots].

*Schnapp*: On this subject, in April 1934 Brancati published *L'urto: Un dramma da rappresentare all'aperto in uno stadio* [Clash: A drama to be performed in an open-air stadium], an interesting experiment in line with the era's fantasies about fusing the new theater and mass athletics.

*Sofia*: The idea for this play was suggested to him by Interlandi, his greatest admirer and supporter. A man of great intelligence and curiosity, Interlandi cast his lot with the regime right up to the bitter end. The odd thing is that he was sheltered and saved by an antifascist. (Otherwise he would have been strung up with Mussolini in Milan's Piazzale Loreto.) In the postwar period, he decided to write a monograph grappling with the question of whether it was he who had erred in his choices or whether others had been double-dealing all along. He reserved the bulk of this ire for Brancati, who, as I noted earlier, was deeply repentant over his political commitments during the period. Brancati responded furiously. The past disgusted him, he said; it made him nauseous.

*Schnapp*: I want to get a better fix on Forzano's influence, whether negative or positive. At the time and despite his popular success, some critics did not hesitate to speak ill of him in public. They hinted that he was a mediocre artist, a protégé, a recycler of well-worn commonplaces. How come Mussolini continued to collaborate with Forzano, albeit in somewhat veiled fashion, on the composition of a trilogy of historical dramas *Campo di maggio* [Champ de Mai], *Villafranca*, and *Cesare* [Caesar].

*Sofia*: I'm afraid I have never seen any of the three performed, so it is difficult for me to judge Forzano's work. But the fact of the matter is that Mussolini's knowledge of the theater was greatly improving thanks to the company of Interlandi. He was always seeking out new avenues, even as he maintained his ties to Forzano. Interlandi gave Mussolini Russian books to read, he talked to him about mass theatrical experiments in the Weimar Republic, all in an effort to stimulate his imagination and to bring him closer to Interlandi's own views. It goes without saying that Mussolini's principal cultural adviser was Margherita Sarfatti. Her influence was also crucial in the domain of the theater. Mussolini's troubles began almost as soon as he broke with Sarfatti.

*Schnapp*: Given that, thanks to Interlandi, Mussolini was acquainted with the Soviet and German political theater, did the formula "the theater for 15,000 or 20,000" have a foreign source? The great German director Max Reinhardt, a two-time participant in the Florentine Maggio Musicale festival, had since the early 1920's been speaking of a "theater for 5,000": a theater realized, or so Reinhardt claimed, in the Berlin Großes Schauspielhaus.

*Sofia*: All I can tell you is that the phrase is consonant with the general lines of Mussolini's thought. He was committed to eliminating a certain Italian individualism and the accompanying personality types. He wanted to forge a unitary nation, to eliminate dialects and regional differences, and to achieve this end he was prepared to borrow. But I strongly suspect that Interlandi spoke to him less about Piscator's Germany than about Meyerhold's Russia. Interlandi's story is an intriguing one. During the first fascist decade, he was a great proponent of [M. A.] Bulgakov and maintained close ties with the Soviet embassy. Then, when the racial campaigns started up, he became as intransigently pro-Nazi as he had been pro-Soviet. This allowed him to receive government subventions and thereby to rescue his newspaper *Il Tevere* from bankruptcy. But he lost the esteem of nearly everybody in the process. I moved on to *La Stampa*, having refused to follow him down this erroneous path. When I turned down an invitation to work for his new magazine *La Difesa della Razza*, he accused me of being either a Jew or a Jew-lover. He was right about the latter. At the time I was in love with a Russian Jewess who had come to Italy to promote the Soviet revolution, but who had instead become sold on Italy (much as in the film *Ninotchka*). In the postwar period, Francesco Lanza and I had hoped to make a film about this eastern seductress seduced by the West.

*Schnapp*: What exactly did Interlandi know about the Russian revolution and about its consequences in the domains of art and culture?

*Sofia*: Before undertaking his career as a newspaper editor, Interlandi had briefly dabbled in acting. He was truly crazy about the theater: a passion that led him to write *La croce del sud* [The Southern Cross]. During the 1920's, he had a Jewish friend who would pass along to him the theatrical works that were in vogue in Russia. He has always maintained an overwhelming interest in things Russian, even from his earliest youth. And he was hardly alone in his admiration for the 1917 revolution. It dazzled us all; we truly thought that it would transform the world.

*Schnapp*: Circling back to Mussolini's theater readings, Anton Giulio Bragaglia had long been spreading the word about the sorts of experiments that were going on in the Weimar Republic and Soviet Russia. Was Bragaglia a prominent figure in the intellectual circles surrounding Mussolini?

*Sofia*: Mussolini took art and culture seriously. He maintained close ties with Marinetti. As a result, he accorded subventions to the Teatro degli Indipendenti, Bragaglia's theater during the mid 1920's. But Bragaglia never achieved any real popular acclaim. And for this reason alone, his influence would remain modest compared with that of Forzano.

*Schnapp*: In 1929 Bragaglia published *Il teatro della rivoluzione* [The theater of the revolution], a collection of essays in which he bitterly criticizes the regime's theater politics.

*Sofia*: The edge to his writings is indicative of the fact that he was regularly thwarted by conservative opponents within the regime, as well as by uncomprehending critics. The Teatro degli Independenti failed for lack of adequate financial support. This despite the fact that Bragaglia had regularly outdone himself in trying to create and disseminate a new culture of the stage. His experiments were remarkably intelligent and imaginative. He employed amateur actors, encouraged improvisation, allowed Aniante to make up stories on the spot. Bragaglia was a spirited and polemical man, not servile enough to suit the tastes of party bureaucrats or of Italy's most powerful critics. The latter tried to block him, claiming that he wasn't up to the challenges he took on so energetically. The contrary was true: he was bubbling over with marvelous ideas. The proof came at an international theater congress held in Paris in the immediate postwar period. France, England, Spain, and many other countries were represented by full delegations, but for Italy there was but a single sign that read "Bragaglia." He embodied the very best of Italian experimental theater during the interwar period. But as far as Italy's youth were concerned, nothing was satisfactory: Bragaglia wouldn't do; certainly not Forzano. Pirandello didn't appeal to the public at large. Indro Montanelli's essay on "Il teatro e l'eroe" [The theater and the hero], published right after the *18 BL* debacle, says it all: Mussolini wanted a theater for the masses, a theater for the people. He wanted the oceanic mob crying out his praises. And, however stimulating, Bragaglia's theater didn't seem up to the task.

## ■ JOURNEYS TO THE SOVIET UNION AND CHINA

*Schnapp*: Let's talk about the period of your first publications, articles, essays.

*Sofia*: I started out on the editorial staff of Interlandi's *Il Tevere*, as the assistant of Vincenzo Cardarelli, whose principal collaborator was Alberto Cecchi. They needed a junior assistant to cover the avant-garde theater, to which they attributed little importance. Neither Cardarelli, an old socialist and contributor to *Avanti*, nor Cecchi wished to stick his neck out, so this became my personal beat.

*Schnapp*: We are talking now about the late 1920's. Your trip to Russia took place in September 1930.

*Sofia*: Yes, it was the first such excursion organized by the Soviet Union, which, after a decade of isolation, had decided to open up its borders to journalists from all over the world. I participated as the correspondent of *La Stampa*, the Agnelli family's newspaper.[1] The newspaper was especially interested given that there were over 200 Fiat technicians already in Moscow teaching the Russians how to build automobiles.

*Schnapp*: Among them was Gaetano Ciocca, a Fiat engineer who would write a book on collectivism *Giudizio sul bolscevismo* [Judgment on Bolshevism] after his reentry and become one of the main champions of the theater of masses.

*Sofia*: I don't believe that I ever met Ciocca. It's important to understand that there was considerable interest in Italian-Soviet trade during the period. Owing to the presence of so many foreign technicians, tourism was beginning to develop in Russia. The Russians were eager to spread the good word about the "heroic conquests" of Stalin's five-year plan and invited three Italian newspapers to join in on the trip: *La Stampa* (chosen because of its connections to the Agnelli family); *Il Giornale d'Italia* (selected because of its status as a state-sponsored journal); and *Il Tevere* (chosen because of Interlandi's close ties to the Soviet embassy). This was the triad of newspapers represented. I received my invitation to participate from Curzio Malaparte, editor-in-chief of *La Stampa*, who was fired soon thereafter and ran off to Paris, where he completed his famous *La tecnica del colpo di stato* [The technique of the coup d'état]. I accepted eagerly and succeeded in obtaining a visa thanks to the efforts of Ermanno Amicucci, the director of *La Stampa*'s rival newspaper, the *Gazzetta del Popolo*. Amicucci was a close friend of the head of Mussolini's press office. He seemed surprised that I would ask him to intervene to the benefit of his principal rival. I had to promise him that, upon my return, I would work instead for *Gazzetta del Popolo*. The promise was kept.

*Schnapp*: Could you describe the itinerary of the journey?

*Sofia*: We were able to tour the entirety of the Soviet Union over two months. But the trip can hardly be described as a propaganda success for the Soviets. At Rostov, for example, our train stopped right in front of a group of exiled convicts who were being led to their execution. Once they heard that foreign journalists were on board, they began shouting that they were innocent victims: an episode recounted in detail in the travelogue compiled by one of our American colleagues. Instead of popularizing a utopian image of communist Russia, the journey raised grave doubts about the true nature of the regime.

*Schnapp*: So you were a mixed group?

*Sofia*: Yes, Japanese, French, Americans, Germans, Italians. Perhaps 30 in all. The Italians were asked to travel in the second-class compartment of the train. This prompted my friend [Francesco] Lanza to protest: "What sort of communism is this!? The Americans travel in

first class and you put the Italians in second!?" Our hosts were embarrassed, and to redeem themselves they arranged a special lunch for us inside the Kremlin. Eaten with the czar's golden cutlery, the meal included two political exiles. One of them was Togliatti, known as Hercules at the time, who accused Italy of preparing for war (and, of course, he was quite right).

*Schnapp*: Aside from your visits to factories, what cultural sites and events were you permitted to experience?

*Sofia*: It was possible to meet only a few selected writers: those who were in the good graces of Soviet officialdom. I would have liked to meet Pasternak, but didn't succeed. Our hosts took us to numerous concerts and plays.

*Schnapp*: Which theaters do you remember?

*Sofia*: The Meyerhold Theater most of all, because of the amazingly interesting shows that were put on there. Most were party comedies featuring actors who would descend from the stage to embrace members of the audience, as if all had been saved and transfigured by the revolution. A dumbfounding spectacle. My main concern, however, was landing an interview with Stalin. Malaparte had begged me: "You simply must write an article about Stalin!" No one seemed to know whether he was dead or alive. It sufficed to name him, however, and everyone would vanish or become mum. Terror was already widespread. No one dared to speak with foreigners, not to mention about a topic as sensitive as internal politics. As a matter of fact, Lanza, an ex-socialist who had converted to fascism because he saw socialism and fascism as extensions of one another, was left deeply disillusioned. He had dreamed of a utopian Russia and found instead a totalitarian state, in which terror had permeated even the churches.

*Schnapp*: Did you meet any of the writers like Valentin Kataev, Boris Pilniak, and company who were involved in the collective drafting of novels under the five-year plan?

*Sofia*: A few of them. I remember Pilniak in particular.

*Schnapp*: Was Gorky in contact with this group?

*Sofia*: Yes. But he was still residing in Italy in the fall of 1930. His definitive return to the Soviet Union took place the following year. One of my very first newspaper articles, entitled "Uno scugnizzo da Gorkî" [An urchin at Gorky's place], recounts the story of a failed attempt to interview him in Sorrento. I did meet him later in Rome.

*Schnapp*: Gorky was quoted by Valentino Bompiani in the article by means of which he launched the "Debate on the Collective Novel" in 1934: a debate that would soon involve Bontempelli, Luigi Chiarini, the Hungarian writer Ferenc Körmendi, and Alberto Moravia. Besides which Bompiani was one of the promoters of debates over the Soviet Union. Between 1930 and 1935, his publishing house churned out a long succession of books on this subject, including Bardi's *Un fascista al paese dei Soviet* [A fascist in the land of the Soviets], translations of Fülöp-Miller and various of H.R. Knickerbocker's books. To what degree do you think that the principal Soviet cultural experiments had an impact upon the Italian literary scene?

*Sofia*: To a considerable degree. A number of articles appeared in Interlandi's newspaper and in *Quadrivio*, among other places, concerning the collective novel. There was also the prize offered by the so-called Dieci [a collective of ten writers that included Marinetti and Beltramelli]. It was a time of cultural-historical transition, and these sorts of proposals seemed conceivable, even if the intellectual circle I traveled in was opposed to the collective or collaborative writing of novels.

*Schnapp*: Back again to the Soviet Union, did you attend many movie houses?

*Sofia*: We were able to view films of a strange and austere beauty, films by famous directors like Sergei Eisenstein. I was especially interested in the Soviet film industry and pestered our hosts with endless questions about the cinema. Stalin, the Soviet film industry, the revolutionary theater: these were the topics that I wanted to write home about.

*Schnapp*: A final question about your trip to Soviet Russia. Were you able to visit the production studios of any of the great directors?

*Sofia*: Despite many requests on my part, it wasn't possible. I suspect they weren't all that well equipped and they didn't want us to see the handicraft methods still being employed. The Soviets were exceedingly careful as regards what they would allow journalists to see and visit. During a second trip many years later, I asked to see the Museum of the Revolution in Leningrad. I was told the museum was closed, but two hours later a group of soldiers was permitted to visit it.

*Schnapp*: After your return to Italy in late 1930, you changed newspapers?

*Sofia*: My 30 or so articles on Russia had appeared in *La Stampa*, with the usual time lag, just as Malaparte was on the verge of being driven out. I ran into Amicucci, who remembered our pact. He asked me if I would be interested in going to China in 1932. I accepted his offer. In a book entitled *Avventure in Cina* [Adventures in China], I describe my sojourn and my encounters with the communists (thanks to the help of the American journalist Agnes Smedley).

*Schnapp*: What was the precise purpose of the trip to China?

*Sofia*: According to Amicucci it was to write at length about Galeazzo Ciano, husband of Edda Mussolini, il Duce's daughter, recently sent as a diplomatic envoy to Shanghai. I didn't do so to Amicucci's satisfaction. From my own point of view, the trip's purpose was to get to know a mysterious world that I had heard about mostly from the Jewish girlfriend I had frequented in the company of men like Paolo Milano, Nicola Chiaromonte, and Alberto Moravia. All were men of the left at heart, even if Moravia was a communist who sometimes reasoned like a right-winger, rejecting fascism on the one hand, but supporting the invasion of Ethiopia on the other.

*Schnapp:* How much was known about the Chinese communist movement during this period?

*Sofia:* In Europe little was known; in Italy even less. The Italian newspapers had completely neglected the Chinese scene. Nearly everything that was known came from the splendid articles published by Smedley in the *Frankfurter Allgemeine Zeitung*. I couldn't read German, so my girlfriend would translate the articles into Italian. Thanks to them, I reached China relatively well informed. After my arrival I was able to contact Smedley, which wasn't all that easy, given that she was forced to change residences constantly in order to escape the scrutiny of Chiang Kai-shek's spies. She accompanied me on several journeys, passed along information, introduced me to several representatives of Mao's group. Ciano was aware of my activities and wasn't exactly pleased. He hadn't understood that I was not a communist and that I simply wished to deepen my knowledge of the developments in question.

### ■ ART THEATERS/MASS THEATERS

*Schnapp:* What did you do after returning from China in 1932?

*Sofia:* In 1932 I was invited by Bottai to join the editorial staff of *Critica Fascista*, where I published articles on cultural issues.

*Schnapp:* What was the tone of Bottai's relation to Mussolini at the time?

*Sofia:* There was much tension in the air. Bottai often spoke out against Mussolini. I suspect that Bottai and Balbo both would have liked to overturn Mussolini. They were well aware of the regime's deficiencies and opposed to its later racial politics. Bottai made sure that I met Balbo, who had been appointed governor of Libya in the wake of the transatlantic mass flights that transformed him into an international media celebrity. Claiming not to know French or English, Balbo would ask me to read articles from foreign newspapers that spoke of him as Mussolini's possible successor. He wanted me to understand his ambitions, knowing full well that I was in no position to spread information of this kind.

*Schnapp:* I want to ask you about an essay entitled "Necessità di un teatro" [The need for a theater] that you published in *Critica Fascista* in June of 1933. The essay replies to Mussolini's SIAE speech with an appeal for the foundation of an "art theater for youth" in Rome modeled after the Moscow art theaters: "a revolutionary theater, where the clash between the old and the new generations can be felt through the performance of works reenacting the most dramatic episodes of the postwar and fascist periods." [2] Several months later, *Critica Fascista* carried favorable responses from Ardengo Soffici, Corrado Alvaro, Corrado Pavolini, Sandro de Feo, Eurialio de Michelis, Silvio d'Amico, and even Bragaglia (whom you had sharply criticized).

*Sofia:* I was close to Massimo Bontempelli at the time. We had wanted to repeat what Bontempelli and Pirandello had done in their mid-1920's art theater in Rome. We hoped to found an avant-garde revolutionary theater for the younger generation. The main obstacle was to locate an appropriate site. We made various inquiries, with the OND among many other public entities, and sought financial support. But our efforts were for naught.

*Schnapp*: Your proposal for the foundation of an art theater seems to link up to numerous initiatives dating back to the mid 1920's far more than it does to Mussolini's call for a "theater for 20,000 spectators."

*Sofia*: First of all, it must be said that it was far from clear just what Mussolini understood by "theater of masses." We still felt a great deal of nostalgia for Bragaglia's experimental theater, which had closed some time before. Bragaglia's audience had simply withered away. His theater had become a demeaning discothèque filled with harlots. Our dream was to found an art theater like the Russian ones: a theater for a sophisticated audience, like the stupendous audiences I had seen in Moscow.

*Schnapp*: Mussolini's speech before the SIAE was delivered on April 28, 1933. In its wake a wide range of often-contradictory positions were formulated. Some argued for the reestablishment of the Teatro degli Independenti. Others, like Luigi Bonelli in *L'Italia Vivente*, seemed to put forward a more "bolshevizing" sort of interpretation of Mussolini's words, explicitly invoking Russian precedents. Their goal was the foundation of an authentic fascist mass theater. Others still, held that there was no "theater of masses" to create. It already existed in the thespian cars and open-air spectacles of the Verona coliseum. What was your impression of this debate?

*Sofia*: A variety of currents and voices were campaigning for a renewal of the Italian theater. The mass theater proposed and desired by Mussolini reflected this multiplicity, as well as the era's contradictions. The intellectual world was in turmoil and demanded a theater that in no way resembled its conventional bourgeois counterpart. Mussolini had become accustomed to the crowd of spectators that cheered him when he stepped out onto the balcony of the Palazzo Venezia. It would seem that the idea was prompted in his spirit by

these regular encounters with the multitudes. For him these oceanic crowds stood for the very essence of the theater. As a result, he could hardly imagine a theatrical revolution except in terms of the great fascist rallies.

## ■ PREPARATIONS FOR THE SPECTACLE

*Schnapp*: Could you tell me the story of how you were invited to become a member of the authorial collective that would write the script for the first (and last) "spectacle of masses for masses"?

*Sofia*: It was Giovanni Poli who first contacted me. Along with Venturini and Sarfatti, he hoped that I would become one of the regime's stage directors. I felt underprepared. I doubted I had the guts or the overbearing character required. Besides, the times were difficult. Like Bontempelli, I believed in the art theater, in a theater like Pirandello's where words are capable of conveying feelings. Instead, Blasetti's spectacle was made up only of lights, noise, gunfire.

*Schnapp*: Poli was the vice-secretary of the GUF at the time. But who were the true initiators of the venture?

*Sofia*: Pavolini and Venturini in the first place. Pavolini inasmuch as he was the organizer of the Littoriali of Art and Culture; Venturini inasmuch as he was an authentic man of the theater.

*Schnapp*: Let's start with Pavolini, who had always cultivated literary ambitions, in part because of his playwright brother and philologist father. In 1929, he published a brief comedy entitled *Le fatalone* [Vamps] not to mention novels like *Giro d'Italia* [Tour of Italy] (1928) and *Scomparsa d'Angela* [Angela's disappearance; 1940].[3] A contradictory character: at once the most odious and the most cultivated of the fascist hierarchs.

*Sofia*: Pavolini was indeed contradictory to the extent that he was simultaneously violent and intelligent. I remember sending a copy of *Giro d'Italia* to the novelist Alfredo Panzini, who had been my teacher. Panzini's reaction was enthusiastic. He saw in Pavolini a politician endowed with a strong literary sensibility. Pavolini was even contradictory in his attitude towards his great friend Galeazzo Ciano, who was responsible for his being named minister of popular culture. In 1937, when I was stationed in Yugoslavia working for the Agenzia Stefani wire service, the two of them came to Belgrade in order to settle a conflict between the Croatians, Serbians, and Bosnians. I remember the enormous respect that Ciano demonstrated towards Pavolini, permitting him to speak in Ciano's name. A few years later, Pavolini signed Ciano's death sentence.

*Schnapp*: So the original core of your group was made up of Venturini, a young director and producer, and Pavolini, a rising star in the PNF. Why did they decide to recruit eight authors for the inaugural spectacle of the Littoriali? Why not choose a single author instead?

*Sofia*: They were thinking both about the collective novel and about the cinema: to be precise, about the collective drafting of screenplays. Venturini was persuaded that the theater of the revolution would be a theater of authorial collectives, a theater of masses of actors *and* spectators.

*Schnapp*: There is a striking absence of anyone from the generation of Bontempelli in the group. Bontempelli, after all, had set the stage for Mussolini's speech and had spread the message, perhaps even beyond Mussolini's own intentions. Why wasn't he even consulted?

*Sofia*: They chose to consult no one: not Bontempelli, Pirandello, Marinetti, or Bragaglia. The goal was to constitute a group of entirely new figures who were untainted by any prior success. The new theater was supposed to arise from down below, from out of the heart and soul of the first fascist generation. Of course, it would have been far better if they had consulted other, more experienced figures. But the choice of new writers is telling. As a mere adolescent, I found work in Interlandi's newspaper right away. I simply walked in off the street with an article on Panzini and asked to see the editor. They told me that he was busy, but the article appeared in print the very next morning. One week later I was on the editorial staff alongside Cardarelli, Maccari, Pavolini, Rodolfo de Mattei, later to be joined by Lanza and Alfredo Mezio. Our contributors included Ungaretti, Zavattini, Stefano Landi (Pirandello's son), and many others who would become famous. Despite its flaws, fascism frequently promoted the young.

*Schnapp*: Gherardi, Bonelli, and Lisi were fairly well known writers in the theater world. Melani much less so.

*Sofia*: Gherardi and Bonelli were well established comic playwrights. Melani was chosen because he was Venturini's friend. Lisi was known as a poet and was meant to contribute a more Catholic poetic coloration.

*Schnapp*: To judge by Lisi's works from the 1920's, for instance, *Il calendario dei pensieri e delle pratiche solari* [Almanac of thoughts and solar practices] and *L'acqua* [Water], he seems an improbable choice for a mass spectacle like *18 BL*.

*Sofia*: Indeed, Blasetti had no idea what to do with his contribution to the script.

*Schnapp*: Speaking of Blasetti, who was it that selected him as director?

*Sofia*: Pavolini and Venturini. They considered him the liveliest, the most modern of Italian directors. The decision to hire a film director to direct a dramatic work was their mistake. A fine film director to be sure, but one who had no experience with theater direction. The outcome

**173**

was predictable: the cinema ended up betraying the idea of the theater.

*Schnapp*: In an interview right before his death, Blasetti claimed that he had been asked by Mussolini to direct *18 BL*.

*Sofia*: I find that unlikely. But Pavolini could well have spoken to Mussolini about Blasetti.

*Schnapp*: How come Mussolini never became actively involved in the preparation of a mass spectacle that was attempting to put into practice one of his own ideas?

*Sofia*: Surely he didn't wish to compromise himself. He was a prudent man. He was awaiting the result before going on record. The idea was his, but, of course, he had many other far more pressing matters to worry about. This said, the renewal of Italian culture was one of his most heartfelt ambitions, which explains in part many of the grandiose initiatives undertaken during the period.

*Schnapp*: Let's turn now to the project chronology. In June, you had published "Necessità di un teatro" in *Critica Fascista*; in September, the responses were published. When did the first meeting take place in Florence?

*Sofia*: I attended two to three meetings towards the end of 1933 and/or at the beginning of 1934. Blasetti wasn't present at any of them. Later, in February, I believe, there was a meeting where he, too, was included. The two of us returned home together on the train to Rome. I remember our conversation well. At the beginning, Blasetti was well disposed towards the authorial collective and its ideas. I was still fresh from my experiences in Russia (where the spoken word played a key role in the revolutionary theater), so I was deeply persuaded of the need for live voices and speech, a conviction I maintain to this day. Without the spoken word, there can be no real theater. Blasetti seemed convinced. He promised de Feo and myself that we would always be at his side. Clearly, others

must have lured him away and he decided to block out a cinema-based spectacle.

*Schnapp*: Early in his career, Blasetti had published several articles sharply critical of the talking cinema, articles in which he asserted that talkies were an American plot to undo the European cinema. Soon thereafter he changed his mind and became the first Italian director to produce a "talkie" [*Resurrectio*, which predated Gennaro Righelli's *La canzone dell'amore* (Love song) by some months]. But do you think it possible that he still felt a lingering aversion to a talk-based cinema and a preference for image-based montage? [A preference shared by Bragaglia and by so many other champions of the avant-garde theater.]

*Sofia*: Your point is well taken. De Feo and myself had been the principal advocates of a truck as protagonist at the first Florence meetings. And for us the truck was above all a carrier of human beings, of human beings engaged in conversation and singing the songs of war and of the squadrist raids. Those human voices were inaudible during the performance. The truck-heroine's movements were accompanied by explosions and machine-gun fire. The action on stage didn't make sense. There was no way to relive the three epochs that *18 BL* was meant to celebrate: World War I, the March on Rome, the land-reclamation projects. Even so, Blasetti was a firm believer in the heroism of the events we had intended to represent.

*Schnapp*: Was Pavolini present during the first meetings of the authorial collective?

*Sofia*: Only at the first. He issued a series of fairly generic directives regarding the importance of the new theater of masses and the bourgeois theater that needed to be overcome.

*Schnapp*: The standard antibourgeois commonplaces?

*Sofia*: Yes, Mussolini's characteristic rhetoric.

**174**

*Schnapp*: I gather that the principal plot ideas were the assassination of Berta and the story of the truck. Or were there other possibilities as well?

*Sofia*: The story of the truck was approved almost right away. We had in mind, not a cold machine, but rather a vehicle that would acquire distinctly human attributes—maternal attributes—by means of the human voices and songs that would emanate from its passengers. Blasetti might have understood better if he had attended the first meeting. Or at least we would have been more forceful in underscoring our commitment to the spoken word.

*Schnapp*: Trucks had already found a privileged place in the iconography of the revolution?

*Sofia*: Yes. They evoked the war and the fascist squadrons' punitive raids in particular. Those squadrons of wild-eyed, inquisitive, courageous youths who would enter towns and beat up trade unionists. At the time these sorts of things enthused us no less than they now repulse us. But, most of all, it was the truck of the revolution. The plot assumed its definitive form once we linked it up to World War I and the *bonifiche* [fascist land-reclamation projects]. Mother Cartridge-Pouch was supposed to embody the history of the era. Even today, after so many years, I don't think that the idea was a bad one for a spectacle of this kind. But it demanded a different sort of approach: a calmer one, more poetic in tone, infused with a typically Italian feeling of humanity.

*Schnapp*: The choice of a truck as protagonist recalled a long tradition of modernist narratives including Octave Mirbeau's *La 628-E8*, Bontempelli's *522: Racconto di una giornata* [522: A day's tale], and numerous other texts belonging to the first and second futurism (whether Russian or Italian). But given fascism's ambivalent attitude towards the machine world, it might also have raised some eyebrows. On the other hand, fascism favored the industrialization and modernization of Italy; on the other, it was dead set against the mechanization of human beings.

*Sofia*: The drive to heroicize machinery was strongly felt during the entire two decades of fascist rule. As a case in point, take Leonardo Sinisgalli, a young poet of the period, who later became famous as the head editor of the magazine *Civiltà delle Macchine*. He even invented the Alfa Romeo emblem! We wanted to reconcile man and machine. From this standpoint, there is simply no denying that the era was unusually lively. I doubt that fascism would have ended as it did were it not for the subsequent colonial wars, the Spanish Civil War, the racial laws and, lastly, as a definitive catastrophic finale, the Great War.

*Schnapp*: A philological curiosity. In some versions of the play, the truck's name is Mother Glory. How was the name Mother Cartridge-Pouch settled upon?

*Sofia*: Mother Glory must have been Blasetti's idea. He had a strong rhetorical penchant in his personality. When he would shoot movie scenes, he would respond to criticisms by seizing a megaphone and shouting out Starace-style: "Citizens! The Italian cinema is being celebrated here!" The name Mother Cartridge-Pouch was meant to evoke something far more human and simple. Not glory with a capital G, but the daily heroism of the humble foot soldier.

*Schnapp*: Another question I have concerns the context within which the spectacle came about. Forzano's *Camicia nera* [Black shirt] had premiered the year before and shares the same tripartite structure with *18 BL* [representing the war, revolution, and land-reclamation projects]. I am well aware of your disdain for Forzano, but did his film have an impact on your deliberations?

*Sofia*: I don't think that we ever spoke about it. I'm sure, on the other hand, that I spoke at great length about the plays and films that I had seen in Russia—something I did frequently during these years. Someone must also have talked about the Weimar theater.

*Schnapp*: Was Blasetti's *Sole* [Sun] mentioned? It, too, rehearses the myth of the fatherland's redemption.

*Sofia*: Perhaps. *Sole* was greatly admired by the Italian intelligentsia. It contained truly extrordinary images. For the first time in the history of the Italian cinema, there appear frames of a beauty that would only be equaled by the great Japanese directors.

*Schnapp*: We have covered the topic of theater and film precedents, so I would like to turn to another possible source of inspiration: the close pairing between mass cultural forms and mass athletics envisaged by figures such as Bontempelli, Bragaglia, and Starace, in their polemics against the bourgeois past. You yourself published an essay on "Cultura e sport nella rivoluzione fascista" ("Culture and sport in the fascist revolution") around this time.[4] To what degree did mass sporting events shape your conception of a future theater of fascist times?

*Sofia*: Bottai expressed a strong interest in this essay; he was enthusiastic about it. It seemed logical to all of us that mass sporting events should permeate the daily life of a modern and reinvigorated Italy. Sports entertained the masses, enlivened them, conferred a new dynamism and strength. Moreover, Mussolini had assigned sports a key role in the forging of a new Italian. So, by all means, we viewed them as important. But from the moment that Starace began to hammer away at Italy's youth with calls for everyone to jump through hoops and to participate in mass gymnastics, a revolt began from within the fascist fold. The first schisms were born, the first open signs of dissent.

*Schnapp*: What was your overall opinion of Starace?

*Sofia*: We viewed him as a stubborn ignoramus. We brought him down on the strength of jokes alone [in October 1939 Starace was dismissed as the PNF's national secretary]. I'm serious. Starace never knew what hit him. He would arrive in the furthest reaches of Calabria and call upon his audience to "Hail il Duce, the founder of the empire," and the peasants would take their hats off. Someone wrote him a letter proposing that Mussolini be referred to instead as the Gran Duce, on the model of the title grand duke! This much can be said to Starace's credit: he was sincere in his athletic vocation. He was even executed in athletic garb.

*Schnapp*: I was curious about Starace, because it seems that, sometime around the end of November 1933, Pavolini was asked to submit his plans for the Littoriali (including the inaugural spectacle) in order to obtain Starace's approval. The latter was granted during the drafting of *18 BL*, which is to say between the time of your first meetings and the February meeting attended by Blasetti. He may even have read and approved Blasetti's final cut of the text.

*Sofia*: Indeed, after the preliminary discussions of 1933, each of us had set to work with relative autonomy. For this reason, the text had to be completely reworked in the wake of our February meetings. Five or six drafts, often in open contradiction with one another, were presented and discussed. They were then handed over to Blasetti, whose responsibility it was to come up with a final edit on the basis of our ideas.

*Schnapp*: The final version was never shown to the authorial collective?

*Sofia*: No. From the minute that he assumed the helm, Blasetti became the sole boss and manager. His first decision was to fold the collective and to seek the help of others, like

Calzavara, who was a cinema technician. He wanted to develop the spectacle on his own, thinking (and sincerely so) that we had already done our part. He wanted to avoid being influenced by our theories, and perhaps feared that our input would end up derailing his plans. We should have reacted, but didn't. You have to understand that none of us wanted to stand in Blasetti's way. Our collective work had been undertaken with the express desire of carrying out a revolution in the theater, and Blasetti was our ally in this battle. We didn't have a contract, there was no money at stake, our trips to Florence alone were reimbursed. Do you know whether Blasetti was paid for his services?

*Schnapp*: Yes—15,000 lire in all: a substantial sum at the time, especially when one considers that Forzano was paid only 12,000 lire for his work as scriptwriter, producer, and director of *Camicia nera*. Ceseri was paid 4,500 lire for his performance. Calzavara, maestro Massarani, the Bonora company, Venturini, Mannucci, and Gatteschi also received very modest payments. Blasetti had asked that 1,000 lire be paid to each of the eight authors, but Pavolini objected.

*Sofia*: This is all news to me.

*Schnapp*: What about the other preparations? Were you consulted as regards the site, the lighting, the musical score, the loudspeaker system, the staging itself, or the choreographies?

*Sofia*: Never. Except for Venturini, who was a key member of the production team, none of us were ever invited to come to the Albereta before the day of the performance. Blasetti took charge of the project as if it were a film production, and, as was his wont, when he went to work, he was the absolute commander, a veritable dictator. Venturini's contribution was mainly in the domain of organizational matters. Aside from the pre-performance advertising and press campaigns, we were mostly forgotten. I remember that de Feo understood right away what the result would be. His was the

most acute and lively intelligence; he was the sharpest critic among us. I remained a believer unto the very end. Hence my rage.

*Schnapp*: I find this hard to believe, given that you had openly expressed skepticism about the work in an anonymous article ["Nel clima dei giovani: Il teatro di masse" (In the clime of youth: The theater of masses)] published in *Il Lavoro Fascista* several days before the performance.

*Sofia*: This was perhaps symptomatic of Blasetti's abandonment of me and de Feo.

■ **THE AUDIENCE AT THE ALBERETA**

*Schnapp*: Did you stay in Florence for the duration of the Lictorial games?

*Sofia*: No. We arrived the night of the show. All the authors were present: Lisi, Melani, Gherardi, Bonelli, de Feo, Venturini, Pavolini, and myself. After arriving at the train station, we reached the amphitheater from the Oltrarno side. We didn't cross the boat bridge, but instead entered along a narrow lane brimming over with students and youths. I remember well the enormous auditorium. After all these years, what remains impressed in my memory is the enormous ruckus, the confusion: masses of people coming and going—a mass spectacle before the true mass spectacle. From the beginning there was mumbling and shouting: a typically Italian uproar. There was not a trace of the magical silence I had encountered in the Russian theaters.

*Schnapp*: How would you characterize the audience? The site was close to San Frediano, a working-class neighborhood.

*Sofia*: All of Florence was there and lots of people from out of town. Everyone expected a grand spectacle, a prodigious event. After all, this was what the entire Italian press had been promising for well over a month.

*Schnapp*: So it was neither a bourgeois public of the sort that one might expect on opening night nor an audience made up entirely of OND, GUF, Balilla, and PNF members?

*Sofia*: No. It was an audience of young people, students, and ordinary Florentine citizens; an audience left to its own devices. There were no rules to follow here. It wasn't like the Piazza Venezia, where, as soon as Mussolini came to the balcony, the group leaders would bark out orders: salute! shout! etc., etc. A genuine audience, in other words, that understood right away that the whole thing didn't hang together and did not hesitate to express its views. This was an era when the Italian public was far more prone to responding vividly and even violently, much as during the famous futurist soirées. Towards the end of the show, I recall one student cursing the mechanical heroine. I think his words were, "Why the hell should we care about this godforsaken truck?"

*Schnapp*: Marcello Gallian, a fellow contributor to the "mass criticism of the mass theater" that appeared in *Quadrivio* after the show, is quite ironic about the audience crossing the boat bridge: an elite audience, he claims, made up of people dressed as if they were attending the opening night of *Tosca*.

*Sofia*: Gallian was close to Bontempelli. Since he had been left out of the authorial collective, he was happy to pan the performance.

*Schnapp*: During the intermissions, there were lighting displays, fireworks, and overflights, which were supposed to include the dropping of broadsheets from *Il Popolo d'Italia* announcing Mussolini's dictatorship and the "conquests" of the first fascist decade. Youths were supposed to run through the audience distributing newspapers. How could they cover such a vast area?

*Sofia*: Corridors divided the long benches up into large seating blocks. As for the airplanes,

I believe only one or, at most, two actually showed up. A single airplane would hardly have made a strong impression. Remember that this was the era of Balbo's transatlantic crossings.

*Schnapp*: Giuseppe Longo, the theater critic for *La Gazzetta di Messina*, has told me that, in the course of *18 BL*'s final act, the actors found themselves unable to push Mother Cartridge-Pouch into the gulch. This caused Blasetti to improvise a trick: he turned off the lights, called a second truck, and turned the lights back on only after the dirty deed was done.

*Sofia*: There were tricks of this sort. The finale was dreadful.

*Schnapp*: Had some of the audience already departed?

*Sofia*: Yes, some had left out of irritation. The end brought neither whistles nor applause. There was only silence.

### ■ THE POLEMIC

*Schnapp*: I would like to discuss your relationship with Blasetti after the performance.

*Sofia*: My disillusionment was enormous. I acknowledge that my criticisms were far too harsh. The alarm sounded as soon as the issue of *Quadrivio* that contained "Il parere di uno degli autori: TRADIMENTO!" [The opinion of one of the authors: TREASON] hit the newsstands. Bottai and de Pirro called me in and dressed me down. But Interlandi had wanted to cause a scandal. He was always eager to undermine Pavolini.

*Schnapp*: Who came up with the subtitle "Treason!"?

*Sofia*: Interlandi, naturally. It was a harsh title and was placed right on the front page alongside Interlandi's own trashing of *18 BL*. The issue of *Quadrivio* made an enormous splash. I know that Mussolini was aware of it. He was well acquainted with my writings and had sent me compliments on several occasions. After the polemic erupted, everything went up in smoke, including the contest for a mass spectacle to be performed at the 1935 Littoriali of Culture and Art.

*Schnapp*: Why was Interlandi so embittered towards Pavolini?

*Sofia*: His main target was Corrado Pavolini. But this didn't prevent him from denouncing all members of the Pavolini family. It was he who encouraged Maccari to draw cartoons and to compose satirical verses for *Il Selvaggio*. Concerning the family patriarch, the academician, Maccari wrote: "Excellency, let us vow/that the grandchildren will be higher brow." About Alessandro, he wrote: "Let it be known to the poet of *Solaria*:/Better to hang out in cafés than at *L'Italia Letteraria*." About Corrado, he wrote: "You too, you too, Corrado/have jumped a grade or two."[5] Maccari was always the jokester.

*Schnapp*: Ditties typical of Maccari's goliardic tastes.

*Sofia*: The feud with Corrado Pavolini arose in 1926–27 over *La croce del sud* [The Southern Cross], a comedy thought up by Interlandi, produced by Pavolini, and directed by Pirandello, with disastrous results. Having once been an actor, Interlandi was deeply sensitive about the fact that he had never made a major contribution to the theater. The flopping of *La croce del sud* decreed the end of his theatrical ambitions. The fault was wholly that of Pavolini (or so he thought), to whom he attributed an inadequate effort. This was the beginning of a ferocious feud, which continued on after Pavolini left his position as art critic for *Il Tevere* and moved on to direct *L'Italia Letteraria*.

*Schnapp*: Luigi Chiarini also joined in on the "mass critique of the mass spectacle," alongside Interlandi, Gallian, and yourself.

*Sofia*: Indeed. It must have been deeply distressing to Blasetti. The blame was his, though; he had refused to listen to me or to de Feo. He had treated the theater as if it were the cinema, with a frivolity that is typically Italian. We reproached him especially for having neglected to take into account the ancient theater as a precedent. The theaters of Siracusa and Epidaurus: we wanted to follow in their path.

*Schnapp*: But if Blasetti had adopted your views, *18 BL* would have been a far less avant-garde experiment.

*Sofia*: It would have meant retracing some well-worn paths; well-worn paths that were no longer accepted, even if still available and valuable. This was the nub of my dispute with Blasetti. He didn't believe that we had anything to learn from the classical tradition. Blasetti wanted instead to create a vast new sort of spectacle. His staging was spectacular but confused. Even I couldn't make heads or tails out of it. I felt personally responsible, implicated in an endeavor that left everyone disconcerted (even if the original idea was valid).

*Schnapp*: In your commentary on the performance, you insisted upon Blasetti's efforts to present the actors at a sharp angle, from bottom to top. You connected this foreshortened perspective with Eisenstein's method of constructing frames. I wonder, however, whether Blasetti was all that familiar with the Soviet cinema at the time.

*Sofia*: You are right. He was curious about what was being done abroad, but not deeply interested. The fact that he had initially been opposed to the sound film, as you noted earlier, may be significant. The loudspeakers that he had placed throughout the audience and on stage were irritating. They deformed the human voice. Everything should have been tested in advance. Blasetti seemed unaware of what would result.

*Schnapp*: Were the songs audible?

*Sofia*: Yes, but poorly so. Overamplified, they were denuded of poetry or pathos. When Blasetti directed films he could, of course, rectify problems in the editing room. In the postwar period, our friendship began anew, and when he came to interview me, I was able to experience firsthand just how meticulously and diligently Blasetti would edit even a single phrase. In the case of *18 BL*, this was out of the question. Yet he somehow believed that cinematic practices would be transferable to the domain of the theater.

*Schnapp*: What were the circumstances of your rapprochement?

*Sofia*: In truth Blasetti was a very fine person. When I returned from my second trip to China, which took place in the 1960's, he attended a public lecture of mine. We became friends once again.

*Schnapp*: Bontempelli also had a violent clash with Blasetti. Even if it isn't quite as harsh as some other reviews, his review of *18 BL* is distinctly lukewarm, especially when one considers his long-standing advocacy of the mass theater. Blasetti was deeply wounded by the fact that Bontempelli deserted the cause. It seems that they didn't talk for three or four months. Beyond which, he had to answer to conservative critics like Ugo Ojetti, for whom the idea of heroicizing machines represented a kind of cultural bolshevism. Did Blasetti encounter difficulties in attempting to relaunch his career?

*Sofia*: He was a man of great courage. Within a month of *18 BL*'s flop, he published two theoretical texts on the mass theater in order to regain some lost ground. Soon thereafter he went back to making excellent films.

*Schnapp*: As a matter of fact, *Vecchia guardia* came out towards the end of 1934 and borrows numerous motifs from *18 BL*. It was highly suc-

cessful. But Blasetti's conflicts with the fascist regime and with Luigi Freddi, head of the cinema division of the Ministry of Popular Culture, were only beginning.

### ■ PIRANDELLO AND THE VOLTA CONGRESS

*Schnapp*: What happened after the debate over *18 BL* died down? What was the fate of all the theories that had been in circulation about the theater of masses or the theater of 20,000?

*Sofia*: The idea of a revolutionary mass theater simply collapsed, and with it, a certain myth of cultural collectivism. The ultimate implications of this collapse have become visible only in the present era, through the collapse of the Eastern European communist regimes.

*Schnapp*: Nonetheless, high-profile figures within the Ministry of the Press and Propaganda like Alfieri and de Pirro (who was directly in charge of the theater sector) continued to make use of these phrases with reference either to the thespian cars or to the open-air spectacles of the Baths of Caracalla, the Verona arena, and the theater of Sabratha.

*Sofia*: In order to please Mussolini, the phrases were preserved but slightly altered in their meaning. They were brought into line with the new emphasis upon *romanità*. But it's difficult for me to talk in detail about events that occurred after 1935, because I departed for Yugoslavia in that year to take up a position with the Agenzia Stefani. I remained there until 1942, and during the intervening years, my contacts with the theater world became ever more occasional.

*Schnapp*: Let's turn back, then, to the beginning of October 1934. You were present, weren't you, at the Volta congress on the dramatic theater?

*Sofia*: I was, although my only contribution was a response from the peanut gallery to a statement of Silvio d'Amico's. Naturally, these unsolicited remarks never found a place in the conference proceedings.

*Schnapp*: D'Amico, perhaps the most influential theater critic of the fascist era, expressed his opposition to the "theater of masses" at numerous junctures during the congress: as, for example, in his negative reactions to Ciocca's presentation of his stadium-theater project (already published in *Quadrivio*). This said, d'Amico's review of *18 BL* was even-handed and nuanced even in its criticisms. Globally speaking, his vision of the theater seems firmly grounded in tradition, even if there is a certain openness to new experiments.

*Sofia*: D'Amico was an active and intelligent man. To him we owe the foundation of the Academy of Dramatic Art. Thanks to his connections to Catholic circles, he always succeeded where Pirandello failed.

*Schnapp*: Pirandello presided over the congress. Although he had been absent at the fateful April 29 performance, he makes an oblique allusion to *18 BL* in his inaugural remarks. This seems all the more surprising given that Bonelli, Bontempelli, d'Amico, and Guido Salvini, all four of whom were present at the Albereta, scrupulously avoided any mention.

*Sofia*: The experiment had failed. No one wanted to talk about it.

*Schnapp*: The inaugural speech expresses reservations about the "theater of masses," reservations that often seem to border on outright criticisms. The crisis of the bourgeois theater, Pirandello claims, can only be addressed by bringing the populace back to the traditional theater. One-time, open-air spectacles offered in public squares, stadiums, or Roman amphitheaters will not do. What is needed instead, he asserts, are modernized facilities that reflect new economic and social needs.

*Sofia*: A professorial sort of stance, out of touch with the times.

*Schnapp*: Did he want to distance himself?

*Sofia*: I know for a fact that he was horrified by Mussolini's speech and by the implementation of its proposals in *18 BL*, about which he was fully informed thanks to newspaper reports. I saw a lot of him at the time and used to attend all dress rehearsals of his works. It was I, as a matter of fact, who brought him the telegram announcing his receipt of the Nobel Prize. I have recounted the episode in my book *Pirandello: Storia di un amore* [Pirandello: A love story; Enna: Il Lunario, 1992]. He took me to the Trattoria il Buco, a hangout popular with intellectuals. It was an oddly asymmetrical friendship: he, the winner of the Nobel Prize in literature; me, a fledgling 28-year-old journalist. He always said that young people had been the first to understand his theater.

*Schnapp*: Was the theater of masses a completely erroneous notion according to Pirandello?

*Sofia*: Not 100 percent erroneous, but close. He feared that it would lead the theater world astray. At the time, he was at work on his final play, *I giganti della montagna* [The mountain giants]: a Pirandello for the masses.

*Schnapp*: But his plays never aspired to the condition of stadium- or Roman amphitheater-dependent works. His was a theater of enclosed spaces, an art theater more than a mass theater. According to [Yvon] de Begnac's notebooks, Mussolini complained frequently about Pirandello's aristocratic intellectualism and about his "theater more of thought than of action." [6]

*Sofia*: They had a hard time making sense of each other. Mussolini was grateful for Pirandello's embrace of fascism right after the Matteotti assassination. But he criticized him openly, heaping scorn on the playwright's platonic adoration of Marta Abba. You are doubtless familiar with Mussolini's witticism, reported in one of Bontempelli's books: "When you love a woman, you toss her on the couch." [7] Only after Pirandello's death did Mussolini understand that his theater was a true antibourgeois theater. We young writers believed in Pirandello. He was our great hope.

*Schnapp*: Pirandello wouldn't have been ill disposed to becoming the chief dramaturge of a state theater under Mussolini's sponsorship.

*Sofia*: This was his great aspiration and dream. It may have even determined his decision to join the Fascist party. In my book I recall the passion with which Marta Abba defended Pirandello's work, claiming for him the status of master of a theater of state.

*Schnapp*: Do you think that the events and episodes that we have been discussing have something to teach us today?

*Sofia*: I think so. A scrupulous examination and awareness of the past, its mistakes included, can help us to shape a different future. And perhaps this future, despite protestations to the contrary, looms brighter than the past. The mass theater imagined by Mussolini had at its origin a desire to educate the great majority of the Italian people. The youth of my era, the era of Pirandello, came to embrace this vision, but their point of departure differed from Mussolini's. They longed for radical new kinds of theater. In his final years, Pirandello himself looked to the cinema as a possible new avenue, as a shortcut to the future. If today's films and television programs often exceed the magic provided by the theater, then new approaches will be necessary. You who teach in California, and who have reconstructed, much like an archeologist, the theatrical experiments of those distant days, whether in Italy, Germany, or Russia, will have to define the avenues that remain available. As for myself, I am convinced that the stakes are considerable, for, as I think it was García Lorca who said, "A nation without a theater is a nation without a future."

# APPENDIX F

The following figures are extracted from "Bilancio consuntivo: Dettaglio del conto dei Littoriali della Cultura e dell'Arte al 28 ottobre 1934 Anno XII," a document found in ACS-PNF-DN-Servizi Vari, ser. 1, b. 660, f. 3, which I have cross-checked with other budgetary documents found in ACS and BA. Because this budget document gathers together most, but not all, expenses incurred and donations received in the course of the Lictorial games, the figures proposed below are incomplete and approximative. This is particularly the case as regards the budget of the inaugural spectacle, it being impossible fully to disentangle the different categories of expenditures covered in the final balance sheet. All figures are in 1934 Italian lire.

The figures do not take into account the many services provided gratis by the Civil Engineering Corps of Florence (equipment, trucks, survey work, boats) and the Italian army (reflectors, airplanes, pilots, trucks, projectors, field telephones).

## ■ I: THE 1934 LITTORIALI OF CULTURE AND ART

### A. Major contributors:

*Public*

| | |
|---|---|
| Presidency of the Council of Ministers | 100,000 |
| Rectorate of the University of Florence | 4,000 |
| Ente Autonomo di Turismo | 50,000 |
| Corporation of Spectacle | 5,000 |
| Movimento Forestieri | 50,000 |
| Italian Royal Academy | 10,000 |
| PNF Directorate | 110,000 |
| PNF Florentine Federation | 10,000 |

*Private*

| | |
|---|---|
| Magona | 500 |
| Fiat | 2,500 |
| Cassa di Risparmio Falassi | 500 |
| *Total contributions* | 342,500 |

### B. Total income (generated by ticket sales, guidebook sales, attendance at performances [including *18 BL*])

161,281

### C. Total expenses incurred by the 1934 Lictorial games (including *18 BL* and the publication costs of the review *I Littoriali*)

721,718

## ■ II: EXPENSES DIRECTLY RELATED TO THE STAGING OF *18 BL*

### A. Materials, Site Preparation, Construction of Theater

—cleaning and preparation of Albereta site and access lanes on both sides of the river Arno — 15,000

—excavation and earthmoving work performed before and after the day of the performance — 19,000

—salaries for construction work performed before and after the day of the performance — 106,898

—gravel and other construction and landscaping materials — 2,989

—construction and installation of bench seating areas and rental of seats for numbered seating areas — 23,700

—construction of boat bridge across the river Arno — 9,600

—construction of on-stage shelter for actors and director's assistant — 700

—signage for mass theater entrances, exits, etc. — 330

—carts and horses for transportation of construction materials — 3,000

—miscellaneous costs (including office expenses, warehousing of equipment, correspondence, repair of well damaged by truck during performance, additional construction materials, etc.) — 34,880

*Subtotal for A* — 216,097

### B. Props, Costumes, Sets

—costumes (rented from the Reale Accademia dei Fidenti, Florence) — 2,400

—boots (for actors) — 1,000

—stage props — 240

—rental of trucks for use in rehearsals — 80

—materials for stage sets — 8,890

—rental of carts and horses employed in spectacle — 1,969

*Subtotal for B* — 14,579

### C. Sound, Lighting, Electrical Systems, Special Effects

—custom sound system including speakers, microphones, wiring, and amplifiers (Philips) — 8,750

—lighting equipment (spotlights, projectors, panels, switchboxes, rheostats, etc.) — 9,475

—construction of ten canvas and wood lighting towers in the form of books and muskets — 1,000

—electricity required during rehearsals and performance — 501

—electrical system installation and equipment — 6,512

—recording and pressing of records for soundtrack (Società Anonima Nazionale Grammofoni, Milan) — 6,000

—fireworks display for interval between Act 1 and Act 2 — 6,769

*Subtotal for C* — 39,007

### D. Advertising for *18 BL*

—design and printing of 3,000 posters and 6,000 banners — 5,320

—posting and distribution of posters and banners in Florence and environs — 2,700

—publicity truck (with loudspeakers) and driver — 723

*Subtotal for D* — 8,743

**E. Personnel Expenses**

| | |
|---|---|
| —Blasetti (salary) | 15,000 |
| —Blasetti (travel, including transportation in Florence back and forth to performance site) | 3,397 |
| —Sofia (travel to Cortina d'Ampezzo to present plans for *18 BL* to GUF secretaries) | 482 |
| —Calzavara (salary for March and April) | 600 |
| —Ceseri (fee for performance of lead role) | 4,500 |
| —Compagnia Bonora (fee for dance performance at beginning of Act 3) | 2,800 |
| —Musicians (fee for performance of fanfares composed by Massarani) | 200 |
| —Stage personnel (payments to ushers, stage hands, helpers, etc.) | 25,000 |
| —Meals (including lunches for actors during rehearsals) | 1,064 |
| —Sick-leave costs resulting from injuries sustained by workers during construction of theater (5 workers injured; 2 out for 20–30 days) | 1,513 |
| —Royalty payments to authors and musicians | 16,332 |
| *Subtotal for E* | 70,888 |
| Approximate total expenditure | 349,314 |

## FOREWORD

1. This points to a paradox of fascism, the elitism of its mass politics, which in turn may point to a difference from communism. An important contribution of this book is its typology of these two political rivals of the 1930's.

2. This fall into the Pontine marshes may echo the plunge into the industrial drain by Marinetti in the 1909 manifesto of futurism, at least to the extent that both are deaths-and-rebirths. Both rebaptisms are allegories of a new modern subject or military-industrial ego. Even Freud once used the reclamation of the Zuider Zee as a metaphor for the carving out of the ego from the id. But what kind of ego is carved out of the Pontine marshes in the last act of *18 BL*, and is it an ego at all? In *Männerphantasien* (cited below, ch. 1, n. 24), Klaus Theweleit notes that this trope of reclamation recurs in proto-Nazi writing, where feminized fluidities threaten the masculinist fetish of the armored body. Does a similar fantasy set up the emergence of Mussolini here?

3. The simple fact that different orders, American capitalist, Soviet communist, Nazi and Italian fascist, all required related origin myths like *Birth of a Nation, October, Triumph of the Will*, and *18 BL*, suggests the need for further comparative work along these lines.

4. Again, *Triumph of the Will* has a similar dynamic, especially in scenes like the one in which the commemorated World War I dead return, resurrected, as the youth of the Nazi movement.

5. For example, in *Reproductions of Banality: Fascism, Literature, and French Intellectual Life* (Minneapolis: Univ. of Minnesota Press, 1986), Alice Kaplan defines fascism in France as a polarity machine whose ideological power lies in its tensed binding of traditional opposites like left and right, revolutionary and conservative, populist and elitist, modern and anti-modern, technological and primitive.

## CHAPTER 1

1. Scott Nearing, *Fascism* (New York: Vanguard Press, 1932), 58.

2. "Where the antithesis between Rome and Moscow is absolute, elementary, and irreduc-

ible is in the domain of the spirit and of moral and religious values, and for this reason the duel between bolshevism and fascism is and *must* remain absolute and eternal, like the duel, not between two economies and political systems, but between two overall conceptions of life and of the world: hence the character of the 'holy war' between fascism, the religion of spirit, and bolshevism, the religion of matter" (Sergio Pannunzio, "La fine di un regno," *CF* 9.18 [Sept. 15, 1931]: 343). This article launched a debate that would last until the end of 1932 and, to mention the pages of *CF* alone, included contributions from Ernesto Brunetta, Carlo Franelli, Luciano Ingianni, Riccardo Fiorini, Mario Rivoire, Alberto Luchini, and Armando Tosti. In 1937 the debate was reopened by Berto Ricci and Tommaso Napolitano (see *CF* 15.8 [Feb. 15, 1937] through 15.23 [Oct. 1, 1937]). This debate has been studied by Giuseppe Carlo Marino, *L'autarchia della cultura: Intellettuali e fascismo negli anni trenta* (Rome: Editori Riuniti, 1983), 70–87.

3. The full passage reads: "Today, before art can recover its sense of the external world and of magic, politics recovers the sense of power and contingency it lost along the democratizing road of the nineteenth century. At the present moment, there are two burial grounds for nineteenth-century democracy in Europe: one in Rome, the other in Moscow. In Moscow the tomb is guarded by mysterious wild beasts scratching the earth. In Rome by young hawks, who, by staring into the sun, may succeed in altering its course." Massimo Bontempelli, quoted from Giuliano Manacorda, *Letteratura e cultura del periodo fascista* (Milan: Principato, 1974), 102.

4. Bruno Spampanato, "La rivoluzione del popolo," *CF* 10.21 (Nov. 1, 1932): 403.

5. Erwin Piscator, *The Political Theater*, trans. Hugh Rorrison (London: Methuen, 1980), 186.

6. Maurice Pottecher, *Le Théâtre du peuple: Re-naissance et destinée du théâtre populaire* (Paris: Ollendorff, 1899), 73. On the revolutionary festivals, see Mona Ozouf, *La Fête révolutionnaire, 1789–1799* (Paris: Gallimard, 1976).

7. Georg Fuchs, "Der Schaubühne der Zukunft," *Das Theater* 15 (Berlin, 1905): 33. "The perfection of naturalism by mechanical means has developed the peep show *ad absurdum*," Fuchs declared elsewhere. "We have come to the end of our wisdom. The conventional theater itself has proved to us that we are encumbered with an apparatus that prohibits all healthy growth. This whole sham world of cardboard, twine, canvas, and gilt is ripe for destruction." Id., *Revolution in the Theater: Conclusions Concerning the Munich Artists' Theater*, trans. Connor Kuhn (Ithaca, N.Y.: Cornell Univ. Press, 1959), 37.

8. Viktor Shklovsky, quoted from Lynn Mally, *Culture of the Future: The Proletkult Movement in Revolutionary Russia* (Berkeley and Los Angeles: Univ. of California Press, 1990), 125.

9. Viktor Shklovsky, quoted in Konstantin Rudnitsky, *Russian and Soviet Theater, 1905–1932*, trans. R. Perman, ed. L. Milne (New York: Abrams, 1988), 41.

10. Platon Kerzhentsev, *Tvorcheskii teatr* (creative theater), quoted in Rudnitsky, *Russian and Soviet Theater*, 45.

11. Boris Arvatov, quoted in Rudnitsky, *Russian and Soviet Theater*, 90.

12. Zeev Sternhell, *The Birth of Fascist Ideology: From Cultural Rebellion to Political Revolution*, trans. David Maisel (Princeton: Princeton Univ. Press, 1994), 6.

13. Palmiro Togliatti, *Lezioni sul fascismo* (1935; Rome: Editori Riuniti, 1974), 15.

14. Camillo Pellizzi, *Fascismo-Aristocrazia* (Milan: Alpes, 1925), 45–46.

15. Cf. Barbara Spackman's insightful analysis in "The Fascist Rhetoric of Virility," *Stanford Italian Review* 8.1–2 (1990): "Fascism seems to

compensate for this refusal (or incapacity) by (over) defining itself semiotically; hence, the need to change calendar and holidays, to eradicate all traces of foreign words and dialect from the 'official' language, to identify the fascist by the clothes he wears and the slogans he repeats and, in general, to attempt a realignment of signifiers and signifieds" (88).

16. Igor Golomstock, *Totalitarian Art in the Soviet Union, the Third Reich, Fascist Italy and the People's Republic of China*, trans. Robert Chandler (New York: Icon, 1990), 91.

17. The phrase "eclecticism of the spirit" is Mussolini's and was used in his inaugural speech to the Italian Academy on October 28, 1929. On this subject, see Marino, *L'autarchia della cultura*, 3–17.

18. Although there are passing references to *18 BL* in some of the postwar secondary literature concerned with the Italian theater during the fascist decades, the present monograph has no real predecessors. Brief but useful discussions may be found in Corrado Sofia, *Pirandello: Storia di un amore* (Enna: Il Lunario, 1992), 46–49; Emanuela Scarpellini, *Organizzazione teatrale e politica del teatro nell'Italia fascista* (Florence: La Nuova Italia, 1989), 238–40; Adriano Aprà's introduction to *Alessandro Blasetti: Scritti sul cinema* (Venice: Marsilio, 1982), 31; Giovanni Lazzari, *I Littoriali della cultura e dell'arte* (Naples: Liguori, 1979), 22–23; Enzo Maurri, *Rose scarlatte e telefoni bianchi: Appunti sulla commedia italiana dall'impero al 25 luglio 1943* (Rome: Abete, 1981), 77–78; and Ruth Ben-Ghiat, "The Formation of a Fascist Culture: The Realist Movement in Italy, 1930–43" (Ph.D. diss., Brandeis Univ., 1991), 225–27. As far as I am aware, the sole article specifically devoted to *18 BL* is Mario Verdone's brief "Spettacolo politico e *18 BL*," in *Futurismo, cultura, e politica*, ed. Renzo de Felice (Turin: Fondazione Giovanni Agnelli, 1988), 483–84, which contains numerous factual errors.

19. Alessandro Pavolini, "Cervelli in allenamento," *ILCA* 1 (Dec. 1933): 18; emphasis added.

20. Benito Mussolini, *Fascism: Doctrine and Institutions* (Rome: Ardita, 1935), 133.

21. For Geertz, "thick description" implies a complex mode of description, characteristic of ethnography, that lays out for analysis the stratified hierarchy of meanings that a given culture permits to coexist, produces, perceives, and interprets. See Clifford Geertz, *The Interpretation of Cultures* (New York: Basic Books, 1973), 6–30.

22. For an instance of reperiodization, see Ben-Ghiat, "Formation of a Fascist Culture." On fascism's powers of interpellation, see Alice Yaeger Kaplan, *Reproductions of Banality: Fascism, Literature and French Intellectual Life* (Minneapolis: Univ. of Minnesota Press, 1986).

23. Perhaps because of his own intellectual affinities with fascism, Bataille's theorization is often stronger and more insightful than that of the Frankfurt school (whether in the version of Benjamin or of Horkheimer/Adorno). As a point of entry, see "The Psychological Structure of Fascism," in Georges Bataille, *Visions of Excess: Selected Writings, 1927–1939*, ed. Allan Stoekl, trans. C. R. Lovitt, D. M. Leslie, and A. Stoekl (Minneapolis: Univ. of Minnesota Press, 1985), 137–60.

24. *Gli annitrenta: Arte e cultura in Italia* (2d ed., Milan: Mazzotta, 1983) documents the 1982 Milanese exhibition of the same name. The full titles of the cited works of Fredric Jameson, Pier Giorgio Zunino, and Victoria de Grazia are, respectively, *Fables of Aggression: Wyndham Lewis, the Modernist as Fascist* (Berkeley and Los Angeles: Univ. of California Press, 1979); *L'ideologia del fascismo: Miti credenze e valori nella stabilizzazione del regime* (Bologna: Il Mulino, 1985); and *How Fascism Ruled Women: Italy, 1922–1945* (Berkeley and Los Angeles: Univ. of California Press, 1992). Giorgio Ciucci's

most recent major contribution has been *Gli architetti e il fascismo: Architettura e città, 1922–1944* (Turin: Einaudi, 1989); Diane Ghirardo has long been one of the leading analysts of fascist architectural modernism, on which subject see her *Building New Communities: New Deal and Fascist Italy* (Princeton: Princeton Univ. Press, 1989); Richard Etlin is author of *Modernism in Italian Architecture, 1890–1940* (Cambridge, Mass.: MIT Press, 1991); among Thomas Schumacher's publications, the most recent is *Surface and Symbol: Giuseppe Terragni and the Architecture of Italian Rationalism* (New York: Princeton Architectural Press, 1991). Emilio Gentile is the author of numerous seminal studies, but I single out *Il mito dello stato nuovo dall'antigiolittismo al fascismo* (Bari: Laterza, 1982) and *Il culto del Littorio. La sacralizzazione della politica nell'Italia fascista* (Rome and Bari: Laterza, 1993) because of their important analysis of the role played by myth in resolving ideological and social tensions. Klaus Theweleit's *Männerphantasien* (1977–78) has appeared in two volumes in English: *Male Fantasies*, vol. 1, *Women, Floods, Bodies, History*, trans. Stephen Conway (Minneapolis: Univ. of Minnesota Press, 1987) and vol. 2, *Male Bodies: Psychoanalyzing the White Terror*, trans. Erica Carter and Chris Turner (Minneapolis: Univ. of Minnesota Press, 1989). For examples of Hal Foster's psychoanalytically inspired approach, see "Postmodernism in Parallax," *October* 63 (Winter 1993): 3–20, and "Prosthetic Gods" (forthcoming, ibid.). Francesco Tentori's *P. M. Bardi con le cronache artistiche de L'Ambrosiano, 1930–1933* (Milan: Mazzotta, 1990) stands as a model of scholarly rigor and accuracy. Laura Malvano's *Fascismo e politica dell'immagine* (Turin: Bollati Boringhieri, 1988) is perhaps the best recent overview of fascism's image politics. Barbara Spackman is the author of a body of essays that includes "The Fascist Rhetoric of Virility," as well as of *Decadent Genealogies: The Rhetoric of Sickness from Baudelaire to d'Annunzio* (Ithaca, N.Y.: Cornell Univ. Press, 1989), the final pages of which describe a now forthcoming book specifically concerned with fascism. Pietro Cavallo's work began with the essay "Culto delle origini e mito del capo nel teatro fascista," *Storia Contemporanea* 18.2 (Apr. 1987): 287–339, which has now reappeared as ch. 2 of *Immaginario e rappresentazione: Il teatro fascista di propaganda* (Rome: Bonacci, 1990).

25. Alessandro Blasetti, quoted in Elaine Mancini, *Struggles of the Italian Film Industry During Fascism, 1930–35* (Ann Arbor, Mich.: UMI Research Press, 1985), 113.

## CHAPTER 2

1. Achille Starace's commitment to the theater seems to have dated back to his military service as a lieutenant in World War I, when he and a second lieutenant named Tramontini founded a small military theater called (with a pinch of irony one would hope) the Trianon. On this subject, see "Il precursore dei carri di tespi" (signed "Tim."), *Comoedia* 13.4 (Apr. 15–May 15, 1931): 45.

2. For the playscripts as well as an account of this collaboration, see Giovacchino Forzano, *Mussolini, autore drammatico: Campo di maggio, Villafranca, Cesare* (Florence: G. Barbèra, 1954). In his magisterial biography, *Mussolini il duce*, vol. 1, *Gli anni del consenso, 1929–1936* (Turin: Einaudi, 1974), 32, Renzo de Felice comments: "There is little doubt that . . . the three historical dramas that resulted from Mussolini and Forzano's collaboration reveal fairly clearly Mussolini's tendency to envisage himself and his actions in a 'historical' perspective: that of a solitary man who, conscious of his pursuit of a grand goal but surrounded by the lack of understanding and moral inadequacy of his circle of associates and conscious also of the need to act taking full advantage of every occasion, is participating in a race more dramatic than the

race against death: that against the 'cycle' [of history]." For an overview of Forzano's work, particularly as a librettist, see the entries by Luigi Baldacci and Carmelo Alberti in *Il Piccolo Marat: Storia e rivoluzione nel melodramma verista*, ed. Piero and Nandi Ostali, Atti del terzo convegno di studi su Pietro Mascagni (Milan: Sonzogno, 1990), 81–112.

3. The full passage reads: "I am certain that further readings will permit you to perfect the text ('Caress your sentence: she will end up smiling back at you'—A. France)." Mussolini, letter dated Dec. 26, 1934, reproduced in *OO* 42.92.

4. Jacques Copeau, "The Absent Deity," in *Copeau: Texts on Theater*, ed. and trans. J. Rudlin and N. H. Paul (New York: Routledge, 1990), 53.

5. The phrase "crisis of the theater" recurs continually in the pages of the principal Italian theatrical journals of the late 1920's and early 1930's. In *Comoedia* alone, I count some 25 articles specifically devoted to the "crisis" between 1928 and 1932. In addition, one must add two publications by the leading theater critic of the era, Silvio d'Amico: *La crisi del teatro* (Rome, 1931), and *Il teatro non deve morire* (Rome, 1945).

6. See Emanuela Scarpellini, *Organizzazione teatrale e politica del teatro nell'Italia fascista* (Theater organization and theater politics in fascist Italy; Florence: La Nuova Italia, 1989).

7. On the history of the Corporazione dello Spettacolo, see ibid., esp. 131–64. The government's policy bias towards regulation of theater producers and not the content of their work has been examined from a sociological standpoint by Mabel Berezin, "The Organization of Political Ideology: Culture, State, and Theater in Fascist Italy," *American Sociological Review* 56 (Oct. 1991): 639–51.

8. Alessandro Brissoni, "Teatro fascista e littoriali dell'arte," *Il Bargello*, Sept. 9, 1934, 3. For an overview with particular relevance to the theatrical initiatives in Florence, see Alessandro

Sardelli, "Appunti per una storia del teatro fascista: 1. Fascismo e origine del teatro di regime, 2. L'organizzazione teatrale 'di massa' a Firenze (1925–35)," *Città e regione* 5.5 (May 1979): 122–39. Useful period discussions are Nicola de Pirro's propaganda pamphlet *Il teatro per il popolo* (n.p., 1938) and Corrado Pavolini, "Per un teatro di domani," in *Storia del teatro italiano*, ed. Silvio d'Amico (Milan: V. Bompiani, 1936), 349–67. The idea of staging government-sponsored contests for new playwrights was adopted also by the Nazi regime during the period of its support for the *Thingspiel* movement (1933–37). It extends back at least as far as the French architect and reformer Eugène Viollet-le-Duc (1814–79), on which subject, see Jacques Rancière, "Le Théâtre du peuple: Une Histoire interminable," in *Esthétique du peuple* (Paris: La Découverte, 1985), 30.

9. The best source for information on the history, internal workings, and teachings of the *filodrammatiche* is the volume *Il teatro filodrammatico* (Rome, 1929), edited by the Ufficio Educazione Artistica della Direzione Centrale dell'OND but largely authored by Antonio Valente. On the movement in general, see Victoria de Grazia, *The Culture of Consent: Mass Organization of Leisure in Fascist Italy* (New York: Cambridge Univ. Press, 1981), 166–68; Scarpellini, *Organizzazione*, 105–9; and Sardelli, "Appunti," 124–26.

10. The philodramatic celebrations of political anniversaries were singled out as disgraceful kitsch by advocates of a "true" fascist theater like Augusto Consorti: "These 'evocations'— they cannot be considered *representations*— ought to be disciplined, and brought into line with the criteria that guided the organizers of [1932] Exhibition of the Fascist Revolution" ("Rievocazione," *LIV* 3.18 [Oct. 28, 1933]: 9).

11. Ufficio Educazione Artistica della Direzione Centrale dell'OND, ed., *Il teatro filodrammatico*, 101, 99, 107. The word *complesso* resists translation, since it simultaneously designates a

"whole," a "complex" in the sense of "industrial complex," a musical "band," and a "set" of factors, instruments, or machines. The central theme of the second part of *Il teatro filodrammatico* (99–146) is the spiritual condition of the modern age and its implications for the theater arts.

12. All the cited figures are from Scarpellini, *Organizzazione*, 249.

13. There is little non-Russian bibliography on the Peredvizhnoi Teatr but, as a point of departure, see Alexander Tairoff, *Notes of a Director*, trans. William Kuhlke (Coral Gables: Univ. of Miami Press, 1969), 20–21, 45; on Gémier's work, see Frederick Brown, *Theater and Revolution: The Culture of the French Stage* (New York: Viking, 1980), 284–303. Mario Corsi conveniently suppresses any reference to non-Italian precedents, so as to be able to claim that the thespian cars represented "the first mobile theater for masses in the world" (Corsi, *Il teatro all'aperto in Italia* [Milan and Rome: Rizzoli, 1939], 265).

14. "The idea for the thespian cars first arose in the context of the OND's philodramatic movement and, if I recall correctly, was thought up and championed by Goffredo Ginocchio. Augusto Turati wanted the thing realized and placed the enterprise under the directorship of Giovacchino Forzano" (*Il Lavoro Fascista* [July 4, 1929], quoted in Giovanni Isgrò, *Fortuny e il teatro* [Palermo: Novecento, 1986], 189). Later in the same article, a certain Bassi is mentioned as the engineer of the first thespian car. On Valente, see Giovanni Isgrò, *Antonio Valente: Architetto scenografo e la cultura materiale del teatro in Italia fra le due guerre* (Palermo: Flaccovio, 1988).

15. Forzano, *Mussolini, autore drammatico*, xx.

16. The repertory of the *carri di tespi* is listed in full in Scarpellini, *Organizzazione*, 365–69.

17. "The work of the thespian cars has in a certain sense one of spiritual and intellectual recla-

mation" (Carlo Lari, "I carri di tespi," *Comoedia* 15.7 [July 15–Aug. 15, 1933]: 36). "The purest accent, words pronounced with perfect tonality, secure rhythm, and with a sense of wise and suggestive expressivity, will serve as pronunciation school in those areas where dialects still hold our marvelous language in the thrall of deformity" (Paolo Orano, *I carri di tespi dell'OND* [Rome: Pinciana, 1937], 17). Orano later refers to the cars as "the most efficacious school of proper speech" (18).

18. Brown, *Theater and Revolution*, 288. The rise to power of the French Popular Front in 1936 was accompanied by a resurgence in mass theatrical experiments (on which subject, see ibid., 390–411).

19. The most complete technical overview of the thespian cars is found in *Carro di tespi*, a pamphlet published by the OND in 1936. Also worth consulting are Corsi, *Il teatro all'aperto in Italia*, 263–88; Orano, *I carri di tespi*; *Gente Nostra* 47–48 (Sept. 13–26, 1937): 1–15; and Scarpellini, *Organizzazione*, 109–115.

20. "The very operation of assemblage and dismantling, carried out in full public view, is presented to spectators as an unusual effect, outside of the ordinary course of life" (Isgrò, *Fortuny e il teatro*, 107). Cf. the OND pamphlet *Carro di tespi*: "The theater's construction constitutes a spectacle unto itself because of the structure's simplicity and of the care with which the enormous building comes about" (40). It should be noted that the actors and musicians almost always traveled by train, so their arrival would have marked a separate moment in the pre-spectacle show.

21. Orano, *I carri di tespi*, 19.

22. On the science of work, see Anson Rabinbach, *The Human Motor: Energy, Fatigue, and the Origins of Modernity* (New York: Basic Books, 1990).

23. Orano, *I carri di tespi*, 19–20.

24. On Fortuny and the cupola, see Isgrò, *Fortuny*, 99–108 and 179–91. Isgrò rightly emphasizes the fact that Fortuny himself remained largely unaware both of the OND's use of thespian cars and of the technical enhancements added after the 1929 season.

25. "This large cloth is manufactured in the shape of a sack so that it can be pulled tight. A powerful electrical vacuum, attached to it by means of a tube, sucks out the air and holds the cloth perfectly taut, eliminating even the slightest crease" (OND, *Carri di tespi*, 21).

26. Describing the first thespian car's inaugural performance—a rendition of Alfieri's *Oreste* held on the terrace of the Pincio in Rome on April 27, 1929—Fortuny wrote: "The 'sky' was designed so that it would be confused with the actual sky. One might well have thought that the backdrop of the stage had been raised up and that the actual sky had been placed on stage" (Isgrò, *Fortuny*, 188–89). Cf. Cipriano Giachetti writing about the theater constructed by Blasetti for *18 BL*: "Here, thanks to the harmonious background furnished by the surrounding hills, nature already provided the ideal backdrop and the Fortuny cupola was replaced by a truer and greater cupola: that of the sky" ("La rappresentazione del '18 BL' ha luogo stasera," *LN* [Apr. 29–30, 1934]: 5).

27. One such episode is recounted by C[orrado] P[uccetti], "I carri di tespi," *Gente Nostra* 47–48 [Sept. 13–26, 1937]: 7): "At the conclusion of the show, while the crowd of 5,000 that had partaken of the harmonies of Giuseppe Verdi's masterpiece was on its feet cheering il Duce, the performers, technicians, and stage workers climbed onto the stage and began loudly intoning 'Giovinezza' and 'The Hymn to Rome.' In that instant the public's enthusiasm could no longer be contained. The crowd joined in on the singing and, as it came to an end, shouted an exalted and vibrant invocation to the Chief." As regards the performance of propaganda poetry from 1936 onward, Orano writes: "During the intermissions between acts, a specially selected actor on each car would read the most significant epic lyrics concerned with the fascist empire" (Orano, *I carri di tespi*, 56).

28. "It is perhaps worth underscoring just how effective, deep, and unique is the propaganda work accomplished by a thespian car. Aside from the spiritual impact of a thespian car performance on the people, the presence of a marvelous reality that surges forth, in a few short hours transforming athletic fields or public squares into theaters perfect in every detail, acts as concrete propaganda. It acts as the full actualization of that notion of creative power that is fascism's own" (P[uccetti], "I carri di tespi," 7).

29. The classic study on this subject remains Corsi, *Il teatro all'aperto in Italia*, who neglects, however, to note the important role played by non-Italian theorists, in particular by men such as Edward Gordon Craig and Sheldon Cheney, in promoting the open-air theater movement. Also worth consulting is Giulio Pacuvio, "Teatro all'aperto," in *Cinquanta anni di teatro in Italia*, ed. Centro di Ricerche Teatrali (Rome: Carlo Bestetti, 1954), 43–52.

30. Corsi, *Il teatro all'aperto in Italia*, 76.

31. Ibid., 101.

32. Ibid., 88.

33. "The truth is that the civil doctrine of which Virgil is both an advocate and magical herald is the same as that under whose auspices the new Italy has taken up once again, after a century of lethargy, its laborious and glorious march across the centuries" (*Virgilio: Discorso pel bimillenario pronunciato in Campidoglio il 15 ottobre 1930*, Celebrazioni e Commemorazioni 2 [Rome: Reale Accademia d'Italia, 1931], 20). The speech closes by evoking the great public works of the empire, including the draining of marshes, and ends: "In these days of new trials and new glories, Virgil is the ancient, the new, the eternal prophet of the Latin

195

folk" (23). It is worth noting that Romagnoli was a signatory to the Manifesto of Fascist Intellectuals.

34. Romagnoli would later be proclaimed the precursor of Mussolini's theater of the 20,000 in Oscar Andriani, "Ettore Romagnoli: Precursore del teatro di masse e ideatore delle rievocazioni classiche all'aperto in Italia," *Giornale dello Spettacolo* 11: 3–8.

35. Carlo Goldoni, *Memorie*, quoted in Corsi, *Il teatro all'aperto in Italia*, 144.

36. A contemporary account of the crisis and its resolution may be found in Giuseppe Silvestri, "All'arena di Verona," *Comoedia* 12.7 (July 15–Aug. 15, 1930): 29–31.

## CHAPTER 3

1. These figures are approximate and include audiences at musical events; they are based on table 3 in the appendix to Emanuela Scarpellini, *Organizzazione teatrale e politica del teatro nell'Italia fascista* (Florence: La Nuova Italia, 1989), 355–60.

2. "The incorporation of performers into the regime's corporative structures was viewed as the first phase of a process that would lead inexorably to the total participation of the worlds of art and culture in the nation's renewed existence. The second phase would entail the creation of an art that would faithfully mirror the values of the new historical era that fascism claimed to have inaugurated" (ibid., 67).

3. Anton Giulio Bragaglia, *Il teatro della rivoluzione* (Rome: Edizioni Tiber, 1929), 7. This letter was originally published in *Il Lavoro Fascista*, Mar. 20, 1929. The fact that Bragaglia's title is doubly borrowed from Georg Fuchs's *The Revolution in the Theater: Conclusions Concerning the Munich Artists' Theater* (1908) and Romain Rolland's *Théatre de la révolution* (1909) may deliberately imply that his is a fascist interpretation of these two

populist theaters. The reference to "Belli" is doubtless meant to refer to Vincenzo Bellini, the composer of *Norma*.

4. Bragaglia, *Il teatro della rivoluzione*, 24.

5. Ibid., 12.

6. The referendum was launched on Sept. 22, 1929, and concluded on Feb. 16, 1930. Participants included Soffici, Titta Rosa, Aniante, Marinetti, Barbaro, Bacchelli, Gallian, Bonelli, Campanile, (Corrado) Pavolini, Marchi, Vergani, Bontempelli, and Alvaro.

7. Quoted in Scarpellini, *Organizzazione*, 149. A typical contemporary view of the Soviet revolutionary theater is that of Adriano Lualdi, "Viaggio musicale nell'URSS," *Nuova Antologia*, Oct. 16, 1933, 541–65, who notes that "the time and space dedicated to overt propaganda and to fiery tirades are so disproportionate, that one has difficulty understanding just how the audience can listen without boredom or annoyance. . . . It's all kid's stuff, you might conclude" (556).

8. Mussolini's view is not unlike that advanced by Goebbels, who faulted communist propaganda, not for being propagandistic as such, but rather for being insufficiently artful. On this subject, see Gerd Albrecht, *Nationsozialistische Filmpolitik: Eine soziologische Untersuchung über die Spielfilme des Dritten Reichs* (Stuttgart: Ferdinand Enke, 1969).

9. Ernesto Forzano, *Rapsodia fascista. Dramma: Prologo, Primo sacrificio, Secondo sacrificio, Olocausto* (Genoa: Studio Editoriale Genovese, 1926). Farinaccci's *Redenzione* (of the same year) belongs, roughly speaking, to the same genre.

10. Vitaliano Brancati, "La mia visita a Mussolini," *CF* 9.15 (Aug. 1, 1931): 293. This brief essay is reprinted in Renzo de Felice, *Mussolini il duce: I—Gli anni del consenso, 1929–1936* (Turin: Einaudi, 1974), 867–71.

11. The bibliographical references are as follows: Vitaliano Brancati, *Everest: Mito in un*

*atto* (Catania: Studio Editoriale Moderno, 1931) and *Piave: Dramma in quattro atti* (Milan: Arnaldo Mondadori, 1932); Saverio Grana, *Il mito di Roma: Cronaca in tre parti della rivoluzione fascista* (Florence: Ed. Sergio, 1927); Mario Bonetti and Lelio Montanari, *L'artefice: Cinque sintesi teatrali per la storia di un grande popolo* (Bologna: Ed. Aldine, 1933), published with a cover featuring a monumental profile of Mussolini (inspired no doubt by Thayaht's famous steel bust).

12. "Discorso per il cinquantenario della Società Italiana degli Autori ed Editori" (Rome), Apr. 28, 1933 (*OO* 44.51). Earlier in the speech, Mussolini had insisted on the special *pathos* of the contemporary era, while calling for writers to dig deep within themselves because "extemporaneous and superficial things are destined to leave no lasting trace" (*OO* 44.50).

13. *OO* 44.50. There are numerous echoes here of Rolland's pages on "The New Theater," in *The People's Theater* (see esp. 99–117 in B. H. Clark's translation [New York: Henry Holt, 1918]; the translator has eliminated the work's original subtitle: *An Essay on the Aesthetics of a New Theater*). Mussolini's attitude towards Rolland was, naturally, complex, given that Rolland had been a favorite author during his early socialist period. (He had even published a translation of "Beethoven's Testament" in *Vita Trentina* [Dec. 4, 1909] from Rolland's *The Life of Beethoven*.) Yet Rolland's pacifist stance during World War I and his later embrace of the Paris expatriate community of Italian antifascists earned him frequent denunciations, as in "Tiro a segno" (*PdI* [July 7, 1921]; *OO* 17.32), where he is referred to as "the unspeakable Rolland," and "Morti che camminano" (*PdI* [June 29, 1937]; *OO* 28.217), where he is described as "the most authentic interpreter of a cowardly decadentism to the point of treason" and as "the opportunist of all -isms, from reformism to anarchism."

14. On Ciocca, see Pietro Maria Bardi's preface to the second edition of *Giudizio sul bolscevismo* (Milan: V. Bompiani, 1933), 14–20; and Francesco Tentori, *P. M. Bardi con le cronache artistiche de l'Ambrosiano, 1930–1933* (Milan: Mazzotta, 1990), 67, 121–22.

15. "Russia and America are the present era's two most authentic representatives of the *class capitalism* that arose during the past century in the wake of the more traditional *caste capitalism*. Their point of departure is identical: the same (excessive) concentration and mechanization of the means of production, all economic questions reduced to matters of accounting. It isn't by accident thus that New York furnished Moscow with the model for its first five-year plan" (Ciocca, *Giudizio sul bolscevismo*, 2d ed., 25, but see also 50–55). In the spring of 1934, Ciocca made a trip to the United States under the dual sponsorship of the Italian government and the Reale Accademia d'Italia in order to pursue his research on economic rationalization. *Economia di massa* was published by Valentino Bompiani in Milan in 1936.

16. In "(Servizi a Mussolini) Progetto di casa rurale," *Quadrante* 26 (June 1935): 6, where he first described this patented project, Ciocca wrote: "The novelty of this project consists in the following: that the rural house is conceived of as if it were a machine." A sample unit was apparently built during the following year. The transport project, which anticipated today's container shipping systems, is documented in *La strada guidata* (Milan: Bompiani, 1939), as well as in several essays published in *Meridiano di Roma*.

17. The full passage reads as follows: "I have championed the guided street because it greatly reduces the amount of labor involved in transportation. But, one might ask, why should labor be conserved through the judicious use of machines? The old economics answers: 'to create wealth.' The new economics responds otherwise: 'to increase the nation's power, a

power measured according to the number of arms, hearts, brains, made available for the pursuit of the highest collective aims by being freed from ordinary economic duties'" (Gaetano Ciocca, *La strada guidata*, vi). Ciocca felt that the technology would prove especially valuable in colonial Ethiopia.

18. Gaetano Ciocca, "La tecnica del teatro di masse," in RAI, *Atti—Convegno di Lettere: Tema—Il teatro drammatico* (Oct. 8–14, 1934): 177–78. Ciocca's views are anticipated in Carlo Goldoni's discussion of the Roman arena at Verona: "forty-five marble tiers encircle it [the arena] and can accommodate 100,000 people with ease. . . . There are no box seats for spectators. The theater's floor becomes a vast enclosure filled with chairs. The lower classes can afford very inexpensive seating along the vast steps that extend across the front of the theater, but, despite the modest ticket prices, there is no more profitable venue in Italy than the arena" (quoted in Mario Corsi, *Il teatro all'aperto in Italia* [Milan and Rome: Rizzoli, 1939], 144).

19. Ciocca, "La tecnica del teatro di masse," in RAI, *Convegno*, 178.

20. Ciocca, "(Servizi a Mussolini) Progetto di casa rurale," 27. The essay is filled with borrowings from Le Corbusier's writings.

21. Ciocca, "La tecnica del teatro di masse," in RAI, *Convegno*, 178.

22. For photographic documentation of Ciocca's theater, see *Comoedia* 16.11 (Nov. 1934); for his evolving concepts, see "Il teatro di masse," *Quadrante* 3 (July 1933): 7–10; "Ancora sul teatro di masse," *Quadrante* 8 (Dec. 1933): 17–18; and "La tecnica del teatro di masse," *Quadrante* 14–15 (June–July 1933): 47–53.

23. Gaetano Ciocca, "(Servizi a Mussolini) Il teatro di masse," *Quadrante* 3 (July 1933): 9.

24. Ibid.

25. Ibid., 10.

26. Ciocca's hybrid understanding of the spec-

tacles to be performed in the new mass theater was shared by the *Thingspiel* movement in Germany. As described by Rainer Schlößer, *Thing* theaters were meant to accommodate: "First, oratorios made up of the interaction between choruses and individual speakers; second, pantomimes in the form of allegories, tableaux vivants, ritual oaths [*Fahnenweihe*], and celebratory rites [*Festakte*]; third, processions in the form of parades, celebratory processions, and rallies; fourth, dance in the form of ballets, processional dances, gymnastics, or athletic celebrations" (*Das Volk und seine Bühne: Bemerkungen zum Aufbau des deutschen Theaters* [Berlin, 1935], 53).

27. Telesio Interlandi and Corrado Pavolini, *La croce del sud: Dramma in tre atti* (Milan: Rizzoli, 1927).

28. Telesio Interlandi, "Domani nuovo spettacolo: Un teatro di masse," *Il Tevere*, June 26, 1933, 3.

29. Ibid.

30. Ibid. The distinction between "shade" and "sun" zones was (and is still) a standard feature of European soccer stadiums.

31. "Price distinctions will be made as a function of the distance of seats from the stage, but they will be slight, just like the differences in visibility and audibility" (ibid.).

32. Le Corbusier and Pierre Jeanneret, *Oeuvre Complète, 1934–1938* (Zurich: Girsberger, 1939), 90. On this period of Le Corbusier's career, see Jean-Louis Cohen, *Le Corbusier and the Mystique of the USSR: Theories and Projects for Moscow, 1928–1936* (Princeton: Princeton Univ. Press, 1992), 223–30.

33. The competition and the prize-winning entries are described and documented in Mario Perniconi, "Concorso per l'Auditorium di Roma," *Architettura: Revista del Sindacato Nazionale Fascista Architetti* 14.2 (Dec. 1935): 671–91. On these projects, see "Tre progetti

dell'Auditorium di Roma," *Quadrante* 25 (May 1935): 6–25; and the special issue on Saverio Muratori of *Storia Architettura: Rivista di Architettura e Restauro* 7.1–2 (Dec.–Jan. 1984): 115–19. I am indebted to Francesco Tentori for this reference.

34. Both quotations are from Perniconi, "Concorso per l'Auditorium di Roma," 686–87. Luigi Vietti's project was presented to the public in "Il megateatro di Vietti," *Ottobre* (June 19, 1935): 5, which claims that his design goals were "equality of all views" and "a large capacity."

35. On these late projects, see Ada Francesca Marcianò's edition of Terragni's *Opera completa, 1925–1943* (Rome: Officina, 1987), 254–55.

36. The writings in question were collected by Bontempelli himself into *L'avventura novecentisa* (Florence: Vallecchi, 1974). On Bontempelli's career, various overviews are available, including Luigi Baldacci, *Massimo Bontempelli* (Turin: Borla, 1967); Antonio Saccone, *Massimo Bontempelli: Il mito del '900* (Naples: Liguori, 1979); Fulvia Airoldi Namer, *Massimo Bontempelli* (Milan: Mursia, 1979); and Carlo Cecchini, *Avanguardia mito e ideologia: Massimo Bontempelli tra futurismo e fascismo* (Rome: Il Ventaglio, 1986).

37. Massimo Bontempelli, "Teatro per le masse (conclusioni)," May 1933, rpt. in *L'avventura novecentista*, 256.

38. Ibid.

39. Ibid., *L'avventura novecentista*, 262.

40. Massimo Bontempelli, "Per il tifo a teatro," May 1933, rpt. in *L'avventura novecentista*, 265. Bontempelli's point was to become a commonplace in contemporary discussions of how to resolve the crisis of the theater. For other examples, see Anton Giulio Bragaglia, "L'inquadramento degli sportivi fra i teatrali," *La Vita Italiana* 22.253 (Apr. 1934): 438–47; and Giorgio

Venturini, "Teatro d'oggi," *ILCA* 1 (Dec. 1933): 36–40.

41. On Heidegger and the intellectual climate of the 1920's, see the closing chapter of Hans Ulrich Gumbrecht's forthcoming *In 1926: An Essay in Historical Simultaneity*.

42. "The mob [*folla*] will frequent this gigantic theater, this theater for mobs, not as tired and cold judge, but as an active protagonist" (Bontempelli, *L'avventura novecentista*, 261).

43. The May 30, 1933, issue of *L'Italia Vivente* (3.9: 6–7) included contributions by Bino Sanminiatelli, Dino Terra, Carlo Betocchi, Giani Stuparich, Enrico Pea, and Camillo Pellizzi; the June 15 issue (3.10: 6–8), contributions by Francesco Bruno, Angelo Silvio Novaro, Guido Piovene, Umberto Barbaro, Aldo Capasso, Pier Maria Pasinetti, Adriano Grande, Bruno Romani, Fabio Tombari, and Luigi Bartolini; the June 30 issue (3.11: 4–5), contributions by Ugo Betti, Elio Talarico, Alfredo Trimarco, and "Uno Qualunque" (probably Nino d'Aroma himself).

44. Augusto Consorti, "Un teatro fascista," *LIV* 3.14 (Aug. 25, 1933): 1.

45. Ibid., 2.

46. "Appunti per un teatro di masse," *LIV* 3.14 (Aug. 25, 1933): 9.

47. Ibid.

48. Pietro Maria Bardi, "(Proposte) Sacra rappresentazione del fascismo," *Quadrante* 7 (Nov. 1933): 4. Bardi's choice of the Stadio Berta is indicative not only of his desire to identify its rationalist architecture with the regime but also of the fact that Berta's murder is featured in the second act of the mystery play.

49. Ernest de Weerth, "Italy Outdoors: Open-Air Theatre Performances," *Theater Arts Monthly* 19.5 (May 1935): 368.

50. The theme is pervasive in Emil Ludwig's famed *Colloqui con Mussolini* (Verona: A. Mondadori, 1932). It can be traced back to such early statements as Mussolini's claim, at the

opening of the 1923 Novecento exhibition, "I, too, am an artist who sculpts a given material in the pursuit of certain ideals" ("Alla mostra del Novecento," *PdI* [Mar. 27, 1923], rpt. in *Il "Novecento italiano": Storia, documenti, iconografia*, ed. Rossana Bossaglia [Milan: Feltrinelli, 1979], 83).

51. Filippo Tomasso Marinetti, "Fondazione e manifesto del Futurismo," in *Teoria e invenzione futurista*, ed. Luciano de Maria (Milan: A. Mondadori, 1983), 11.

52. In late 1930, the Movimento Nazionale dei Giovani had founded the Italian Youth Theater (Teatro Italiano dei Giovani) in an attempt to remedy the perceived crisis of the Italian theater—this in the midst of a polemic in *Comoedia* between Sabatino Lopez and Mario Buzzichini regarding the role of the fascist state, of public institutions, and of theater professionals in shaping and giving encouragement to the next generation of playwrights. In subsequent months, the issue was debated by Giovanni Cavicchioli ("Il teatro dei giovani," *Comoedia* 13.1 [15 Jan.–15 Feb., 1931]: 53–54); Silvio d'Amico ("Autori giovani e autori nuovi," *Comoedia* 13.3 [Mar. 15–Apr. 15, 1931]: 5); Luigi Antonelli, Gian Capo, Anton Giulio Bragaglia, Guido Salvini, Cipriano Giachetti (all in "Opinioni sui giovani," ibid., 6–8); Carlo Veneziani ("Autori giovani, vecchi e così così," ibid., 17–18); Giacomo Sipari ("Parlo per esperienza," ibid., 20); and Gherardo Gherardi, Luigi Bonelli, and Buzzichini (all in "Ancora sui giovani," *Comoedia* 13.4 [Apr. 15–May 15]: 17–18).

53. On Pavolini's career, see Arrigo Petacco, *Pavolini: L'ultima raffica di Salò* (Milan: A. Mondadori, 1982); and esp., Marco Palla, *Firenze nel regime fascista, 1929–1934* (Florence: Olschki, 1978), 171–230.

54. Palla cites the following testimony from Piero Calamandrei, who at the time was a student of Salvemini's: "It was the eyes of Alessandro Pavolini that were to remain indelibly impressed in my memory, amid the deafening uproar. At the time a law student, he stared at me silently with a gaze that communicated such acute hatred that I was transfixed as if by a reptile's eyes" (*Firenze nel regime fascista*, 174).

55. In *Critica Fascista*, see, e.g., Alessandro Pavolini, "Nostranità di Pirandello," *CF* 5.11 (June 1, 1927): 210–12. Pavolini's play *Le fatalone: Un atto tropicale* was published in *Comoedia* 11.3 (Mar. 15–Apr. 15, 1929): 47–49; *Giro d'Italia: Romanzo sportivo* was published in Foligno in 1928.

56. Palla, *Firenze nel regime fascista*, 180–81.

57. Alessandro Pavolini, "Rivoluzione di popolo," *Il Bargello*, June 12, 1932, 1.

58. Ojetti's criticisms did not stick. Reinhardt would go on to direct *The Merchant of Venice* in 1934 and Copeau was invited back to direct *Savonarola* and *As You Like It* at the Maggio Musicale festivals of 1935 and 1938 respectively. Reinhardt had been slated to produce a musical spectacle for the 1932 Los Angeles Olympic games and later, in 1934, presented his production of *A Midsummer Night's Dream* in the Hollywood Bowl, as the opening performance of the California Theater Festival.

59. "Importanza del Maggio," *Il Bargello*, Apr. 30, 1933, 1.

60. Ibid. The principal bones of contention were Sironi's designs for Donizetti's *Lucrezia Borgia* (directed by Guido Salvini) and the presence of Reinhardt and Copeau.

61. The Littoriali competitions were divided between "colloquia" (*convegni*) and "contests" (*concorsi*), the former requiring participation in a debate; the latter, the submission of a work. On this subject, see G. Silvano Spinetti, *Difesa di una generazione* (Rome: O.E.T. Polilibraria, 1948), 129–66. On the Littoriali in general, see Ugoberto Alfassio and Marina Addis Saba, *Cultura a passo romano: Storia e strategie dei Littoriali della cultura e dell'arte* (Milan: Feltrinelli,

1983); Giovanni Lazzari, *I Littoriali della cultura e dell'arte*; and Tracy H. Koon, *Believe, Obey, Fight: Political Socialization of Youth in Fascist Italy, 1922–1943* (Chapel Hill: Univ. of North Carolina Press, 1985), 202–7. Two detailed and sharply conflicting memoirs concerning them are Ruggero Zangrandi's classic *Il lungo viaggio attraverso il fascismo: Contributo alla storia di una generazione* (Milan: Feltrinelli, 1962), esp. 381–87; and Nino Tripodi, *Italia fascista in piedi!: Memorie di un Littore* (Milan: Le Edizioni del Borghese, 1961). However useful, many of these publications claim that the Lictorial games were antifascist breeding grounds, a view put forward by many Lictorial participants during the postwar period. Although true in part, this is at odds with much of the historical record. The entire matter needs to be reopened from a perspective that is neither motivated by the desire for self-apology (whether on the right or the left) nor founded on reductive definitions of fascist or antifascist ideology.

62. Achille Starace, letter to Mussolini, Mar. 19, 1935, in response to a proposal by Cesare Maria de Vecchi, head of the Ministry of Public Instruction, that the GUF and Littoriali be placed under the supervision of his ministry (Mussolini, personal papers, MF 815, Reel 230 #1222B), 9. Starace called this "the greatest problem haunting the revolution's future: that of youth, their education and political and military training" (ibid., 3).

63. I am indebted to Francesco Tentori for pointing out that the 1932 Littoriali hinged upon the connection between mass athletics and architecture.

64. Bragaglia's gloss on this reform is telling: "The inclusion of professional athletes within the Corporation of Spectacle bears out (even in a juridical sense) the coherence of the new theatrical genres that are now emerging in order to convey allegories and heroic fables" ("Lo spettacolo per masse," *La Vita Italiana* 22.256 [July 1934]: 69). But see also his "L'inquadra-mento degli sportivi fra i teatrali." It is essential to note that the linkage just described was upheld just as strongly on the revolutionary left as it was on the right: a case in point being Berthold Brecht's polemics in favor of an athletic theater during the 1920's.

65. Composed in 1931, prompted by Interlandi, Brancati's *L'urto* was published in *Quadrivio* 2.25 (Apr. 15, 1934): 1–4, accompanied by photomontages by Vinicio Paladini.

66. Alessandro Pavolini, "Cervelli in allenamento," *ILCA* 1 (Dec. 1933): 18.

67. "University youth is indeed fascist, but not in the way il Duce intended. I would describe them as fascist when considered as a mass, but they need to become an aristocracy of command" (Carlo Scorza, report, ACS, Segreteria Particolare del Duce, Carteggio Riservato, b. 31, fasc. 242r ["Riunione del direttorio 14 luglio 1931"], sottofasc. 2, 20).

68. The inquiry was launched in the March 1932 issue of *Il Saggiatore* and concluded with "Conclusions Concerning the Inquiry on the New Generation," *Il Saggiatore* 3.2 (Jan. 1933): 437–64, apparently authored by the review's editorial board members, Domenico Carella, Luigi de Crecchio, Giorgio Granata, and Nicola Perrotti.

69. The full questionnaire read as follows: "(1) Every new generation arises in conflict with that which preceded it. In the case of the present generation, is it possible to speak, not of this ordinary kind of conflict, but rather of a decisive and definitive gap? (2) Do you think that the new generation possesses a well-delineated spiritual vision that could bring a new spirit to culture and life? (3) What would you identify as the telltale signs of this complete spiritual renewal?" ("Quesiti sulla nuova generazione," *Il Saggiatore* 3.4 [June 1932]: 169). There have been several excellent studies of this, including Mario Sechi, *Il mito della nuova cultura: Giovani, realismo e politica*

*negli anni Trenta* (Manduria: Lacaita, 1984), esp. 147–213.

70. Summation by the editors, "Contributo per una nuova cultura," *Il Saggiatore* 4.6–8 (Aug.–Oct. 1933): 379. The contributors to this special issue included many of the leading lights of the period: Luciano Anceschi, Carlo Belli, Romano Bilenchi, Eurialo de Michelis, Mario Pannunzio, Francesco Pasinetti, Roberto Pavese, Berto Ricci, Alberto Sartoris, Elio Talarico, and Sigfrido Wolfango. On this subject, see Pasquale Voza, "Il problema del realismo negli anni Trenta: *Il Saggiatore, Il Cantiere*," *Lavoro Critico* 21–22 (Jan.–June, 1981): 65–105.

71. Filippo Burzio, "Personalità e collettivismo: Orientamenti pericolosi," *Corriere Padano*, May 1, 1934, 1.

72. The first phrase is from "Punti fermi sui giovani," PNF—Foglio d'ordini 64 (Jan. 20, 1930), quoted from *OO* 37.358. The second is from ibid., *OO* 37.359; emphasis added.

73. *Critica Fascista* had featured the "youth question" in its first 1930 issue, running Giuseppe Bottai's "Giovani e più giovani" on its lead page. Subsequent articles by Gian Paolo Callegari, Dionisio Colombini, Carlo Curcio, Cornelio di Marzio, Cesare Marroni, Domenico Montalto, Agostino Nasti, Sandro Volta, and, in 1931, Ugo Manunta, Domenico Rende, and Carlo Giglio, among others, continued the discussion.

74. Carlo Scorza, report dated July 11, 1931, in ACS, Segreteria Particolare del Duce, Carteggio Riservato, b. 31, fasc. 242r ("Riunione del direttorio 14 luglio 1931"), sottofasc. 2, 18.

75. Ibid., 20.

76. Ibid.

77. The full passage reads: "To give every individual not only the religious conscience and responsibility that derives from feeling as if one embodies the thought and even the Person of the Master (much like the Apostles), but also the luminous pride of participating in so glorious a mission. The Mussolini Myth equals LOYALTY-COURAGE-THOUGHT-LIGHT-BEAUTY-HEROISM-ETERNITY" (ibid., 22).

78. Starace to Mussolini, Mar. 19, 1935, 4; Mussolini, personal papers, MF 815, Reel 230 #1222B.

79. Alessandro Pavolini, "Fascisti giovani al lavoro: Lo spettacolo di masse," *Il Bargello*, Apr. 1, 1934, 1.

80. Giovanni Poli, national vice-secretary of the GUF, also appears to have sat in on these early meetings. The first evidence of Alessandro Blasetti's participation, however, is found in a letter from Venturini to Corrado Pavolini dated Feb. 5, 1934, requesting that the film director be alerted "not to miss the meeting concerning the mass spectacle scheduled for Thursday 8th at 9 P.M. at our federation" (BA, Littoriali letterhead). Sofia would later insist that Blasetti "was unaware of how the discussions took shape and was not present at any of the meetings. There wasn't even any talk about his possible participation" ("Il corago immaginario," *Quadrivio* 2.29 [May 13, 1934]: 2).

81. Alessandro Pavolini, "Fascisti giovani al lavoro," 1.

82. "We need engineers who build living quarters. We need engineers who build automobiles and tractors. But we need engineers just as much who build men's souls. You, writers, are engineers who are building men's souls!" (Joseph Stalin, speech to the newly formed Union of Soviet Writers, 1934, quoted in Gary Browning, *Boris Pilniak: Scythian at a Typewriter* [Ann Arbor, Mich.: Ardis, 1985], 65). Solzhenitsyn's observation is drawn from *The Gulag Archipelago*, trans. Thomas P. Whitney (New York: Harper & Row, 1973), 1: xii.

83. "Today a familiar device can offer us the infinitely vast and the infinitely minute, the voice of the individual and the howl of the mob, and that device is the radio" (Valentino Bom-

piani, "Invito editoriale al romanzo 'collettivo,'" *GdP* [Mar. 14, 1934]: 3). Following the publication of Bompiani's invitation, the debate on the collective novel raged for several months in the pages of the *Gazzetta del Popolo, Corriere della Sera, L'Ambrosiano* and *Quadrivio*, among other places. Participants included Massimo Bontempelli, Luigi Chiarini, and the young Alberto Moravia. On collectivism and 1930's fascist culture, see Ruth Ben-Ghiat, "The Formation of a Fascist Culture: The Realist Movement in Italy, 1930–43" (Ph.D. diss., Brandeis Univ., 1991), 210–18.

84. From a radio interview with Giulio Ginnasi, reprinted as "Dietro le quinte dei Littoriali di cultura e arte," *Il Bargello*, Mar. 25, 1934, 2.

85. In an article published late in 1933, Venturini appears to have been the first to merge the labels "theater of masses" and "theater for masses" into the single phrase that would appear subsequently on *18 BL*'s publicity posters: "Here then are some of the enormous advantages of a Theater of Propaganda, a Theater of Masses for Masses" (Giorgio Venturini, "Teatro d'oggi," *ILCA* 1 [Dec. 1933]: 38). "It is essential to recall that our revolution has imbued the people with new ideas and, God willing, a new spirit," he goes on. "In Italy we can and must do just this. Only then will we be able to say that we have resolved the [theater's] crisis. Let us push aside the endless criticisms and polemics, and go to work instead. It was Russia that first felt this need and developed a theater of propaganda and of masses: a theater that, after much hard work and sacrifice, has yielded truly magnificent results."

86. Berta, son of the owner of the Berta foundries, was slain for daring to appear in a black shirt before the population of San Frediano (Florence's traditional proletarian neighborhood) in the immediate wake of the fascists' cold-blooded murder of Spartaco Lavagnini, a communist leader and publisher. Long immortalized as a "martyr of the revolution" in fascist

myth and song—hence the presence in Room N of the 1932 Exhibition of the Fascist Revolution of the bridge from which he fell to his death—Berta would still be remembered in the central episode of Act 2 of the spectacle-to-be (as had been the case also of Bardi's *Sacra rappresentazione*), in which a solemn commemoration of the fascist dead is accompanied by the singing of "They Have Murdered Giovanni Berta," a ballad promising faith in Mussolini and the defeat of Lenin. For the lyrics to this song, see *Canti dell'Italia fascista, 1919–1945*, ed. A. V. Savona and M. L. Straniero (Milan: Garzanti, 1979), 89.

87. Although Pavolini had long been engaged in myth-making around this truck, the immediate source for this idea may have been an article by Blasetti's friend, Leo Bomba, which appeared in the midst of *L'Italia Vivente*'s campaign for a revolutionary fascist theater. Bomba, a fascist squadrist, had fondly recalled and, indeed, humanized the trucks of the revolutionary squadrons: "I don't remember who it was that proposed that a truck be placed in one of the rooms of the Exhibition of the Fascist Revolution. Whoever he was, he was surely a squadrist. For it is impossible to divorce the recollection of our past from this fast and noisy hulk that, for us, was never just a means of transportation" ("Il vecchio camion," *LIV* 3.18 [Oct. 28, 1933]: 6–7). This article seems to have provoked Bardi's "Camion veterani," which appeared less than a week later in *Il Lavoro Fascista*, Nov. 2, 1933, 3.

88. On the Camion theater, see Edoardo Fadini and Carlo Quartacci, *Viaggio nel Camion dentro l'avanguardia ovvero la lunga cinematografia teatrale, 1960/1976* (Turin: Cooperativa Editoriale Studio Forma, 1976). Tom Wolfe's *The Electric Kool-Aid Acid Test* was first published by Farrar, Straus & Giroux in 1968.

89. "They plod forward slowly, hunched over, but do not quit. They hold to the road with dignity. They are the disinherited, the proletarians,

**203**

the poor of the world of automobiles" (Bardi, "Camion veterani"). The myth of the "proletarian nation" was, of course, one of Enrico Corradini's key contributions to fascist discourse.

90. The entire passage reads as follows: "*The subject?* Anonymous: a truck during the war, the revolution, and the reconstruction of our Italy. *Who are the authors?* Anonymous: a group of youths, authentic youths, who sat around a table one night and discussing the mass theater came up with a bunch of ideas and names—the Rubicon . . . the Legionnaire . . . Caesar Augustus . . . the Victory. But they gave birth instead to a humble truck: a hero that gained the sympathy of all right from the start. It was the idea of everyone, and was discussed, written up, and approved by all. *Who are the creators?* They too are anonymous: all Italian soldiers, all fascist squadrists, all the youth of the new Italy—in short, Mussolini's entire people" (Ginnasi, "Dietro le quinte dei Littoriali").

91. See, for instance, Sironi's multiple versions of *The Truck* (1919, 1920); his 1919 collage *The Yellow Truck* (in which the words of Marinetti's *Zang Tumb Tuuum* can be read against the truck's side panels); his various urban landscapes with trucks from the 1920–23 period; and his *Great Panel with Trucks* (Fiat Pavilion, International Exposition, Paris, 1937). Sironi's famous urban landscapes from the early 1920's feature trucks precisely inasmuch as the landscapes in question are usually transitional spaces on the city's industrial edge, with the truck serving as an iconographic hinge to outlying rural spaces.

92. Alessandro Pavolini, "2 Mostre del Fascismo" *Il Bargello*, May 15, 19932, 1; emphasis added.

93. Ibid.

94. The full text reads: "Filmmakers, men of the theater, strive to understand the aesthetic [consequences] of these great events. Painters, con-

sider not only that the physiognomy of the countryside and of its crops [*culture*] is changing, but also that the meaning of these crops [*culture*] is changing. A lucid and passionate impulse and inspiration animates them. As for writers, we await an Oriani who will dedicate pages of an epic timbre to the *bonifica integrale*, to the entire agricultural battle fought by fascism, just like those in [Oriani's] *Lotta politica* that recount the building of the Italian railway system: that rare gesture of accelerated courage and constructive energy on the part of nineteenth-century Italy, the closing act of the Risorgimento, our unitary revolution" (ibid.).

95. Vasco Patti, "La visita del Duce all'Agro Pontino," *La Conquista della Terra* 3.4 (Apr. 1932): 10.

96. Ibid.

97. Ibid.

98. "During the penultimate meeting, several of us were asked to develop portions of the plot that had been elaborated collectively. At the final get-together, these scripts and drafts were read aloud, modified, and then, as clearly and explicitly requested by the Honorable Alessandro Pavolini, they were handed over to the director, whose responsibility it was to draft (and draft he did) a definitive script bearing all of the modifications he felt to be essential" (Corrado Sofia, "Il parere di uno degli autori: TRADIMENTO!" *Quadrivio*, May 6, 1934, 3). In his tirade against collective authorship, Sofia subsequently claims that he produced a full screenplay of his own, even though the script preserved in the BA contains only five of the nine tableaux referred to in its title *18 BL: Mistero in 9 quadri*.

99. Many decades later, Blasetti would assert that Mussolini had personally chosen him to direct the spectacle: "[Mussolini] imagined a show for a crowd of 20,000 spectators and he wanted me to direct it. I made a show called *18 BL*, the name of a truck. . . . It was the biggest

fiasco in the history of international theater. This was . . . the only time Blasetti received the congratulations of Mussolini. . . . He said: 'This has demonstrated a power of initiative, of force, of resistance, of steadfastness. Extraordinary" (quoted in Elaine Mancini, *Struggles of the Italian Film Industry During Fascism, 1930–35* [Ann Arbor, Mich.: UMI Research Press, 1985], 113). Since Blasetti somewhat distorts Mussolini's concept of mass theater and omits any mention of the other occasions on which il Duce had intervened in his favor, there are reasons to doubt this claim. Archival records indicate that it was Pavolini who organized *18 BL* and made the key personnel decisions. (Mussolini was, no doubt, kept informed about plans for the Littoriali through Poli, but his relative disengagement is attested to by his decision not to attend the performance of *18 BL*.) Pavolini elected to involve Blasetti only in late January 1934 when the compositional process had long been under way.

100. All the scripts seem to have been preserved in the BA, if one can rely upon Gherardi's account: "[Blasetti] consulted four, five, or six scripts. He tried to fuse them together" (Gherardo Gherardi, "Difendo Blasetti," *Il Resto di Carlino*, May 26, 1934, 3). The authors are de Feo, Lisi, Melani, Sofia, and Venturini—the latter two serving as Blasetti's principal source texts. (Another fragment may have been composed by Bonelli, although the extant copy is in Blasetti's hand.) The exact degree to which Blasetti took it upon himself to introduce thematic elements from his prior films into the final screenplay is hard to determine, since the authorial collective was familiar with most of his films (*1860* in particular) and Pavolini had selected him as director back in January 1934, with the result that some of the scripts already seem to contain Blasettian motifs. This much, however, is certain: the key additions and modifications of the various scripts resulted from the practicalities of staging *18 BL*. "The script

was manipulated and modified by him, according to the results of his experiments in the early phases of the production" (Pavolini, "Fascisti giovani al lavoro," 1). Despite his later complaints that Blasetti had "chopped up" his work, Sofia concurs: "Blasetti . . . drafted the definitive script, which included all those changes he felt were warranted given the practical demands of the production" (Corrado Sofia, "Nel clima dei giovani: Il teatro di masse," *Il Lavoro Fascista* [Apr. 28, 1934]: 3).

101. The quotations are from Alberto Boero's first screenplay as reproduced in *Sole: Soggetto, sceneggiatura, note per la realizzazione*, ed. Adriano Aprà and Riccardo Redi (Rome: Di Giacomo, 1985), 27.

102. "The temptation to rely upon a kind of emblematic German-style heroism, present in *Terra madre* even in the names of the protagonists (the Duke, Emilia), is transformed into the individuation of the group. The collectivity appears through the interplay between a protagonist-guide (almost a figure of the spectator himself) and the towering figure of a Garibaldi who is so distantly portrayed against immense fields of Quarto and so fully absent in the course of the battle of Calatafimi that he can appear as the true Father: a dictator because of his actual absence and virtual presence, a vocal presence more than a bodily one" (Adriano Aprà, introduction to Alessandro Blasetti, *Scritti sul cinema* [Venice: Marsilio, 1982], 22). The most recent English discussions of *1860* are Angela dalle Vacche's in *The Body in the Mirror: Shapes of History in Italian Cinema* (Princeton: Princeton Univ. Press, 1992), 96–120, and Marcia Landy's, *Fascism in Film: The Italian Commercial Cinema, 1931–1943* (Princeton: Princeton Univ. Press, 1986), 183–87. But see also Mancini, *Struggles of the Italian Film Industry*, 108–13.

103. Filippo Sacchi, review of *18 BL*, in *Corriere della Sera*, Mar. 30, 1934, quoted in Aprà, introduction to Blasetti, *Scritti sul cinema*, 23. Other

**205**

connections between *18 BL* and *1860* include the nearly identical opening battle scene, the constant recourse to chiaroscuro, the use of sloped hilltops as stages, the equestrian portrayals of Garibaldi, the theme of regional and class collaboration in the forging of the Italian nation, and the use of roll calls.

104. On the filming of *Camicia nera*, see Giovacchino Forzano, *Come li ho conosciuti* (Turin: Edizioni della Radio, 1957), 102–8.

105. The enterprise was carried out with the assistance of the city and the military: "Workers recruited from among the rolls of unemployed fascists excavate the immense stage, altering the profile of the hills, completing roads, working side by side with workers and machinery from the Comune of Florence. On this occasion, the Comune leaders and offices have offered us a consummate example of how an extremely up-to-date mentality now pervades local government. Likewise, the military authorities have provided their always cordial cooperation and understanding, assisting in a thousand ways, making available backhoes for the excavations, photoelectric equipment, machine guns, artillery batteries, and a great deal of additional human and mechanical matériel" (Pavolini, "Fascisti giovani al lavoro," 1). Pavolini's claim that the authorities were cooperative is belied by numerous documents in the BA indicating Blasetti's despair at their slowness and incompetence, on which subject, see Appendix D.

106. "Early on [Blasetti] had thought of building a new kind of theater, based on an inversion of the shape of Greco-Roman theaters, with the audience seated in the middle and with a circular stage extending around on all sides" (Giuseppe Isani, "Nascita d'uno spettacolo," *LIL*, Mar. 18, 1934, 4). This proved impossible "for the obvious practical reasons: the problem of locating an appropriate crater-shaped site that could accommodate the public down below and a stage up above, time restric-

tions, etc." (ibid.). Isani also mentions an even earlier project (put forward by Sofia): "At one time . . . a stage was envisaged that would be made up of two large planar components, one fixed and the other mounted on wheel-tracks and, therefore, movable against the backdrop. The idea was rejected because, in point of fact, it was too much like the stages found in conventional theaters." Ibid.

107. Other sites were considered as well: "The shore of the Anconella that lies upstream from the city was considered for a time. But, soon thereafter, the Albereta of the Isolotto was chosen. In both cases the architectural possibilities offered by a riverside site were crucial factors. The theater would face the silence and tranquillity of the river Arno; at its back there would loom the sweet grassy expanses of the Tuscan countryside" (B. F., "Esperimento di teatro per ventimila persone: Rombante epopea del *18 BL*," *CdS*, Apr. 20, 1934, 5).

108. "A 250-meter-wide hillside was employed as a stage; another, almost entirely artificial, across from the first and alongside the riverbank, was used as an auditorium. Between the two lay a deep gully that performed various functions: orchestra pit, supply area, prompter's box, and director's cabin" (Cipriano Giachetti, "Il teatro ai Littoriali di Firenze," *Comoedia* 16.6 [June 1934]: 8).

109. Romain Rolland, *The People's Theater*, trans. I. H. Clark (New York: Holt, 1918), 108.

110. Gherardo Gherardi's estimate is even larger: "The stagefront was 200 meters long and 300 meters deep" ("Difendo Blasetti").

111. "The fine telephone engineers of the Seventh Corps set up twenty fully interconnected telephone lines in order to link up the ten projector emplacements and to facilitate their coordinated movements; a group from the Nineteenth Field Artillery Corps provided the equipment" (Ruggero Orlando, "Che cos'è '18 BL,'" *La Tribuna*, Apr. 20, 1934, 3). Blasetti's

stage drawings indicate that the network switchboard was located at position 1 (figs. 31–33) in the gulf between the stadium and the stage.

112. Blasetti, "Prime considerazioni e proposte dopo i primi esperimenti: Tempi della rappresentazione" (BA, typescript; Mar. 1934). Cf. "The lights projected across from the audience will have the function of lowering a sort of curtain over one part or another of the spectacle. Selected zones will be illuminated as the action unfolds in such a way as to allow the careful preparation of successive scenes on the darkened portions of the stage without the audience's knowledge" (C[ipriano] G[iachetti], "I preparativi del teatro di masse: Alessandro Blasetti all'opera," LN, Apr. 12, 1934, 5).

113. "Three fundamental points have been deemed essential: (1) the audience in attendance must be seated below the level of the stage; (2) the action must unfold upon an elevated platform, such that figures and objects appear cut out against the sky, appearing and disappearing in perspective; (3) the field of action must be enormously vast, so as to allow the grouping of scenes by means of lighting and so that the succession of scenes is distributed over a succession of locales" ("Per lo spettacolo di masse," Il Bargello, Mar. 4, 1934, 3). Much of the post-performance polemic would hinge on the links to Eisenstein. "Blasetti wanted all figures to be profiled against the sky. In so doing, he adopted the usual Eisensteinian trick of presenting everything from the bottom up, treating the audience just like those geese that inspired Eisenstein's now completely dated cinematographic style. The result was that the spectators saw little and heard even less" (Sofia, "Il parere di uno degli otto autori," 7).

114. Adolph Appia, "Comments on the Theatre," in Adolph Appia: Essays, Scenarios, and Designs, trans. Walter R. Volbach, ed. Richard C. Beacham (Ann Arbor, Mich.: UMI Research Press, 1989), 181–82.

115. Some ten lighting sketches are preserved in the BA. In addition to his directorial commitments, Blasetti faced enormous difficulties in getting various authorities to deliver the promised lighting equipment. On March 14, he wrote to Giovanni Poli noting that the Comune was unable to furnish the needed searchlights. On March 22, he was still pleading for help: "First, the medium-range lights still haven't reached the performance site and nobody seems to know when they will arrive. Second, of the six military (photoelectric) searchlights that were requested, the local engineering corps can only furnish me with two. A third is available, but there is no one to man it. As for the remaining three, which are absolutely essential, they appear nonexistent" (BA, Blasetti to Poli, protocol #39). The problems were solved thanks to help from the Cines company and from other sectors of the army.

116. "Sound effects will be achieved by switching back and forth between extended silences and powerful noises like the shouting of crowds and the din of machinery" (Isani, "Nascita d'uno spettacolo di masse," 4).

117. "Among the many difficulties, there is also this one: that all these men, soldiers, and youth have to work in absolute silence because there are microphones planted everywhere. The spectacle can succeed if the noises that are heard—there is an abundance of them already—are limited to those that are strictly necessary and intended" (Ruggero Orlando, "Prove di 18 BL," La Tribuna, Apr. 26, 1934, 3).

118. In an unsigned article published several days before the spectacle, Sofia had already expressed reservations and noted the alternatives Blasetti had rejected: "The music and choruses have been recorded on records and will be transmitted over a loudspeaker system. It is hard to foresee the results that will be obtained

**207**

by means of this novel theatrical and musical device. Corrado Sofia, one of the creators of this 'mystery play,' had proposed an alternate solution to the many difficulties posed by such a large audience. He had wanted to 'normalize' the higher pitched voices and to assign to newspaper sellers the role of commenting upon the scenic action, much like the chorus in an ancient Greek tragedy. A town crier would have announced events of capital importance. In allegorical and satirical scenes, like the parliamentary banquet of Act 2, the actors would have addressed the audience through megaphones. During the rest of the play, there would have been live choruses and voices allowing for the direct expression either of the distance separating diverse groups of actors or of the spiritual elation of the person crying out. The plot was conceived of and developed with the performance site in mind. Nonetheless, the director chose instead to transmit even the choruses over loudspeakers by means of recordings. Should these mechanical means permit him to obtain the same emotional resonance that would have resulted from recourse to actual human voices and song, he will have established a remarkable precedent that could be followed in subsequent performances" ("Nel clima dei giovani: Il teatro di masse," 3).

119. In his notes, Blasetti would write: "Choruses, various noises, voices, the marching of military columns, music, etc. must all be recorded and transmitted over loudspeakers. This because: (1) The already difficult work of preparing the spectacle will be eased by eliminating the need to rehearse the choruses[;] (2) On the evening of the performance, the requisite sound effects can be achieved with absolute certainty by adjusting the level of amplification. Missed notes, miscues, tonal mistakes, etc. will be eliminated[;] (3) Because this will make it possible to create highly effective and shifting sonic landscapes[;] (4) Because this will alleviate the crowding of masses and ma-

chines on a stage that is already overloaded with linguistic problems" (BA, "Prime considerazioni e proposte dopo i primi esperimenti: Parte Sonora," 2).

120. "Blasetti . . . had a special loudspeaker system built. Distributed along the sides of the auditorium to considerable effect, they will transmit, much as happens in a cinema, artificially produced noises. By this means it will be possible to hear the actions of machines and the mob's cries on different sonic planes but at the same time" (Isani, "Nascita," 4).

121. Sergio Codelupi, "Un teatro per ventimila persone a Firenze," *Il Telegrafo*, Apr. 1, 1934, 7.

122. "His words [i.e., those of Ceseri] and those of the small number of companions who will be responding to him, will be faithfully picked up by microphones and amplified irrespective of where they are spoken on stage. When necessary, his voice will be more powerful than that of a cannon" (Orio Vergani, "L'elogio di Starace agli organizzatori e ai vincitori dei Littoriali: Stasera il *18 BL* rivivrà la sua eroica epopea—Prove col megafono," *CdS*, Apr. 29, 1934, 3).

123. The phrase is employed by "B. F." in "Esperimento di teatro per ventimila persone": "Against that backdrop it is truly poetic that the snippets of dialogue should take on an unusual grandeur over the loudspeakers, thanks to a kind of vocal gigantism. The cries, the phrases want to be enormously real, supremely symbolic, because in *18 BL* the individual speaks and acts for an entire people."

124. Orlando, "Prove." The political meaning of such an arrangement had been understood at least since Rolland: "The essential point is that all seats be equally good. . . . Nor shall we achieve true brotherhood among men or develop any truly universal art until we have done away with the stupid system of orchestra seats and boxes, and the resultant antagonism be-

tween classes" (Rolland, *People's Theater*, 107–8).

125. Orlando, "Prove."

126. As far as I am aware, there is no detailed record of who was in the audience. Giulio Bucciolini claims that "all of intellectual, thinking, working Florence gathered together at the experiment organized by Italy's youths" ("Felice realizzazione del primo esperimento del teatro di masse: Cronaca della serata," *Il Nuovo Giornale*, Apr. 30, 1934, 11). Others note the presence of the *podestà* and prefect of Florence, Renato Ricci (undersecretary for physical and youth education), Giacomo Paulucci di Calboli (president of the Istituto LUCE), and Arturo Marpicati (vice-secretary of the PNF). As for writers and critics, Guido Piovene mentions the presence of "a large number of directors and critics from every nation" ("Dalla gloria della trincea al tempo di Mussolini: Lo spettacolo di masse a Firenze con duemila attori e ventimila spettatori," *L'Ambrosiano*, Apr. 30, 1934, 1). An anonymous article in *La Nazione* claims that "all of Italy's theater critics, as well as 25 correspondents from European and North American newspapers will be present at the show" ("I Littoriali della Cultura e dell'Arte," Apr. 19, 1934, 5). The notice is correct, since there exist several foreign eyewitness accounts of *18 BL*, including that in de Weerth's "Italy Outdoors: Open-air Theatre Performances," 374.

127. As noted above, the original plans were for a double boat bridge, as indicated in Mannucci and Tempestini's drawings and in documents contained in the BA. As late as March 22, Blasetti had begged Poli: "The Engineering Corps tells me that it has 40 meters worth of boats available, when 105 are needed for even a single bridge. You are well aware, as indicated in your quite accurate reflections concerning the difficulties of ensuring access for the public, that my request for a double boat bridge is well founded. Rome thus needs to issue an order for the immediate departure (ei-

ther from Piacenza or Verona) of the personnel and materials necessary for building 200 meters of bridges made up of yoked-together boats" (BA, Blasetti to Poli, protocol #39, 1). The dearth of boats ensured the adoption of a single bridge solution.

128. Giachetti, "La rappresentazione del '18 BL' ha luogo stasera," 5. It is worth noting that, however novel, the boat bridge harkened back to numerous early modern precedents, the river Arno having occasionally been employed as a stage from the time of Giovanni Villani through Alessandro Adimari, who, during the reign of Grand Duke Cosimo II (1609–21), recreated the stories of Hero and Leander, and of the seizure of the Golden Fleece at Colchis.

## CHAPTER 4

1. Pavolini to Blasetti, postcard, dated Apr. 11, 1934, BA.

2. Anon., "Fatti e argomenti," *Il Cantiere: Settimanale di Cultura Politica* 1.7 (Apr. 14, 1934): 1.

3. This information was diffused via numerous newspapers, including *Il Popolo d'Italia* and *La Nazione* (see the Apr. 13, 1934 issue).

4. "I Littoriali di Cultura e d'Arte: Concorsi per soggetti di spettacoli di masse," *Il Nuovo Giornale*, Apr. 13, 1934, 4.

5. Ibid.

6. Alessandro Pavolini, "Fascisti giovani al lavoro: Lo spettacolo di masse," *Il Bargello*, Apr. 1, 1934, 3. Cf. Blasetti: "It is to be hoped that this mass theater will become a school for shaping the young directors of tomorrow, who will have to ensure its vitality and continuation" (quoted in Cipriano G[iachetti], "I preparativi del teatro di masse: Alessandro Blasetti all'opera," *LN*, Apr. 12, 1934, 5). Sofia would later accuse Blasetti of having aspired to a state pension: "The fact of the matter is that Blasetti was yearning for a state pension, thinking that he had ensured for himself the permanent di-

rectorship of this theater" (Corrado Sofia, "Il corago immaginario," *Quadrivio* 2.29 [May 13, 1934]: 2).

7. Cipriano Giachetti, "La rappresentazione del *18 BL* ha luogo stasera," *LN*, Apr. 29–30, 1934, 5.

8. The full passage from Marcello Gallian's sometimes mocking description reads: "But as soon as one reached the river's edge, an unheard-of spectacle greeted the eye: ladies dressed to the nines, wearing dancing shoes, young [*sic*] and delicate furs, and gold and silver baubles, marched in single file across a boat bridge extending from one bank to the other. The legendary audience of opening nights [at the opera], appareled in its usual manner, but heading out into the open fields under a sky enshrouded in darkness" ("Una notte d'aprile," *Quadrivio*, May 6, 1934, 3).

9. The two best descriptions of the pre-spectacle spectacle are those of Guido Piovene ("Dalla gloria della trincea al tempo di Mussolini: Lo spettacolo di masse a Firenze con duemila attori e ventimila spettatori," *L'Ambrosiano*, Apr. 30, 1934, 1) and Gallian ("Una notte d'aprile"). All accounts emphasize the audience's sense that it was participating in a mass rally.

10. Raffaello Franchi, "*18 BL* spettacolo di masse," *LIL*, May 6, 1934, 1. The point is repeated by Piovene in "Dalla gloria della trincea al tempo di Mussolini," 1: "The audience felt that it was the protagonist, the protagonist of an event dear to the heart of all Italians and of solemn significance."

11. Maximilien de Robespierre, "Man Is the Greatest Object," quoted in Frederick Brown, *Theater and Revolution: The Culture of the French Stage* (New York: Viking, 1980), 76.

12. The opening movement of *Squilli e danze per il 18 BL* is designated as *solenne*, consisting of a series of trumpet calls accompanied by tam-tams and slow drumming. Massarani's

score was published in 1937 by Edizioni G. Ricordi in Milan. A transcription for bands was produced by Salvatore Pappalardo and published by Ricordi in 1938.

13. This opening scene must have been nearly identical to the opening scene of *1860*, with its crosscut scenes of cavalry, ruined buildings, running figures, and blazing fires.

14. In Blasetti's script, published as "*18 BL*: Spettacolo di masse per il popolo," *Gioventù Fascista* 4.8 (Apr. 15, 1934): 12–14, the truck was named Mother *Glory* (Mamma *Gloria*) and not Mother *Cartridge-Pouch* (Mamma *Giberna*). Some time in April, Blasetti must have decided to switch to the latter name, which is not found in any of the scripts in BA.

15. Alessandro Blasetti, "Prime considerazioni e proposte: Tempi della rappresentazione," 1, BA.

16. Cited from the second part of Corrado Sofia's typescript entitled "Mistero in 9 quadri," in BA. Sofia was the principal author of Act 2, scenes 2 and 3, and seems to have selected most of the songs.

17. Blasetti, "*18 BL*: Spettacolo di masse per il popolo," 13.

18. On Littoria, see Tommaso Stabile, *Latina una volta Littoria: Storia di una città* (Latina: Arti Grafiche Archivio, 1982), and Silvana Cardosi, "Il mito di Littoria durante il Fascismo" (diss., Magistero Maria SS. Annunziata, Rome, 1973). On the fascist new towns, see Diane Ghirardo, *Building New Communities: New Deal and Fascist Italy* (Princeton: Princeton Univ. Press, 1989), and Riccardo Mariani, *Fascismo e "città nuove"* (Milan: Feltrinelli, 1976).

19. The original plan was for two entire air squadrons to overfly the crowd. For reasons that may have to do with the one-week postponement of the performance, these two squadrons were reduced, according to some accounts, to a few airplanes; according to

others, to a single one: "Vasco Magrini's airplane—the only one that appeared, despite the two squadrons that had been promised—performed three extremely brief laps around the stadium. Young fascists then began moving about the audience announcing Mussolini's seizure of power while distributing copies of the October 28, 1922, issue of *Il Popolo d'Italia*" (Giuseppe Longo, "*18 BL* a Firenze: Non è nato il teatro di masse," *Gazzetta di Messina*, May 4, 1934, 3). The original plan had been described in Blasetti's notes as follows: "Crisscrossed by the multicolored beams of the searchlights, the airplanes will drop broadsheets from *Il Popolo d'Italia*. . . . After they have flown over the audience for the proper amount of time, they will vanish to the right and left sides of the auditorium. When they are far enough removed, the auditorium lights go off and, accompanied by a lively orchestral prelude, the stage lights illumine the athletes who mark the beginning of the third act or moment of the spectacle" ("Prime considerazioni," 2, BA).

20. Another element borrowed from Blasetti's film *Sole*.

21. Blasetti, "*18 BL*: Spettacolo di masse per il popolo," 14.

22. Ibid.

23. "A hilltop pushes forward against the horizon all lit up in the ode of dazzling transfigurations or of Moses's head" (Gallian, "Una notte d'aprile," 4).

24. Blasetti, "*18 BL*: Spettacolo di masse per il popolo," 14. This messianic portrayal of Mother Cartridge-Pouch relies upon the christomimetic components that make up the cult of the Virgin Mary.

## CHAPTER 5

1. As noted later, 1930's culture in Italy, whether fascist, apolitical, or antifascist, was deeply haunted by the sense that the future of art would hinge upon the resurgence of myth. In the words of Massimo Bontempelli: "The most urgent task to be undertaken by our art is the creation of new myths" (*L'avventura novecentista* [Florence: Vallecchi, 1974], 261). *18 BL*'s commitment to forging a modern revolutionary myth was thus part of a mainstream that included everything from the magic realism of Bontempelli to the metaphysical paintings of de Chirico and Savinio.

2. Cipriano G[iachetti], "I preparativi del teatro di masse: Alessandro Blasetti all'opera," *LN*, Apr. 12, 1934, 5.

3. Ibid.; the statement is again Blasetti's.

4. Corrado Sofia, "Verso i Littoriali della Cultura: Teatro di masse, *18 BL*," *La Stampa*, Feb. 21, 1934, 3. Sofia had made a parallel argument a month earlier in "Cultura e sport nella rivoluzione fascista," *CF* 12.2 (Jan. 15, 1934): 21–23.

5. On this subject, see Philip Cannistraro, *La fabbrica del consenso: Fascismo e mass media* (Bari: Laterza, 1975), 273–322, as well as his essay "Cultural Funding and Public Taste: The Case of Film in Fascist Italy," *Essays in Arts and Sciences* 12.2 (May 1983): 17–46. An interesting period document by Giuseppe Domenico Musso, entitled *Le possibilità della cinematografia come mezzo di propaganda e di educazione* (Rome: Luzzetti, 1932), puts forward a complete program for the use of the medium as a political tool, via the Michetti projector: a projector combining a record player (for the playing of "hymns, marches, and nationalist songs" [11]) and a radio (for the broadcast of Mussolini's speeches [ibid.]).

6. "By 1937 the OND reported a well-developed traveling cinema consisting of thirty-eight film trucks equipped for silent films and fifty-six with sound projectors. Its urban network, which was comprised of 334 permanent theaters and 288 summer movie programs with a total of 170,856 seats (1937), supplemented the commercial networks by offering what were for the

most part weekend or holiday showings" (Victoria de Grazia, *The Culture of Consent: Mass Organization of Leisure in Fascist Italy* [New York: Cambridge Univ. Press, 1981], 160).

7. The connection is made by Cipriano Giachetti: "Here nature's harmonious backdrop of hillsides already furnished an ideal setting and the Fortuny cupola was replaced by a truer and greater dome: that of the heavens ("La rappresentazione del *18 BL* ha luogo stasera," *LN*, Apr. 29–30, 1934, 5).

8. In a contemporary debate, Anton Giulio Bragaglia had defined the paucity of words (and their mechanical transmission) as the defining attributes of the new mass theater: "Blasetti himself told me that the number of words required for his staging will not be large. And they will probably be transmitted in part over loudspeakers, as a result of which even the remaining vestiges of the [traditional] theater will be transformed into mechanical representations. Besides which, we are well aware of the difference between mechanical and material words. This verbal 'deficiency' will become the defining and animating feature, as well as the good fortune of the spectacle for 20,000 (since even movies share the same verbal proportions as the theater of words). Given the 20,000 to 30,000 words employed in conventional theater works, this deficiency will make the mass spectacle unrecognizable with respect to what we now refer to as 'theater'" ("La parola nel teatro 'per ventimila,' *Il Giornale d'Italia*, Apr. 28, 1934, 3).

9. Earlier in the same essay, Sofia writes: "No stage, no stars, no dialogues contained within the three standard cardboard walls. Not that the conventional theater ought to vanish entirely, for it has long been in need of a revolution. But our hope is that the passions unleashed by the new theater will be felt as much by the masses of spectators as by the young actors on stage. Then there will be no gap between the one and the other" (Sofia, "Verso i Littoriali della Cultura," 3).

10. "The Mass Theater . . . aspires to become an exalted form of propaganda and [expression] of the collective interest, a means of raising up the mass of spectators to partake of unmediated sensations and meanings, the fusion of thousands and thousands of souls within a single framework of ideas and events" (Ruggero Orlando, "Prove di *18 BL*," *La Tribuna*, Apr. 26, 1934, 3).

11. The full passage reads: "Where the rational conventions that governed polite theater (or what has come to be known as 'the closed stage') maintained, however gauzily, a barrier between actor and role, between audience and dramatis personae, between language and nature, with perspective lines theoretically vouchsafing the king an absolute viewpoint, the Terrorist festival laid low that barrier, sanctifying the mass of its celebrants, the collective body, or the universal *presence* that had no need to look beyond itself" (Frederick Brown, *Theater and Revolution: The Culture of the French Stage* [New York: Viking, 1980], 77).

12. Given that Johst had since the early 1920's been promoting the cause of a cultic popular theater, and given the important leftist models developed by Piscator, Toller, and Brecht, it is difficult to establish the precise degree to which *18 BL* or Italian debates on the mass theater might have shaped the *Thingspiele* movement, officially sanctioned in January 1934 when the Reichsdrammaturg Rainer Schlößer defined the genre's fundamental features in his speech on "The Coming Folk Spectacle" ("Von kommenden Volksschauspiel"). The enterprise found early support in Joseph Goebbels's Ministry of Propaganda and Enlightenment. Some 40 authors contributed to the genre, the most important, perhaps, being Kurt Eggers and Eberhard Wolfgang Möller, who together produced some fourteen works. The *Thing* plays— the archaism *Thing* refers to the open-air gath-

ering places of archaic Teutons—and *Thing* theaters underwent rapid diffusion throughout Germany from around the time of *18 BL* through 1937, when they lost Goebbels's support. To judge by *Thingspiele* preserved on film (such as Kurt Heynicke's *Der Weg ins Reich* and *Neurode*), and by numerous textual remains, their effort to recreate historical events, ancient Teutonic rites, or Nazi ceremonials involved the elaborate use of choral chants and masses of actors, in settings that were always rather explicitly liturgical. Like Italian aspirations to forge a genuine fascist theater, they died out because of the absence of an adequate repertory, despite active efforts on the part of the Nazi regime (at least through 1937). On this topic, see George Mosse's seminal *The Nationalization of the Masses: Political Symbolism and Mass Movements in Germany from the Napoleonic Wars Through the Third Reich* (New York: New American Library, 1977), esp. 113–18; Henning Eichberg, Michael Dultz, Glen Gadberry, and Günther Rühle, *Massenspiele: NS-Thingspiel, Arbeitweihespiel und olympisches Zeremoniell*, Problemata 58 (Stuttgart–Bad Cannstatt: Frommann-Holzbuog, 1977); and Johannes M. Reichl, *Das Thingspiel: Über den Versuch eines nationalsozialistischen Lehrstuck-Theaters (Euringer–Heynicke–Möller)* (Frankfurt am Main: Mißlbeck, 1988). For full bibliography, see Eichberg et al., *Massenspiele*, 22–26 (a listing of the entire repertory of known *Thingspiele*), 252–64; Reichl, *Das Thingspiel*, 123–28.

13. These writings appear in Bontempelli's *L'avventura novecentista* under the rubrics "Il vecchio spettacolo" (223–69) and "Il nuovo spettacolo" (270–94). It goes without saying that *historical* precedents were also invoked by *18 BL*'s creators and critics. Sofia, for instance, does not hesitate to call the work a "sacred representation," akin to a medieval mystery play: "We are attempting to create a *sacred pageant* [*sacra rappresentazione*] with modern means,

lights, machines, and radios, with the objective of bringing back into theaters the people's passion, kindled by its political faith" ("Verso i Littoriali della Cultura," 3; emphasis added). Insisting on the novelty of *18 BL*, Alessandro Pavolini rejected all links to ancient Roman and renaissance pageantry, insisting instead that there was only one sufficiently worthy predecessor: the "great theater of the ancient Greeks" ("Fascisti giovani al lavoro: Lo spettacolo di masse," *Il Bargello*, Apr. 1, 1934, 3).

14. Guido Piovene, "Dalla gloria della trincea al tempo di Mussolini: Lo spettacolo di masse a Firenze con duemila attori e ventimila spettatori," *L'Ambrosiano*, Apr. 30, 1934, 1.

15. Guido Salvini, "Spettacoli di masse e *18 BL*," *Scenario* 3.5 (May 1934): 254.

16. Cipriano Giachetti, "Il *18 BL*," *LN*, May 1, 1934, 5.

17. Enrico Rocca, "Ventimila persone assistono a Firenze alla prima rappresentazione del *18 BL*," *Il Lavoro Fascista*, May 1, 1934, 1.

18. Bontempelli, *L'avventura novecentista*, 265 (the article originally appeared as "Il *18 BL* rappresentato a Firenze," *GdP*, Apr. 30, 1934, 3). Bontempelli's anguish is surely a function of the close connection between *18 BL* and his theses regarding the new theater.

19. Luigi Chiarini, "*18 BL*," *Quadrivio* 2.28 (May 6, 1934): 3. Chiarini later adds: "Last Sunday it was impossible for *18 BL*'s audience not to sense the spectacle's poverty and what one is tempted to call its 'insubstantiality.' All men who fought in the war and directly experienced its monstrous tragedies, all men who participated in the heroic struggles of fascist squadrism and in the March on Rome, who have seen with their own eyes the miracles of Littoria and Sabaudia, couldn't avoid the sense of poverty that permeated the realistic reconstruction of these events. Anyone who has participated in fascism's imposing rallies and seen Italy's new and generous youth in the nation's

streets, stadiums, and athletic fields; anyone, that is, who has taken in the moving everyday spectacles resulting from [Italy's] remarkable collective life and who is deeply aware of the masses' enthusiasm and fervor, was fated to be left cold and disillusioned" (ibid.).

20. Giuseppe Longo, "18 BL a Firenze," 3; emphasis added. In a personal letter, dated June 18, 1992, the author notes that he was fired from the newspaper as a result of the regime's reaction to his sharp attack.

21. Vittorio Torti, cited approvingly in the anonymous "18 BL e fascisti . . . all'amido," Ottobre, May 16, 1934, 4. The fact that Gravelli's "universalist" journal should have lifted a piece out of La Ciurma, the local newsletter of the Alessandria chapter of the GUF (to which Torti belonged), is probably indicative of the embarrassment felt by fascist radicals like Ottobre's editor Gravelli (and perhaps also by men close to him, like Marinetti and Bragaglia) at the experiment's failure.

22. Raffaelo Franchi, "18 BL spettacolo di masse," LIL, May 6, 1934, 1. See also Piovene, "Dalla gloria della trincea al tempo di Mussolini"; Giulio Bucciolini, "Felice realizzazione del primo esperimento del teatro di masse: Cronaca della serata," Nuovo Giornale, Apr. 30, 1934, 11; "S.," "La rappresentazione del 18 B.L.," Il Popolo d'Italia, May 1, 1934, 5; Filippo Baraldi, "I goliardi ferraresi ai Littoriali della cultura e dell'arte," Corriere Padano, May 8, 1934, 7; and the anonymous review "Teatro fascista per il popolo fascista," in Gioventù Fascista 4.9 (May 1, 1934): 8–9. Even the harshest reviewers were willing to grant that 18 BL had achieved notable lighting effects in its opening acts.

23. "Gran successo di 18 BL," Roma, May 1, 1934, 3.

24. "Lo spettacolo di masse 18 BL," Corriere del Lunedì, Apr. 30, 1934, 2.

25. Enzo Maurri, "Il 'fiasco' delle Cascine," Il Tempo, May 4, 1984, 18.

26. Orio Vergani, "Lo spettacolo di masse del 18 BL," CdS, Apr. 30, 1934, 3.

27. Alessandro Pavolini, "Si chiudono domani," Il Bargello, May 6, 1934, 1.

28. Corrado Sofia, "Il parere di uno degli otto autori: TRADIMENTO, 3–4. The entirety of page 3 of the journal was placed under the rubric "Mass Critique of a Mass Spectacle" and, in addition to Sofia's piece, included Luigi Chiarini's sharply negative review, "18 BL," and an ironic account of the evening by Marcello Gallian, "Una notte d'aprile."

29. See, for instance, "Verso i Littoriali della Cultura," where Sofia states: "I am in the process of coordinating, along with Sandro de Feo, the ideas developed by a specially appointed commission of squadrists, writers, students, and set designers" (3). The manuscripts and typescripts contained in the BA suggest that the roles of de Feo and Sofia in the drafting process were important, but no more so than Giorgio Venturini's. Leo Bomba would make a similar point in his response, "Tradimento . . . tradimento!" LIV 4.7 (May 10–24, 1934): 7. In an unsigned piece entitled "Nel clima dei giovani: Il teatro di masse" (3), Sofia had described the ideas of "one of the youngest inventors of this theater" (himself), given a mixed appraisal of Blasetti's achievement in 1860, and concluded with a detailed account of the alternative to Blasetti's recorded soundtrack he had proposed.

30. "Given our staunch opposition to machine-worship, you can hardly imagine how painful it was to sit through this spectacle. . . . Nor can we forgive Blasetti the use of records and loudspeakers. This contamination of the human with the mechanical is neither normal nor edifying for youth" (Sofia, "Il parere," 3).

31. "In a mere month or so, Blasetti wanted to revolutionize everything, but revolutions are

perilous when unnecessary. Every revolution must be prepared even in its minute particulars" (Sofia, "Il parere," 4). Sofia also claimed that critics were guilty of a cover-up: "Critics and journalists—with few exceptions—have been inaccurate. They have wasted an opportunity to tell the truth. They were left disoriented by the confusion, depressed by the exploding bombs, lost in that vast panorama. Whether out of benevolence or on principle, they have not been as intransigent as we would have liked" (ibid., 3).

32. Alessandro Blasetti, "Passaggi a livello: *18 BL*," *La Tribuna*, May 9, 1934, 3.

33. Corrado Sofia, "Il corago immaginario," *Quadrivio* 2.29 (May 13, 1934), 1–2.

34. Blasetti's response, "Passaggi a livello: Ancora sul *18 BL*," *La Tribuna,* May 15, 1934, 3, appeared shortly after the publication of Bomba's "Tradimento . . . tradimento!" It provided a brief final blast from Sofia, "Ultimi bagliori del *18 BL*," *Quadrivio* 2.30 (May 20, 1934): 4, and an even-handed essay by Gherardo Gherardi: "Difendo Blasetti," *Il Resto di Carlino*, May 26, 1934, 3.

35. "Why did the realization of this simple and deep idea succeed in leaving us with a sense of emptiness, depression, and coldness?" (Bontempelli, *L'avventura novecentista*, 265).

36. Private letter from the theater historian Mario Verdone to the author, Apr. 2, 1991.

37. Maurri, "Il 'fiasco' delle Cascine."

38. Ibid.

39. The best description of the closing moments is that of Giuseppe Longo: "Men push hard but aren't strong enough. Blasetti sends others, to no avail. Then, in order to keep the public from seeing what he is about to do, he turns off the lights and makes use of a cinematic trick: he has Mother Cartridge-Pouch pushed over the brink by another truck. This was not part of the original plan (but three-quarters of the audience had already departed). In the end, other trucks arrive and dump loads of dirt on top of the carcass" ("*18 BL* a Firenze: non è nato il teatro di masse," *Gazzetta di Messina*, May 4, 1934, 3).

40. Maurri, "Il 'fiasco' delle Cascine."

## CHAPTER 6

1. The anecdote is reported by Silvio d'Amico, "Teatro di masse: *18 BL*," in *Cronache del teatro 2*, ed. E. Ferdinando Palmieri and Sandro d'Amico (Bari: Laterza, 1964), 285. Such hostility does not seem to have been prevalent, however. In a letter to the author dated Apr. 14, 1992, Luigi Preti (who at the time was a teenager) reports: "Although I remember *18 BL* somewhat vaguely, I recall that it was very well put together, in part because Pavolini was a man of real intelligence. . . . Young people were, on the whole, enthusiastic about the performance (owing to the quality of [Blasetti's] work as director), even if they didn't fully understand it."

2. Ugo Ojetti, *I taccuini, 1914–1943* (Florence: Sansoni, 1954), 435. The point is repeated by Giuseppe Longo: "There is always a danger when one places an inanimate being at the center of a heroic action. . . . For temperamental reasons we Latins are not prone to exalting machinery" ("*18 BL* a Firenze: Non è nato il teatro di masse," *Gazzetta di Messina*, May 4, 1934, 3), and by Nicola Manzari, who had won the drama criticism prize at the Littoriali: "It was also a mistake to have designated a machine as the protagonist of our history and epic struggle, given that machines are blind instruments without the brain that directs them. . . . Nor let it be claimed that the authors viewed the truck as a symbol. Our best minds view the disrupted equilibrium between man and machine, and all fetishistic attitudes towards this inhuman deity, as one of the main causes of the crisis being faced by that contemporary civilization. In

short, to have placed machine values on a higher plane than human values in a work of this kind was not a felicitous idea" ("Il teatro di masse," *Il Messaggero*, May 8, 1934, 5).

3. Claudio Massenti, "L'esperimento fiorentino dello spettacolo di massa," *La Tribuna*, May 15, 1934, 3. Massenti doubtless had in mind works like Emile Schreiber's *Rome après Moscou* (Paris: Plon, 1932), a critical examination of fascist Italy against the backdrop of the Russian precedent. In his preface, Schreiber characteristically notes: "Despite the violent conflict between their core components, they display numerous common traits in actual practice. They even cultivate a secret feeling of indulgence towards one another which sometimes verges on outright sympathy" (i).

4. Pietro Maria Bardi's *Un fascista al paese dei Soviet* (Rome: Edizioni d'Italia, 1933) was a compilation of travelogues published in *L'Ambrosiano* during late 1932, to which was added a preface by Ciocca. Gaetano Ciocca's *Giudizio sul bolscevismo: Com'è finito il piano quinquennale* (Milan: V. Bompiani, 1932) was reprinted in 1933, with prefaces by an anonymous reviewer from *Il Popolo d'Italia* (probably Mussolini) and Bardi. Emile Schreiber's *Come si vive in Rùssia* (Lanciano: Carobba, 1933) and Waldemar Gurian's *Il bolscevismo* (Milan: Vita e Pensiero, 1933) were both translations. But by far the most influential translated work was René Fülöp-Miller's *Il volto del bolscevismo*, trans. Giacomo Prampolini (2d ed., Milan: V. Bompiani, 1931), published with a preface by Curzio Malaparte. Fülöp-Miller's book's wide-ranging impact on fascist perceptions of Soviet Russia would be worthy of a separate study, but suffice it to note that its account of the Russian revolutionary theater (70–99) was repeatedly echoed in period debates on fascist theater (see, e.g., Luigi Bonelli, "Fare un teatro di propaganda," *LIV* 3.14 [Aug. 25, 1933]: 6–7); and that its discussion of collective authorship may have provided the impetus, not only for the collaborative drafting of *18 BL*, but also for Bompiani's launching in March 1934 of the debate on the collective novel (see 108–11).

5. "The imitation of machines has been raised to the status of a religious sacrament, comparable to the imitation of Christ. . . . Just like pious mystics once strove to transform themselves into images of God and to dissolve into His essence, so today the modern fanatics of rationalism strive to transform themselves into machines, to reduce themselves to an assemblage of drive belts, connecting rods, valves, and steering wheels" (Fülöp-Miller, *Il volto del bolscevismo*, 20–21). Cf. Ciocca: "Having made mechanization into its distinctive idol, bolshevism has denatured a healthy idea: that of planning production according to actual needs. In order to avert a crisis, it has relied upon the crisis's principal cause. By reducing all social questions to a crude economic calculation (forgetting the infinity of other factors that are involved), Russia has made the same error as other nations, and America in particular. The coincidence is hardly astonishing (even if Russia did so in the name of a sovereign state and America in the name of the sovereign individual). Russia, on the one side, and the great plutocratic nations, on the other, share the same materialistic conception of life, albeit for opposite reasons. They are both under the spell of the same faith in miracles [*illusione miracolista*], believing that progress will be limitless and that it occurs naturally, as if by inertia" (Ciocca, *Giudizio sul bolscevismo*, 55).

6. Eisenstein's films never underwent general distribution, with the result that cinema clubs became their principal venue. To judge by the films exhibited at the fascist Littoriali, their influence was nonetheless considerable. As for his theoretical writings, *L'Italia Letteraria*, for instance, ran a two-part essay of his entitled "Della forma cinematografica" in its May 28 and June 4, 1934, issues.

7. Press coverage of *18 BL* consistently refers to these experiments, although not always by name. One post-performance essay by Guido Salvini, who had been responsible for the controversial production of Donizetti's *Lucrezia Borgia* at the 1933 Maggio Musicale, even proposed a detailed comparative study ("Spettacoli di masse e *18 BL*," *Scenario* 3.5 [May 1934]: 251–56). On the Soviet revolutionary festivals, the principal English language sources are *Street Art of the Revolution: Festivals and Celebrations in Russia, 1918–1933,* ed. Vladimir Tolstoy, Irina Bibikova, and Catherine Cooke (London: Thames & Hudson, 1990); Szymon Bojko, "Agit-prop Art: The Streets Were Their Theater," in *The Avant-Garde in Russia, 1910–1930; New Perspectives*, ed. Stephanie Baron and Maurice Tuchman (Los Angeles: MIT Press 1980), 72–76; and James R. Von Geldern, "Festivals of the Revolution, 1917–1920: Art and Theater in the Formation of Soviet Culture" (Ph.D. diss., Brown Univ., 1987).

8. A detailed eyewitness account of the spectacle can be found in Huntley Carter, *The New Theatre and Cinema of Soviet Russia* (New York: Arno/N.Y. Times, 1970), 106–9; but see also Fülöp-Miller, *Il volto del bolscevismo*, 96–97, who notes that the spectacle was developed by "a collective of authors and directors" (96).

9. Fülöp-Miller, *Il volto del bolscevismo*, 97.

10. See, e.g., Anton Giulio Bragaglia, "Il teatro di Piscator," *Comoedia* 13.1 (Jan. 15–Feb. 15, 1931): 33–35, where, despite some sharply critical comments regarding Piscator's communist faith, Bragaglia did not shy away from stating, "this is a true man of genius" (35); and Corrado Alvaro, "Si discorre ancora del teatro," *La Fiera Letteraria*, Aug. 25, 1929, 1, one of seven essays surveying the Weimar cultural scene. The best English-language source manual on Piscator is *Erwin Piscator: The Political Theater*, trans. and ed. Hugh Rorrison (London: Eyre Methuen, 1980). For a comparative study of mass theater in Soviet Russia, the Weimar Re-

public, and Nazi Germany, see Hannelore Wolff, *Volksabstimmung auf der Bühne? Das Massentheater als Mittel politischer Agitation*, Europäische Hochschulschriften, ser. 30: Teater, Film- und Fernsehen (Frankfurt: Peter Lang, 1985). But see also George L. Mosse, *The Nationalization of the Masses: Political Symbolism and Mass Movements in Germany from the Napoleonic Wars Through the Third Reich* (New York: New American Library, 1977), 110–26.

11. This doubling extends even to the songs chanted by the actors portraying the fascists. The song "They Have Murdered Giovanni Berta" ("Hanno ammazzato Giovanni Berta"), for instance, would have been familiar to the audience of *18 BL* in both black and red versions. In the version recorded into the soundtrack of *18 BL* the first stanza read:

> They have murdered Giovanni
>   Berta
> a fascist's fascist
> revenge, yes revenge
> will be had upon the reds.
>
> (Hanno ammazzato Giovanni Berta
> fascista tra i fascisti,
> vendetta sì vendetta
> farem sui comunisti.)

In the communist version it read:

> They have murdered Giovanni
>   Berta
> son of a capitalist bloodsucker:
> long live the communist
> who stomped on his hands.
>
> (Hanno ammazzato Giovanni Berta
> figliol d'un pescecane:
> viva quel comunista
> che gli pestò le mani.)

A. V. Savona and M. L. Straniero, eds., *Canti dell'Italia fascista, 1919–1945* (Milan: Garzanti, 1979), 89–90. Such doublings are characteristic:

"The fascist repertory doesn't succeed in differentiating itself from the repertory of antifascist and democratic songs to nearly the degree that it would have liked. It frequently adopts the same expressive tonalities, the same linguistic devices, and sometimes even the same melodies (with minor variations)" (ibid., 5).

12. "Our struggle is for a global revolution, which is to say, for a universal revolution. Rome and Moscow alone are vying for the leadership role. . . . The battle is for universal revolution, and the victors will not be those who are more 'right-minded' [*i meglio pensanti*]. Rather, the victors will be those who, simply and sempiternally, are more universal and more revolutionary" (Berto Ricci, "Chiarezza," *CF* 15.8 [Feb. 15, 1937]: 127). Ricci's piece was followed by several clarifications ("Mosca e il Direttorio," *CF* 15.11 [Apr. 1, 1937]: 170; "Del *più* e del *meno*," *CF* 15.15 [June 1, 1937]: 269; and "Quelli che si meravigliano," *CF* 15.18 [July 15, 1937]: 319), as well as by two longer articles authored by Tommaso Napolitano: "Il fascismo di Stalin" (*CF* 15.18 [July 15, 1937]: 317–19) and "Il *fascismo* di Stalin ovvero l'URSS e noi" (*CF* 15.23 [Oct. 1, 1937]: 396–98).

13. Ruggero Orlando, "Che cos'è *18 BL*," *La Tribuna*, Apr. 20, 1934, 3. The most detailed account of the tone and character of the rehearsals for *18 BL* is Franco Fedele Bozzi, "Ronda in città: Dopo il *18 BL*—Note retrospettive ovvero: Quello che i 20.000 non hanno visto," *Il Bargello*, May 15, 1934, 5.

14. Ruggero Orlando, "Prove di *18 BL*," *La Tribuna*, Apr. 26, 1934, 3.

15. Orio Vergani, "L'elogio di Starace agli organizzatori e ai vincitori dei Littoriali: "Stasera il *18 BL* rivivrà la sua eroica epoea—Prove col megafono," *CdS*, Apr. 29, 1934, 3.

16. Yambo [Giulio Enrico Novelli], "Fervida preparazione dei Littoriali della cultura e dell'Arte: Lo spettacolo di masse," *Il Nuovo Giornale*, Apr. 13, 1934, 1.

17. Ibid. The notion of Blasetti as commander, or *duce*, is a commonplace of contemporary press accounts, such as the following: "Alessandro Blasetti, wearing a turquoise colored overcoat and beret, a heavy gray sweater, riding boots, and always with a cigarette hanging from his mouth, looks just like battlefield commander who is preparing fortifications and studying battle plans" (Cipriano G[iachetti], "I preparativi del teatro di masse: Alessandro Blasetti all'opera," *LN*, Apr. 12, 1934, 5).

18. Since Florentine municipal records for this period are incomplete, it is difficult to establish the precise contribution made by the city authorities. According to documents found in Florence's Archivio di Storia, the Azienda Autonoma di Turismo di Firenze (whose president was Pavolini) contributed at least 100,000 lire to the budget of the Littoriali. The Comune of Florence also covered the electrical bill at the Parterre San Gallo, and allocated 35,000 lire for "the repair of several stretches of Argin Grosso, Mortuli, and Isolotto streets, along which the inaugural spectacle of the Littoriali of Culture and Art will be taking place on April 21" (document dated Mar. 2, 1934, signed by the *podestà*, Paolo Pesciolini, Archivio di Storia, Prefettura di Firenze, Affari Generali, ser. 2, 1934: f. 87, b. 2202).

19. Alessandro Blasetti, "Prime considerazioni e proposte: Ufficio," BA.

20. "One more day of feverish, exhausting work and the theater for 20,000 spectators will become a reality" (Giulio Bucciolini, "I Littoriali della Cultura e dell'Arte: Una visita all'Albereta," *Il Nuovo Giornale*, Apr. 17, 1934, 1).

21. "There is no special box seat for the authorities and, naturally, no free tickets will be distributed: the latter was affirmed in a communiqué issued by the party secretary, who was the first to purchase a ticket. . . . The morality exemplified by such sound administrative practices provides an excellent indication of the

true nature of this new kind of spectacle. It is, in its very essence, for the people, and therefore should not be tainted by inopportune contradictions or privileges" (Orlando, "Prove di *18 BL*," 3). Orlando also mentions that 10,000 unreserved seats were sold within hours of the opening of ticket sales, suggesting large block purchases by the various fascist organizations.

22. The metaphor of "metallization," central to Marinetti's early writings, is cited in the epilogue to Walter Benjamin's "The Work of Art in the Age of Mechanical Reproduction": "War is beautiful because it initiates the dreamt-of metallization of the human body" (in *Illuminations*, ed. Hannah Arendt, trans. Harry Zohn [New York: Schocken Books, 1976], 241). The metaphor also figures prominently in the writings examined by Klaus Theweleit in *Male Fantasies* (cited in ch. 1, n. 24, above) and in works such as Ernst Jünger's *In Stahlgewittern (aus dem Tagebuch eines Stoßtruppführers)* (Berlin: E. S. Mittler, 1931); *Der Arbeiter: Herrschaft und Gestalt* (Stuttgart: Klett-Cotta, 1982); and *Das Kampf als inneres Erlebnis* (Berlin: E. S. Mittler, 1933). For a fine discussion of Jünger's view of machines, see Jeffrey Herf, *Reactionary Modernism: Technology, Culture, and Politics in Weimar and the Third Reich* (New York: Cambridge Univ. Press, 1984), 70–108.

23. One contemporary press account (written, not surprisingly, in Fiat's hometown, Turin) insists on presenting the *18 BL* as the founding ancestor of Italian mass transportation: "The first Fiat trucks were produced to address the nation's military needs, but they were never merely instruments of battle and victory. Rather, they were always also the progenitors of freight-carrying rigs. They were the original rootstock that gave rise to the family of trucks that today fills the streets of Italy with traffic" (C[urio] M[ortari], "Teatro di masse: Lo spettacolo di stasera a Firenze," *La Stampa*, Apr. 29, 1934, 4).

24. Vergani, "Lo spettacolo di masse del *18 BL*."

25. Alessandro Pavolini, "Rivoluzione di popolo," *Il Bargello*, June 12, 1932, 1.

26. Salomé was, of course, already fully codified as one of the turn-of-the-century's key misogynist myths, on which subject, see Bram Dijkstra, *Idols of Perversity: Fantasies of Feminine Evil in Fin-de-Siècle Culture* (New York: Oxford Univ. Press, 1986), 379–401. The myth carries over into the iconology of the "Red menace," as studied by Theweleit in vol. 1 of his *Male Fantasies*.

27. The full passage reads: "To respond to the aesthetic mayhem unleashed by commercial culture, the fascist propaganda machine, with Mussolini's approbation, championed its own standards of female beauty: one ideal, the 'crisis woman,' was negative; the other, whom we might call 'authentic woman,' was positive. The former was a masculinized plaything, a false and alien creature, the product of Paris and Hollywood; the latter was homegrown—broodmare, mother, and mate" (Victoria de Grazia, *How Fascism Ruled Women: Italy 1922–1945* [Berkeley: Univ. of California Press, 1992], 212). It goes without saying that Salomé is clearly identifiable with the so-called *donna crisi*, contrasted with the *donna madre* embodied by the lead truck.

28. Pavolini, "Rivoluzione di popolo."

29. Debate over the term "realism" became a central preoccupation in the wake of *Il Saggiatore*'s 1932 "Inquiry on the New Generation," after which there appeared a slew of articles detailing or criticizing the notion. For an introductory sampler one may consult: "Critica Fascista," "Esortazione al realismo," *CF* 4.10 (Feb. 15, 1932): 61–62; Berto Ricci, Ottone Rosai et al., "Manifesto realista," *L'Universale* 2.2 (Jan. 1933): 1–2; Domenico Carella, "Nostro realismo," *CF* 7.11 (Apr. 1, 1933): 133–34; Mario Pannunzio, "Realismo," *Oggi* 1.2 (May 28,

1933): 1; Giorgio Granata, "Realismo," *Il Saggiatore* 4.9 (Nov. 1933): 389–93; Sigfrido Wolfango, "Il realismo moderno," *Oggi* 1.32 (Dec. 31, 1933): 12; Bruno Corra, "Realismo fascista," *PdI* (Mar. 7, 1934): 1; Arnaldo Bocelli, "Aspetti della letteratura d'oggi: Realismo," *Corriere Padano*, Apr. 26, 1934, 3; and Enzo Paci, "Il nostro realismo storico," *Il Cantiere* 4 (Mar. 24, 1934): 4. On this topic, the best discussions are those of Mario Sechi, *Il mito della nuova cultura: Giovani, realismo e politica negli anni Trenta* (Manduria: Lacaita, 1984), esp. 63–108; and Pasquale Voza, "Il problema del realismo negli anni Trenta: *Il Saggiatore*, *Il Cantiere*," *Lavoro Critico* 21–22 (Jan.–June 1981): 65–105.

30. As noted earlier, in *1860* Blasetti had employed this same principle to even greater effect. Garibaldi, the true protagonist of the film, appears in only a handful of frames and, when he does, his presence is fleeting. Indeed, the film subjects him to a kind of disappearing act: "The mythical leader remains invisible, except for two quick shots. The first time, we get a glimpse of Garibaldi on top of a hill eating bread and cheese; the second time, we see him parading troops before the battle of Calatafimi. During a critical moment of this battle, another choreography of convergence takes place. Various soldiers rushing from left and right and the dynamic editing of shots with opposite screen directions convey the excitement of the counterattack and the charisma of the godlike Garibaldi. His disembodied voice exhorting his men 'To win or to die!' acquires the same resonance as Scipio's phantasmatic presence [in Carmine Gallone's 1937 film *Scipio Africanus*]" (Angela Dalle Vacche, *The Body in the Mirror: Shapes of History in Italian Cinema* [Princeton: Princeton Univ. Press, 1992], 100–101).

31. On Mussolinian iconography and myth, see Jeffrey T. Schnapp, "Heads of State," *Art Issues* 24 (Sept.–Oct. 1992): 23–28; Luisa Passerini, *Mussolini immaginario: Storia di una biografia, 1915–1939* (Bari: Laterza, 1991); Caterina Bian-chi, "Il nudo eroico del fascismo," and Mario Isnenghi, "Il corpo del Duce," both in *Gli occhi di Alessandro: Potere sovrano e sacralità del corpo da Alessandro Magno a Ceaucescu*, ed. Sergio Bertelli and Cristiano Grottanelli (Florence: Ponte alle Grazie, 1990), 154–83.

## CHAPTER 7

1. For a parallel formulation of this constitutive set oppositions in the work of Mario Sironi, see my own essay (written in collaboration with Claudio Fogu) " 'Ogni mostra realizzata è una rivoluzione,' ovvero le esposizioni sironiane e l'immaginario fascista," in *Mario Sironi, 1885–1961*, Galleria Nazionale di Arte Moderna (Rome: Electa Editrice, 1993), 48–61.

2. From Goebbels's famous November 15, 1993, speech before the Reich Chamber of Writers, quoted in Igor Golomstock, *Totalitarian Art in the Soviet Union, the Third Reich, Fascist Italy and the People's Republic of China*, trans. Robert Chandler (New York: Icon Editions, 1990), 183. On "steely Romanticism," see Jeffrey Herf, *Reactionary Modernism: Technology, Culture, and Politics in Weimar and the Third Reich* (New York: Cambridge Univ. Press, 1984), 195–216.

3. On ancient tragedy and the military training of boys, see John J. Winkler's "The Ephebes' Song: *Tragōidia* and *Polis*," *Representations* 11 (Summer 1985): 26–62.

4. Indro Montanelli, "Il teatro e l'eroe," *Gerarchia* 14.6 (June 1934): 504.

5. Georges Bataille, "The Psychological Structure of Fascism," in *Visions of Excess: Selected Writings, 1927–1939*, ed. Allan Stoekl, trans. C. R. Lovitt, D. M. Leslie, and A. Stoekl (Minneapolis: Univ. of Minnesota Press, 1985), 154. On this subject, see also Paolo Valesio's essay "The Beautiful Lie: Heroic Individuality and Fascism," in *Reconstructing Individualism*, ed. T. C. Heller, M. Sosna, and D. E. Wellbery (Stanford: Stanford Univ. Press, 1986), 162–83. Cf. Mon-

tanelli: "Restore to this hero his totalitarian and human essence, keep him from being disjoined from the context that surrounds him (whether moral or spiritual), and the masses will miraculously return [to the theaters] and, for dialectical reasons, will be absorbed within his magical halo. They will return and automatically reassume their role as a choral element both complementary and necessary to the hero himself, who needs them in order not to fall prey to the Nietzschean and d'Annunzian *absurdum* of the entirely unique, deracinated individual, engaged in a tragic conflict with society" ("Il teatro e l'eroe," 503).

6. The most synthetic study on this subject remains Philip Reif's "Aesthetic Functions in Modern Politics," in *The Feeling Intellect: Selected Writings*, ed. Jonathan B. Imber (Chicago: Univ. of Chicago Press, 1990), 175–94.

7. Montanelli, "Il teatro e l'eroe," 503; emphasis added.

8. Isaiah Berlin, "Joseph de Maistre and the Origins of Fascism," *New York Review of Books* 37.14 (Sept. 27, 1990): 57–64; 37.15 (Oct. 11, 1990): 54–58; 37.16 (Oct. 25, 1990): 61–65.

9. Elias Canetti, *Masse und Macht* (Hamburg: Claasen, 1960).

10. Georg Simmel, "The Metropolis and Mental Life," in *Classic Essays on the Culture of Cities*, ed. Richard Sennett (New York: Appleton-Century-Crofts, 1969), 52. The insight is much more elaborately developed out in Simmel's masterpiece *The Philosophy of Money*, trans. Tom Bottomore and David Frisby (Boston: Routlege & Kegan Paul, 1978).

11. Honoré de Balzac, "De la cravate, considerée en elle-même et dans ses rapports avec la société et les individus," in id., *Traité des excitants modernes*, ed. Jean-Jacques Brochier (Paris: Le Castor Astral, 1992).

12. Charles Baudelaire, "Oeuvre et vie d'Eugène Delacroix," in id., *Curiosités esthétiques: L'Art romantique et autres oeuvres critiques* (Paris: Garnier, 1986), 438: "un cratère de volcan artistiquement caché par des bouqets de fleurs." The passage culminates a long description of Delacroix's savage interior, which begins with a comparison to Prosper Mérimée: "His was the same apparent coldness with a trace of affection, the same icy coat worn over a chaste sensibility and a burning passion for the good and the beautiful; under the same hypocritical egotism, his was the same devotion to secret friends and treasured ideas." All translations from Baudelaire are my own.

13. Charles Baudelaire, "Les Foules," *Petits poèmes en prose (Le Spleen de Paris)* (Paris: Flammarion, 1967), 61–62.

14. The words "unexpected" (*imprévu*) and "unknown" (*inconnu*) are given in the masculine in Baudelaire's text, whereas the word "soul" (*l'âme*) is of feminine gender; hence the effectiveness of the gender switch.

15. Mark Seltzer, *Bodies and Machines* (New York: Routledge, 1992). On this subject, the best historical overview is Anson Rabinbach, *The Human Motor: Energy, Fatigue, and the Origins of Modernity* (New York: Basic Books, 1990).

16. Seltzer, *Bodies and Machines*, 168.

17. Adolf Hitler, *Mein Kampf* (New York: Reynal & Hitchcock, 1941), 616.

18. Filippo Tommaso Marinetti, *Let's Murder the Moonshine: Selected Writings*, ed. and trans. R. W. Flint (New York: Farrar, Straus & Giroux, 1971; rpt. Los Angeles: Sun & Moon, 1991), 167. The Italian original reads as follows: "Quando s'alza per parlare tende in avanti la testa dominatrice, proiettile quadrato, scatola piena di buon esplosivo, cubica volontà di Stato. Ma l'abbassa, per concludere, pronto a colpire nel petto o meglio sventrare la questione con la forza di un toro. Eloquenza futurista bene masticata da denti d'acciaio, plasticamente scolpita dalla sua mano intelligente, che sbriccola la plastilina inutile degli argomenti

avversarî" (from the opening of id., *Marinetti e il Futurismo* [Rome and Milan: Edizioni Augustea, 1929], quoted from id., *Teoria e invenzione futurista*, ed. Luciano de Maria [Milan: A Mondadori, 1983], 502).

19. On this subject, see Theweleit's *Male Fantasies* (cited in ch. 1, n. 24, above).

20. For the full question, see n. 12 above.

21. Again cf. Baudelaire's portrait of Delacroix: "Another point of resemblance to Stendhal was his propensity to adopt simple formulas, brief maxims . . . healthy, strong, simple, and hard maxims that can serve as a breastplate and shield for him who is fated to endure perpetual battle because of his genius" ("Oeuvre et vie d'Eugène Delacroix," 438).

22. See A. W. von Schlegel, *Lectures on Dramatic Art and Literature* (1808), trans. John Black, 2d ed. (London: Bell, 1909).

23. See Gilles Deleuze and Félix Guattari, *One Thousand Plateaus: Capitalism and Schizophrenia*, trans. Brian Massumi (Minneapolis: Univ. of Minnesota Press, 1987), 3–25.

24. Georges Sorel, *Reflections on Violence*, trans. T. E. Hulme and J. Roth (New York: Collier Books, 1950), 50.

25. In "Epic Demonstrations: Fascist Modernity and the 1932 Exhibition of the Fascist Revolution," in *Fascism, Aesthetics, and Politics*, ed. R. J. Golsan (Hanover, N.H.: Univ. Press of New England, 1992, 1–37), I have formulated this paradox in terms of its links to the Petrarchan lyric.

## CHAPTER 8

1. "In the wake of *18 BL*'s realization, some have tried to completely destroy the mass theater. We repeat, however, that the theater of masses remains the only solution available today that can adequately address the abnormal condition in which the theater finds itself" (Giampiero Giani, "Vita dei GUF: Dal teatro di masse allo sperimentale dei GUF," *Gerarchia* 14.12 [Dec. 1934]: 1052).

2. Nicola Manzari, "Il teatro di masse," *Il Messaggero*, May 8, 1934: 5: "Supported by a majority of participants, our position was that il Duce had in mind a theater *for* the masses in his speech: a theater, that is, able to create a sense of communion with the crowd, but not requiring the presence on stage of another crowd. The power of this sort of theater derives neither from the greater or lesser number of actors, nor from the vast scale of the stage, but rather from a poetic nucleus tied to the eternal values that fascism has restored and, therefore, capable of ensuring a mass communion." Manzari goes on to criticize the truck-protagonist and "the metallic, inhuman, cosmic voice surging forth between the stage and the audience." Ironically, Blasetti himself had once been a fierce defender of the silent cinema against sound technology and had argued that the latter was little more than a Hollywood plot to destroy the European cinema.

3. "Orchestrina," *Corriere Padano*, June 23, 1934, 3.

4. Edoardo Anton, "Problemi attuali: Teatro di masse e teatro fascista," *Corriere Padano*, Jan. 16, 1935, 3.

5. Alessandro Blasetti, "Teatro di masse, teatro per ventimila," *LIV* 4.7 (May 10–24, 1934): 6–7; 4.8 (June 10, 1934): 9.

6. Blasetti to Bontempelli, letter dated Aug. 8, 1934, Getty Center for the History of Art and the Humanities, Bontempelli Archive, box 4, correspondence "B."

7. Corrado Pavolini, *Storia del teatro italiano*, ed. Silvio d'Amico (Milan: V. Bompiani, 1936), 347–67. The volume was based on a series of talks given at the newly inaugurated Teatro Sperimentale dei GUF in Florence during the fall 1935 and contained an introduction by Luigi Pirandello.

8. Ibid., 357–58.

9. Ibid., 365.

10. Indro Montanelli, "Il teatro e l'eroe," *Gerarchia* 14.6 (June 1934): 502–4.

11. Bragaglia's main contribution to the pre-spectacle debate was a highly favorable essay linking up certain features of *18 BL* to his own experiments, entitled "La parola nel teatro 'per ventimila,'" *Il Giornale d'Italia*, Apr. 28, 1934, 3. For an introduction to his own position in contemporary debates on the crisis of the theater, see Anton Giulio Bragaglia, *Il teatro della rivoluzione* (Rome: Edizioni Tiber, 1929).

12. Anton Giulio Bragaglia, "Lo spettacolo per masse," *La Vita Italiana* 22.256 (July 1934): 67. He goes on to point out the continuities between the debates of the prefascist and fascist eras: "The old advocates of the people's theater—some will recall the socialist projects and the lessons learned twenty years back—advanced the same arguments" (68). The essay was republished on the one-year anniversary of the Lictorial games as "Il teatro per masse I: Dopo l'esperienza di Firenze," *Ottobre*, Apr. 13, 1935, 3; "Il teatro per masse II: Vedere e sentire," *Ottobre*, Apr. 19, 1935, 3; and "Il teatro per masse III: Il problema materiale," *Ottobre*, May 11, 1935, 5.

13. See Jeffrey T. Schnapp, "Politics and Poetics in F. T. Marinetti's *Zang Tumb Tuuum*," *Stanford Italian Review* 5.1 (1985): 75–92.

14. Bragaglia, "Lo spettacolo per masse," 75. The phrase "*teatro-spettacolo* politico, dell'Era Fascista" is employed on p. 71. The call for a broader historical frame of reference was put into effect by Bragaglia himself in a bipartite essay concerned with ancient theater architecture: "Gli antichi teatri di massa I: Le dimensioni," *Ottobre*, June 29, 1935, 3; and "Gli antichi teatri di massa II: Visibilità e acustica," *Ottobre*, July 6, 1935, 3.

15. Other invitees included Jacinto Benavente, Paul Claudel, Noël Coward, Federico García Lorca, Maxim Gorky, Jean Giradoux, Vsevolod Meyerhold, Eugene O'Neill, Bernard Shaw, K. M. Stanislavsky, and Stefan Zweig. Their "letters of support" are reproduced in the published acts, 8–14. It would appear that Pirandello did little more than suggest a couple of names of invitees, leaving d'Amico in full charge of the participant list, the conference structure, and the intellectual program.

16. RAI, *Atti—Convegno di lettere: Tema—Il teatro drammatico* (Rome: Reale Accademia, 1935), 20.

17. Ibid., 21.

18. "This speech presents itself as a commentary upon a phrase of Mussolini's that was pronounced in May of last year. . . . While he [Ciocca] and some of our foreign guests will be shedding light on the technical and engineering aspects of what has come to be referred to as 'the theater for 20,000,' I shall attempt instead to penetrate the Mussolinian phrase's spiritual content, which is extremely profound" (ibid., 139).

19. Ibid., 147.

20. I have discussed Gropius's appearance at the Convegno Volta, as well as the Total Theater project, at far greater length in "Border Crossings: German/Italian Peregrinations of the Theater of Totality," *Critical Inquiry* 21.2 (Summer 1994): 80–123.

21. On the *Totaltheater*, see Erwin Piscator, "Das Totaltheater," and Walter Gropius, "Vom modernen Theaterbau, unter Berücksichtigung des Piscatortheaterneubaus in Berlin," both in *Erwin Piscator: Eine Arbeitsbiographie in 2 Bänden*, ed. Knut Boeser and Renata Vatková (Berlin: Hentrich, Frölich & Kaufmann, 1986), 1: 146–51; and, for further bibliography, Stefan Woll, *Das Totaltheater: Ein Projekt von Walter Gropius und Erwin Piscator*, Schriften der

Gesellschaft für Theatergeschichte e.V. 68
(Berlin: Gesellschaft für Theatergeschichte e.V.,
1984).

22. Gropius's presentation is reproduced in
RAI, *Atti—Convegno*, 154–62. Both quotations
are from p. 157. Many other examples could be
offered.

23. See László Moholy-Nagy, "Theater, Zirkus,
Varieté," in *Die Bühne am Bauhaus*, ed. Oskar
Schlemmer, László Moholy-Nagy, and Farkas
Molnár (Munich, 1925; rpt. Mainz and Berlin:
Neue Bauhausbücher, 1965), 45–57.

24. RA, *Atti—Convegno*, 159.

25. Winfried Nerdinger, *Walter Gropius* (Berlin:
Bauhaus Archiv, Busch-Reisinger Museum,
Gebr. Mann Verlag, 1985), 94. My trans.

26. Ibid., 98. Gropius's reputation remained
very much intact in Italy after his flight from
Nazi Germany, as evidenced by a lecture tour
that took him to Milan and Rome in 1935, and
by the publication of Italian versions of numerous essays, including "Razionalizzazione nella
economia edile," *Quadrante* 24 (Apr. 1935): 13.

27. "The new theater will be a theater of optimism and of initiative. The gigantic protagonists of the no less gigantic ancient Greek stage
were the blind force of destiny and the will of
the gods. Equally gigantic, the protagonists of
the theater of tomorrow will be the enlightened
will of mankind and the creative power of labor" (RAI, *Atti—Convergo*, 190). Ashley Dukes
would later recall Ciocca's presentation as follows: "I understand why the Italian delegates at
the Volta Theatre Congress in Rome, a year or
two back, were always talking of 'the playhouse
of the twenty thousand,' or the largest conceivable playhouse with a roof and walls. In defi-
ance of architects, directors and actors, not to
speak of small fry like dramatists, they continued to insist that the mass-theatre offered the
only fulfillment of the popular and instinctive
dramatic demand. They may get their monstrous building in the course of time, for anything is possible in a Rome that tolerates the
new-style forum with its concrete colossi; but
for the present the mass-theatre, whether political or spectacular, is in the open air. The next
generation, thanks to microphonic and illumi-
native effect, will see this institution more and
more firmly established under the noonday
skies or starry firmament" ("The Scene in Europe: Open Air Theater," *Theater Arts Monthly*
20.10 (Oct. 1936): 771–72).

28. RAI, *Atti—Convegno*, 216.

29. See esp. 216–18.

30. "I believe in the possibility that out of that
'study-theatre' will grow plays as noble as the
ecclesiastic mystery in the Churches, which still
stirs us after being carried on for twenty long
centuries. So I anticipate the new theatre to
contain the festivals which earthbound healthy
people will hold there. Laughter and joy and
humour will be just as much a part of the plays
as the symbolic offerings by which life is dedicated to an all governing idea, reflecting our
temporal life in the infiniteness of the Cosmos"
(ibid., 219).

31. "If they could throw overboard all the superfluous scenery and stage machinery, the
healthy foundation of a new study-theater
could be laid; for the fundamental-idea is good.
The beauty of the construction is only spoiled
by covering it all with cloth and rags" (ibid.,
475).

32. RAI, *Atti—Convegno*, 172.

33. "They are ignorant of preceding doctrines,
like socialism: an ignorance that constitutes a
serious handicap when it comes to understanding how corporatism, which evolved out of syn-
dicalism, is a legacy of ideas and institutions
created by the working class in the prior period" (Giovanni Poli, "Rapporto sui Littoriali di
Firenze," May 23, 1934, ACS-PNF-DN-GUF,
b. 12, f. 119, p. 6).

34. The original reads as follows: "Notevole, in particolare, la reazione che incontrava ogni riferimento a Roma e alla Romanità. Provocava regolarmente interiezioni quasi ironiche. Vi erano in fondo a tale atteggiamento, il desiderio e la convinzione che i giovani non debbano assidersi sulla storia, ma *farla*" (ibid.).

35. The competition announcement read as follows: "Competition for a comedy to be performed either in an enclosed or an open-air theater. The play must be inspired by an episode from the fascist revolution" (PNF, "Littoriali della Cultura e dell'Arte—Anno XIII," pamphlet in ACS-PNF-DN-GUF, b. 12, f. 123). The major reforms in the theatrical domain are discussed in Alessandro Brissoni, "Teatro fascista e Littoriali dell'Arte," *Il Bargello*, Sept. 9, 1934, 3.

36. On the 1935 Lictorial games, particularly as regards the architectural competition, see "Littoriali 1935—XIII," *Architettura: Rivista del Sindacato Nazionale Fascista Architetti* 14.5 (May 1933): 257–75.

37. Roberto Ducci, "I Littoriali," *Il Cantiere*, May 11, 1935, 3.

38. The ACS's documentation concerning the earliest Littoriali della Cultura is often inconclusive and offers relatively few insights into the behind-the-scenes discussions that took place within the PNF regarding Pavolini's experiment. So I have often found myself obliged to reconstruct these sorts of debates on the basis of published materials. As regards the sufficiently or insufficiently "fascist" character of the Littoriali, the latter are abundant enough, since the games provoked some heated exchanges in journals such as *Critica Fascista*.

39. Letter, GUF stationery, July 6, 1934, ACS-PNF-DN-GUF, b. 12, f. 120.

40. "Riportiamo le modalità del concorso per il Teatro di Masse," found in ACS, PNF-DN-GUF, b. 12, f. 520 (Littoriali: Proposte). I would like to thank Claudio Fogu for his help in locating this document.

41. Ibid.

42. RAI, *Atti—Convegno*, 206.

43. The full passage reads: "We must insist that *18 BL*, despite its defects, is not to be fully condemned. Considerable effort went into its realization and, even if the endless controversy contributed to its demise, there is no reason for us to stand still. The new theater willed by the DUCE, and for which we all feel the need, must defy all risks because it is the daring and warlike fascist theater that knows not difficulty and overcomes all obstacles, no matter how insuperable. The courageous must engage in combat and lay bare their ideas" ("Riportiamo le modalità del concorso per il Teatro di Masse").

44. Ibid.

45. "In short, the theater of masses that we [would] like to bring into existence, inasmuch as it is a form of pure art, does not require gigantic material means as much as it does gigantic artistic ones" (Giani, "Vita dei GUF," 1052). Giani goes on first to speak of "the Mussolinian spectacle, the beginning of an amphitheatrical/theatrical era" (1052), and then to affirm "so this is why the experimental mass theaters of the GUF ought to come about, for they represent the only means to furnish the regular mass theater with works and dramatic concepts of sufficient dignity" (1053).

46. Cases in point are Vittorio Zincone, "Dal cinema al teatro di massa," *ILRM* 2.3 (Feb. 1935): 16–17; and Filippo Pontani, "Teatro di masse," *ILRM* 2.4 (Mar. 1935): 24–27.

47. "Il teatro sperimentale dei GUF," *Rivista Italiana del Dramma* 1.1 (Jan.–May 1937): 108.

48. In the discussions that preceded the theater's creation, Nicola Manzari, one of the members of the commission of students who drafted the founding documents, declared: "[It will be] a theater for the people, but not a 'pop-

ular theater' . . . its avant-garde calling will be interpreted with moderation. Works will be performed that mirror the yearning for faith, heroism, and poetry that is felt by the masses of today, but not the literary or exceptional repertory that doesn't resonate with a large theater crowd" ("Il teatro sperimentale dei GUF," *Il Lavoro Fascista*, May 15, 1934, 3). Pietro Ingrao had originally proposed the title "Teatro Sperimentale Rivoluzionario"; see id., "Sul teatro sperimentale dei GUF," *Il Lavoro Fascista*, May 19, 1934, 3.

49. On this subject, see Pietro Cavallo, *Immaginazione e rappresentazione: Il teatro fascista di propaganda* (Rome: Bonacci, 1990).

50. Quoted in Emanuela Scarpellini, *Organizzazione teatrale e politica del teatro nell'Italia fascista* (Florence: La Nuova Italia, 1989), 277.

51. On this subject see George L. Mosse, *The Nationalization of the Masses: Political Symbolism and Mass Movements in Germany from the Napoleonic Wars Through the Third Reich* (New York: New American Library, 1977), 73–126; Henning Eichberg, Michael Dultz, Glen Gadberry, and Günther Rühle, *Massenspiele: NS-Thingspiel, Arbeiterweihespiel und olympisches Zeremoniell*, Problemata 58 (Stuttgart-Bad Cannstatt: Frommann-Holzboog, 1977); Hannelore Wolff, *Volksabstimmung auf der Bühne? Das Massentheater als Mittel politischer Agitation*, Europäische Hochschulschriften, ser. 30: Teater, Film- und Fernsehen (Frankfurt: Peter Lang, 1985); Klaus Vondung, "Bückeberg—Feier des nationalsozialistischen Erntdankfestes 6 Oktober 1935," *Publikationen zu Wissenschaftlichen Filmen*, Sektion—Geschichte/Publizistik 6.1 (1984), and *Magie und Manipulation. Ideologischer Kult und politische Religion des Nationalsozialismus* (Göttingen: Vanderhoeck & Ruprecht, 1971).

52. Mario Corsi, *Il teatro all'aperto in Italia* (Milan and Rome: Rizzoli, 1939), 160.

53. Ibid., 178.

54. Ibid.

55. The tour is lavishly documented in *Il duce in Libia* (Milan: Mondadori, 1938).

56. Corsi, *Il teatro all'aperto in Italia*, 181.

57. Ibid., 180. Most of this account is borrowed from dispatches Corsi had published in *Gazzetta del Popolo*: in particular, "Nel teatro romano di Sabratha si prova l'*Edipo Re*," Mar. 19, 1937, 4; and "L'*Edipo Re* di Sofocle in una indimenticabile rappresentazione alla presenza del Duce," Mar. 20, 1937, 2. Corsi's fantasy that members of the Roman senatorial elite would have ventured out into colonial outposts like Sabratha to take in open-air performances is of course laughable.

58. Corsi, "Nel teatro romano di Sabratha."

59. In 1945–46, after a lapse of over ten years, Blasetti made a new theatrical debut, directing plays by J. B. Priestley, Pirandello, and Robert E. Sherwood.

60. Alberto Spaini, "Blasetti parla di *Vecchia guardia*," *Il Resto di Carlino*, Nov. 5, 1934, 3.

61. Alessandro Blasetti, *Scritti sul cinema*, ed. Adriano Aprà (Venice: Marsilio, 1982), 345.

62. On Venturini's later career and on Hitler's visit to Florence, see Sardelli, "Decorazione murale, architettura e coreografia nelle parate del regime fascista: Il caso di Firenze durante la visita di Hitler," *Biblioteca Teatrale* 19–20 (1990): 189–204.

63. Dino Alfieri, "Il primo teatro di masse," in *Il teatro per il popolo: Estate Musicale Milanese, Giugno–Agosto 1939* (Milan: Il Popolo d'Italia, 1939), 5.

64. "Il primo 'teatro di masse' dell'Italia fascista era creato" (ibid.).

65. Carmelo Musumurra, "Teatro di masse: Problema di popolo, ma (prima di tutto) di costruzione," *MdR*, Aug. 29, 1937, 9, emphasis added. Bardi's editorship of the journal would come to an unhappy end some months later.

## APPENDIX E

1. The Agnelli family were (and remain) the principal owners of the Fabbrica Italiana Automobili Torino, otherwise known as Fiat.

2. Corrado Sofia, "Necessità di un teatro," *CF* 11.12 (June 15, 1933): 240.

3. *Le fatalone* was published in *Comoedia* 11.3 (Mar. 15–Apr. 15, 1929): 47–49.

4. Corrado Sofia, *CF* 12.2 (Jan. 15, 1934): 21–23.

5. These squibs are printed in *Il Selvaggio* 9.8 (Sept. 15, 1932): 1. Given their aphoristic character, my English translations are approximations at best.

6. "The world of the revolution doesn't concern him at all. Perhaps it frightens him. In any case, he refuses to become its citizen. He looks upon some of us as unfinished characters, unfinished according to the terms of his theater more of thought than of action" (Yvon de Begnac *Taccuini mussoliniani* [Bologna: Il Mulino, 1990], 355).

7. "Quando si ama una donna la si butta sul divano."

**233**